Richard Beatniffe

The Norfolk Tour

Or, Traveller's Pocket Companion... Fifth Edition

Richard Beatniffe

The Norfolk Tour
Or, Traveller's Pocket Companion... Fifth Edition

ISBN/EAN: 9783744767897

Printed in Europe, USA, Canada, Australia, Japan

Cover: Foto ©Andreas Hilbeck / pixelio.de

More available books at **www.hansebooks.com**

THE NORFOLK TOUR:
OR,
Traveller's Pocket Companion.

BEING
A CONCISE DESCRIPTION
OF ALL THE

PRINCIPAL TOWNS,
NOBLEMENS AND GENTLEMENS SEATS,
And other REMARKABLE PLACES.

IN THE

COUNTY of NORFOLK.

Compiled from the moſt authentic Hiſtorians and modern Travellers, and corrected to the preſent Time.

TO WHICH ARE ADDED,

An INDEX VILLARIS for the COUNTY,

AND A

Short Account of the chief Towns in
SUFFOLK.

The Fifth EDITION, greatly enlarged and improved.

Neſcio qua natale ſolum dulcedine cunctos
Ducit, et immemores non finit eſſe ſui.

NORWICH:
Printed and Sold by R. BEATNIFFE, in Cockey-Lane,
M.DCC.XCV.

PREFACE.

THE Histories of Norfolk, and its principal Towns, are comprised in so many folios, quartos, and books of all sizes, as collectively are too voluminous and expensive, and several of them too scarce, to be easily procured. These, amongst other reasons, have induced me to compress into as small a compass as possible, to be useful to a Gentleman Traveller, an epitome of what seemed worthy of particular notice in the county; compiled from the labours of Camden, Spelman, Blomefield, Parkin, Swinden, Mackrell, Browne, Martin, and others of less consequence. In this edition much has been added to the former descriptions of Norwich, Lynn, Yarmouth, Thetford, and almost every other place in the county. The distances in measured miles, of every town in the county from Norwich, has been corrected in more than two hundred and fifty places, and with the

Post

Poft Roads, to many of the principal cities, and manufacturing towns in England, will, I am perfuaded, prove extenfively ufeful, and very exact. The Parochial Lift of the inhabitants at different periods, and the Tables of Baptifms and Burials in Norwich, from 1719 to 1743 and 1784 to 1794, have been extracted from manufcript papers, and regular returns for the laft eleven years. The Lifts of Knights of the Shire, and Reprefentatives for the City, from the Reftoration to the prefent time, with the ftate of the poll at each contefted Election, have in part been taken from different MS. copies, compared with each other, and I believe are not to be found complete in any other printed book. The Biography has been *confiderably enlarged*; and in fhort, from the new materials interfperfed through almoft every part, fince the publication of the Fourth Edition, in 1786, THIS may perhaps more properly be called a new work, than the revifal of an old one.

If in making thefe numerous additions, corrections and emendations, and endeavouring to notice thofe changes which the

deftroying

PREFACE.

deftroying hand of Time, or the improvement of modern Ingenuity daily occafion, it fhould be thought that I have felected fome things which might as well have been omitted, and neglected others of greater importance, I plead in excufe, that I do not flatter myfelf fo far as to imagine, that out of fuch an heterogeneous mafs of materials as I have turned over, I can have chofen thofe parts only which will be approved of by every reader; I know 'tis impoffible; but having exerted my beft endeavours to compile an ufeful, and in fome inftances, an entertaining Book, I am perfuaded that the fmaller defects, of inelegance of expreffion, or literal error, will be cheerfully overlooked, and that the NORFOLK TOUR will merit a continuance of that favourable reception which the former editions have fo amply experienced.

THE EDITOR.

NORWICH,
MARCH 25,
1795.

ERRATA.

Page 22. line 14. for fall, *read* fail.—p. 70. l. 16. for Oct. 21, *r.* Oct. 17.—p. 77. l. 14. for 33,00, *r.* 33,000.—p. 119. l. 8. *dele*, of.---p. 124. l. 22. after *eſt*, add *præful*.—p. 143. for indifputable, *r.* indifputably.—p. 151. l. 4. for proffeſſions, *r.* proceſſions, and l. 17. for, rode on horfeback in a failor's habit, *r.* rode in a Phaeton drawn by 4 horfes.—p. 250. l. 16. for contraſt, *r.* contract.—p. 290. l. 14 for PHALRIS, *r.* PHALARIS; l. 20. for SETACCA, *r.* SETACEA; and l. 31. for HOLESTEUM, *r.* HOLOSTEUM.—p. 292. l. 21. for HYPOPIYHYS, *r.* HYPOPITHYS.—p. 294. l. 4. for CREPJS, *r.* CREPIS.

Page 26. line 13 *for*, Sir Edmund, *read*, John.

CONTENTS. vii

	Page.
AYLSHAM	272
Burgh Castle	55
Blickling	216
Caister next Yarmouth	43
Castor near Norwich	56
Castle Rising	264
Cromer	269
Cockthorpe	236
Coffey	172
Dereham, East	259
Denton	234
Felbrigg	229
Fakenham	266
Fastolff, Sir John	48
Gunton Hall	233
Gaywood	273
Houghton	173
Holkham	188
Holt	268
Kimberley	232
Knights of the Shire	298
Langley House	231
LYNN REGIS	238
St. Margaret's Church	243
St. Nicholas Chapel	244
Theatre — Assembly-Room	245
Tuesday Market-place	246
Red Mount	248
General Trade	249
Cure for Witchcraft	250
Mariner's Compass	251
Life of Wm. Watts	252
Melton Constable	227

	Page.
NORWICH	60
Destroyed by the Danes	*61
It's antiquity	62
State of Cities at the Conquest	*62
Present State of Norwich	65
Wards	69
Boundary	70
Parochial List	72
Baptisms and Burials	*71
Manufactures	74
General Trade	77
Representatives from 1701	79
Castle	81
St. Andrew's-Hall	89
Mingay's Guild-feast	92
Guild-Hall	94
Assembly-House	96
Theatre	97
Black Friar's Bridge	98
Duke's Palace	99
Bishoprick	100
Cathedral	102
Cloister	108
St. Peter of Mancroft	111
St. Laurence's Church	113
Norfolk Hospital	115
Bethel	117
Public Library	118
Summary View	119
Origin of Printing	120
Ditto of Cards and Paper	114
Keels and Wherries	115
Kett's Rebellion	117
Life of Bishop Losinga	124
———— Bp. Bateman	126
———— Archbishop Parker	129
———— Bishop Hall	131

CONTENTS.

	Page.		Page.
Life of Bishop Cosin	139	Wolterton -	216
——— Dr. S. Clarke	140	Westwick - -	231
——— Dr. Kaye -	142	Warnam - -	235
——— Dr. Cunningham -	145	Walsingham -	265
——— Sir T. Browne	146	**YARMOUTH**	1
——— Dr. E. Browne	149	Origin of, by Swinden	6
——— John Skelton	150	Present State - -	8
Pageant of Bp. Blaize	151	Privileges -	10
Remarkable Events	152	Fishing Fair -	11
Members from 1660 to 1700 -	172	Boulter's Museum	14
		Yarmouth Cart -	15
		The Quay -	17
NARFORD -	219	Bath and Public Room	18
Norfolk Plants -	289	St. Nicholas Church	19
		Expences of the Haven	22
Post Roads from Norwich to various places - -	331	Admiral Perebourne	24
		Yarmouth Navy -	25
		Yarmouth Island -	27
Rainham -	226	Attacked by the Insurgents -	28
Raveningham -	234	Plagues at - -	29
Remarks on the County -	281	The Roads -	30
Rivers and Broads	290	Address to Richard Cromwel -	32
Swaffham -	261	Plants on the Beach	34
St. Bennet's Monastery - -	276	Passage of Herrings	37
		Manner of Fishing	38
Thetford - -	253	Origin of the Herring Fishery -	41
Towns and Villages in Norfolk -	323	Nashe on Fish and Fishermen - -	42

SUFFOLK.

BUNGAY -	315	Newmarket -	320
Bury St. Edmund's	300	Sudbury -	317
Ipswich - -	309	Woodbridge -	319

THE

NORFOLK TOUR.

THE moſt uſual Route taken by travellers, intending to make the Tour of Norfolk from the Metropolis for pleaſure, is by way of Chelmsford, Witham and Colcheſter, in Eſſex; Ipſwich, Woodbridge, Saxmundham, Yoxford and Loweſtoft, in Suffolk, to

YARMOUTH.

THE Saxon name of this town was *Jiermud*, that is the mouth of the River Garienis or Yare: the preciſe time of its being firſt built, and whether it was the ancient Garianonum of the Romans, where the Stableſian Horſe lay in garriſon, to protect the coaſt from the predatory incurſions of the Northern pirates, has employed the pens of our moſt reſpectable topographical hiſtorians, without ſatisfying candid inquiry.

The Romans after remaining in poſſeſſion of England near 400 years, were in the year 420 withdrawn from theſe and other diſtant provinces, to the more

immediate

immediate defence of Italy and Rome, against the furious incursions of those barbarians, who under the various names of Goths, Vandals, Hunns and Normans, in prodigious swarms, issued from the forests of the uncultivated frozen regions of Denmark, Norway and Sweden, now so thinly inhabited;. over-ran the most civilized States of Europe, and with savage barbarity destroyed those monuments of antiquity, which the riches and elegant taste of an enlightened people had been collecting for a thousand years.

 The Britons and Romans after living together in the same island for near four hundred years, had so far assimilated as in a great measure to become one people, and accordingly, it has been said, that when the Roman Legions were withdrawn from these distant, and perhaps unprofitable possessions, many of the younger and most valuable natives accompanied them. England thus deprived of its best defenders, presented a fair and inviting field of plunder to every bold and necessitous adventurer. Foremost of persons of this description stood Cerdick, called the warlike Saxon, who with his son Cenrick, and as many of their forces as could be brought over in five ships, landed in the county of Norfolk, then constituting a part of the province of the Iceni, and subduing its inhabitants, set sail from Yarmouth for the West, where they founded the kingdom of the West Saxons, and returning from this expedition about the year 495, instead of settling at Garianonum, (Burgh Castle according to Camden) built a new town upon the moist and watery field on the west side of the river Garienis, and called it Jiermud, or Yarmouth, but

the

THE NORFOLK TOUR.

the situation proving unwholesome, the inhabitants removed to the opposite side of the river, then from the same Cerdick, called Cerdick-sand, and there built the present Yarmouth, wherein according to *Domesday-book, there were seventy Burgesses who were Merchants and Traders at sea, in the time of Edward the Confessor, i. e. between the years 1042 and 1066.

The story preserved by Sir Henry Spelman, in the *Icenia*, respecting Lothbrock, being by a sudden tempest driven from the coast of Denmark, in a boat by himself; his entering the Yare; his passing by the place where Yarmouth now stands, and landing at Reedham, where the court of Edmund King of the East Angles then was kept, is well known. But the conclusion

---

* The ancient Notitia of England, called Domesday-book was begun in 1081, and finished in 1086; it contains an exact survey of all the cities, towns and villages in the several counties, except Northumberland, Cumberland, Westmoreland, Durham, and part of Lancashire, which it is said were never surveyed. It does not only account for the several Baronies, knights' fees and plough lands, but gives all the number of families, men, soldiers, husbandmen, servants and cattle; how much meadow, pasture, woods, tillage, common heath, mash, &c. every one possessed. In the front of each county stands a list of the Lords of the soil; that is the King and a few of his Nobles. In the year 1785 this book was handsomely printed in two volumes, royal folio, with a FAC SIMILE type; and, a copy being given to each Member of both Houses of Parliament and the principal Officers of State, there is no longer any danger of its being lost or destroyed. The second volume contains Essex, Norfolk and Suffolk, the first comprehending the remaining counties, thirty-three in number.

conclusion drawn from this apparently fabulous tale, does not seem warranted by the premises, for granting that he entered the Yare and passed by the place where Yarmouth now stands, undiscovered, it does not necessarily follow that no such town then existed: for, the breadth of the river, or æstuary, as it then was, joined to the darkness of a night; or the tempestuous agitation of the winds and waves, may easily be supposed sufficient impediments to his being heard, whatever efforts he might make.

Swinden modernising Sir Henry Spelman's History of Yarmouth, as given in the Icenia, compared with manuscript authorities in the Town, says, " All the
" Records of Yarmouth universally agree, that the
" place where Yarmouth now stands was originally a
" sand in the sea, which by degrees appeared above
" water and became dry land; that Fishermen from
" different parts of England, especially the Cinque
" Ports, resorted here annually during the Herring
" Fishery, and finding the place very convenient for
" their business, they erected temporary Booths or
" Tents; and he thinks this to have been the state
" of Yarmouth at, or soon after the arrival of Cer-
" dick the Saxon, and his companions, in five ships,
" in the year 495. That after this it became fa-
" mous for the resort of Fishermen from Norway,
" Holland, France, &c. That the first Settlement
" or appearance of a Town was upon the western
" bank of the River Yare, whence they removed
" because it was unhealthy and perhaps inconveni-
" ent, and began to build houses on Cerdick-sand,
" but the time of this removal is not precisely ascer-
                                                " tained

"tained. The first houses are said to have been built upon Fuller's Hill, near where St. Nicholas Church now stands, proceeding northerly towards the Haven at Caister. About the year 1066, the Yare at Caister began to be choaked up with sand, which induced the inhabitants to remove towards the South Channel, near Burgh-Castle, the present harbour, by which means the Northern became in a great measure deserted." This the same author says, "happened at the time when Bishop Herbert began to build St. Nicholas Church, that is, about the year 1123; that upon the entire stoppage of the North Haven, the town increased very rapidly towards the South, and had not the inclosing it with a wall (began about 1284 and finished 1338) prescribed the limits, in all probability, St. Nicholas Church would have been at this time standing alone."

In the 9th year of the reign of King John, that is 1208, leave was given to the Burgesses to choose a Provost or chief Magistrate from amongst themselves, but to be approved of by the King, and was made a Free Borough upon paying to the King, 55l.* per annum, in lieu of customs arising from the Port of Yarmouth. The date of this Charter may properly be stiled the grand Æra of Yarmouth, as hence, by gradual degrees,

---

* In consequence of Kerkeley Road being added to the bounds of Yarmouth; (in the 44th Year of the Reign of Edward III. 1370) it now pays 60l. annually into the Exchequer, except the Land-tax.

grees, it has become one of the firſt Sea-ports in the Kingdom.

Naſhe, a native of Loweſtoft, publiſhed a pamphlet in 1599, entitled "Naſhe's Lenten Stuff, containing "the deſcription and firſt Procreation of the Town "of Great Yarmouth, with a new Play of the Praiſe "of Red Herrings." In his account of what he calls the firſt *Procreation* of the Town, there is nothing but what is more fully detailed in the two preceding paragraphs: In noticing the Haven, he ſays, 'in the laſt 'Fiſhing ſeaſon (1598), when I was there, 600 barks 'and veſſels of good burden, and of various nations, 'were at once in the harbour between the bridge and 'the ſouth gate.'

YARMOUTH is a pleaſant Sea-port town, at the Eaſtern extremity of the county of Norfolk, built in the form of an oblong quadrangle of 133 acres, on a peninſula; it is encompaſſed on the South and Eaſt by the ſea, on the North by the continent, and on the Weſt by the Yare, over which there is a handſome draw-bridge,* (re-built in 1785 at the expence of 2,150l.) which divides it from Suffolk. It extends rather more than a mile [1770 yards] along the river from North to South, and is near three furlongs in breadth [603 yards] from Eaſt to Weſt, ſtands near two miles from the Haven's mouth to the S. and about half a mile from the ſea Eaſtward, has four principal ſtreets running from North to South, and 156 narrow lanes

---

* The firſt bridge was built in 1427, before which there had been a ferry boat only. In 1553 the firſt draw-bridge was built.

lanes or *rows*, interfecting them in the oppofite direction; is encompaffed with a wall on the Eaft, North, and South fides, 2,240 yards in length, having ten gates and fixteen towers; extends along the Eaft bank of the river 2,030 yards, the whole circuit being 4,270 yards, or two miles and 75 yards; is faid to contain 16000 inhabitants, and formerly to have been one of the Cinque-ports. It is 123 miles N. E. of London, and 22 miles E. of Norwich, long. 1, 42 W. lat. 52, 46, N.

Queen Anne by charter dated March 11, 1702, being the 25th granted to this town, fettled the form of government as it continues to this day, that is, in a Mayor annually elected out of the 18 Aldermen, on the 29th of Auguft, and fworn into office September 29th, upon which day an elegant entertainment is given at the Hall, on the Quay, to the Corporation, and the Mayor's particular friends.

The Corporation confifts of a Mayor, High-Steward, Recorder, Sub-fteward, 18 Aldermen, including the Mayor, and 36 Common Councilmen, with a Town Clerk, 2 Chamberlains, a Water Bailiff, and other inferior officers. The Mayor, High-fteward, Recorder, Sub-fteward, and fuch of the Aldermen as have ferved the office of Mayor, are Juftices of Peace for the Borough, during their continuance in their refpective offices.

The fingularity of the mode of electing the Mayor of this place feems to merit a fhort defcription. An Inqueft of twelve perfons, chofen out of the Common-Councilmen,

Councilmen, are shut up close in a room in the Town Hall, without meat, drink, fire or candle, till there be a majority of one mind. On these occasions a variety of shifts have been frequently practised by the contending parties, to starve or tire out their opponents.

Yarmouth sent representatives to parliament in the reign of Edward I, (Ed. reigned from 1271 to 1307) which is as early as Norwich and Lynn: they are chosen by the Freemen, in number about 800, who are free by inheritance, servitude or purchase, and the returning officer is the Mayor. The arms are, *per pale gules and argent, three demy lions empaling three herrings tails*. The corporation has particular and extensive privileges; here is a Court of Record and Admiralty, and the Mayor and Magistrates are conservators of the Waveney to St. Olave's Bridge, 10 miles; the Yare to Hardley-crofs, 10 miles; and the Bure to Weybridge, 10 miles; within which limits the laws of distress and attachment can be executed by their officers only: Up to one of these boundaries, there is a grand aquatic procession in July every year, when it is usual particularly to drink to the Gentleman who it is intended should serve the office of mayor for the ensuing year. A fair is annually held here on Friday and Saturday in Easter week. The markets on Wednesday and Saturday, are plentifully supplied, particularly with fruits and vegetables, which are remarkably good. The polite amusements of the Theatre, Assembly-room, and Concerts, during the bathing season, render the residence of strangers perfectly agreeable; and those who are fond of fishing,

shooting,

shooting, sailing or bowling, will find ample opportunities of gratifying those inclinations.

The herrings come by the North East off Scotland in prodigious shoals, and arrive on the coast of Yarmouth about the 20th of September,* at which time the fishing fair begins, and continues till the 22d of November; when the herrings are no longer fit for merchandise, at least not those that are taken hereabouts. Every vessel that comes to fish for the merchants, from any part of England, is allowed to catch, bring in, and sell their fish, free of all duty or toll. The average value of the Yarmouth fishing boats completely fitted for the sea, may be estimated at 600l. each, some of the largest cost near 1000l: A single boat has been known to bring in 12 last of herrings at one time; a last is 10 barrels, or 10,000 herrings, and when cured, are worth about 16l. In the year 1784 fifty-five boats were fitted out from Yarmouth, forty from Lowestoft, fifty from Whitby, Scarborough, &c. and sixty-two came from Holland. In 1788 eighty-seven Dutch Schuyts came to this fishery. Each boat carries eleven hands.

To those who take delight in seeing others pleased, without themselves being particularly interested in what is going forward, it must give much pleasure to behold the cheerful activity of the fishermen on the beach, when landing and carrying off the herrings. In 1580 two thousand last of herrings were brought into the Haven

* The Dutch are obliged to be at Sea, and wet their Nets on the 21st of September. The Yarmouth Fishermen seldom go out before the 26th.

Haven in one tide ; and in 1593 the fishing nets were valued at 50,000l.

The veſſels fitted out by the Merchants of Yarmouth for the Herring Fiſhery, are decked boats of 40 or 50 tons burden; thoſe which come from Scarborough, Whitby, and other Northern Ports, and engage to fiſh for the Yarmouth Merchants and Tradeſmen, during the ſeaſon, are open boats called Cobles, of about 20 tons burden, and generally bring in two or three laſts of herrings every trip. Some years back ſeveral veſſels called Barks uſed to come to this fiſhery from the coaſts of Kent and Suſſex, but they have not lately appeared.

About one hundred and fifty veſſels, are employed in this fiſhery, and between 30 and 40 in the exportation; and when it is confidered what numbers of people are always buſy on ſhore, in ſalting, drying and packing in the time of the fiſhery, as alſo the employment it occaſions during great part of the year to the coopers and ſhip-wrights, it may eaſily be imagined that this Fiſhery is of the firſt confequence to the town of Yarmouth. In the beginning of the reign of King Charles II. Yarmouth employed 155 boats and barks, *communibus annis*, in the North Sea and Iceland Fiſheries. Fifty thouſand barrels or 5000 laſts, containing 50,000,000 of herrings are generally taken and cured here in one year. Theſe herrings are for the moſt part exported by the Merchants of Yarmouth, the reſt by thoſe of London, to Italy and Spain.

Mackrel

*Mackrel arrive upon the Yarmouth coaft the latter end of April and beginning of May, where they continue about fix weeks, during which time large quantities are caught and fent principally to the London and Norwich markets, where they meet with a ready fale:

Thefe fifheries, together with another to the North Seas for white fifh, called North Sea Cod, a brifk trade to Holland, France, Norway and the Baltic, for deals, oak, pitch, tar, and all other naval ftores; the exportation of corn, malt, and flour which often amounts to † three hundred and 33 thoufand quarters a year; the fhipping of the greater part of the ftuffs manufactured at Norwich for foreign markets; the importation of coals, which is allowed to amount to 70,000 chaldrons annually, with other articles of merchandife from the North, and the heavy goods from London, configned to Norwich, Bungay, Beccles, &c. all together occafion much bufinefs, and employ abundance of hands and fhipping.

Befides fifhing veffels, upwards of 300 fhips belong to this port; and the feamen, as well mafters as mariners, are juftly efteemed amongft the ableft and moft expert navigators in England.

The fituation of this town is very commodious for trade, the river Yare being navigable hence to Norwich, which is 32 miles, for keels of fifty tons burden; befides, there is a navigation by the Waveney

---

* A Mackrel fent from Yarmouth in 1792, meafured 17 inches from the fnout to the tip point of the tail, 8 inches 1-half round the thickeft part, and weighed 25 ounces. This is to be confidered as one of the largeft fize.

† The average export of the years 1791, 1792 and 1793 was 267,378 quarters; value 446,796l. 11s.

to Bungay, the South parts of Norfolk, and the North of Suffolk.

After viewing the Church, St. George's Chapel, the Quay, Assembly-house, the Fort and Batteries, with perhaps a fleet of 50 or 60 merchant ships under sail, in various directions; which is not at all an uncommon prospect; there is nothing in the town more worthy of notice than Mr. BOULTER's Museum in the Market-place, who by great industry, with much taste, and at a considerable expence, has collected a curious assortment of English and foreign birds, shells, corals, corallines and sea fans; an assortment of spars, fluors, chrystals, agates, onyxes, sardonyxes, porphyries, and other beautiful stones; petrified shells, corals, woods, ferns and other antediluvian remains; many specimens of ores, metals, sulphers, salts and fossils; fish dried and in spirits. British, Roman, Saxon and English coins and medals in gold, silver and copper; antique bronzes; carvings in wood, stone and ivory; old seals, rings, amulets, fibulas, keys and spurs; old paintings on ivory, copper, wood and canvas; ancient weapons of war, and warlike habiliments; antique illuminations on vellum and paper: pieces of ancient stained glass; brass figures and inscriptions; British celts, Roman urns, pateras and lachrymatories, many warlike instruments, dresses, fishing tackle, &c. brought from Otaheite and other islands in the great South Seas by the ships who went that voyage under the command of Captain Cook. The whole commodiously disposed in a convenient room for view: and his shop may perhaps, not inaptly be called, a neat magazine of modern niceties.

Mr.

Mr. J. D. Downes has a large collection of valuable Pigeons, and other Birds, well worth the notice of the curious.

A traveller wishing to see this town to advantage, with respect to amusement, should make it a visit in the bathing season, during the months of July, August or September, when a great deal of genteel company from London, most parts of the county, and Suffolk, assemble here, either for the purpose of health or pleasure.

A cart of a singular construction, adapted to the narrowness of the *rows* of this place, and used in no other town in England, merits a short description; especially as it is said that more work may be done with it, and at less expence, than with any other carriage, in the same space of time. The length from the tip of the shafts, or strings, to the extreme of the seat is twelve feet, the breath three feet and a half; the wheels being two feet nine inches high, are sometimes made of one solid piece of poplar or ash, five inches thick, without tire; but these are not so much in use as formerly: they are now generally made with spokes and fellies; shod with tire, the spokes being mortised into the axletree, which is a cylindrical piece of oak twelve inches thick, having an iron pin of about an inch diameter, drove through the whole length, and projecting about four inches at each end; these work in two strong staples fixed into the under part of the strings or shafts behind. Over the wheels the seat is placed, upon which the company ride for pleasure. The driver, with a short whip, standing before upon the crofs ftaves of the cart, guides the horfe with a rein. Thefe carriages are never drawn by more than one horfe, the fhafts being faftened to a collar on the top of his fhoulders, the horfe having a cart-faddle on his back, over which goes the back-band. There are a number of thefe carts daily employed in carrying goods to and from the fhipping, and about the town; they are varioufly conftructed according to the feveral purpofes of pleafure and bufinefs, the brewers having them of greater length, and thofe ufed for pleafure being lighter than the common work carts, which have two iron pins ftanding upright through the feat, about nine inches long for the conveniency of faftening goods to; upon the feat and crofs ftaves at the bottom, the whole about fix feet in length, all kinds of goods are placed. In Summer, and particularly during the bathing feafon, a number of thefe vehicles, which the people of Yarmouth dignify by the name of *coaches*, are let out to company who vifit the town, and chufe an excurfion to the Fort, an airing upon the Denes, or a jaunt into the country. The carriages for thefe purpofes are generally painted red, green or blue, and may be had for a few hours for two fhillings, horfe and driver included. The Horfes ufed here are remarkable good trotters; but from the uncouth conftruction of the carriage, they feem to go thundering and blundering down the narrow rows, which the carts fo exactly fit as not to be overturned, and along the ftreets, in a very difagreeable manner. In excurfions to the Fort, you are drove over the Denes nearly all the way, from

whence

whence there is a most charming prospect of the Sea. For a company to have been at Yarmouth, and not to have rode in one of these carts, to the haven's mouth, the bath and the whole length of the quay, is to lose perhaps one of the greatest pleasures this town is able to afford. Upon the whole the Yarmouth cart-coach is the most convenient, useful and whimsical carriage used in the kingdom.

The Quay is allowed to be the longest and handsomest in Europe, that of Seville in Spain only excepted, being 1014 yards from the South gate to the bridge, above which, for smaller vessels, it extends 1016 yards, i. e. the whole length is one mile 270 yards, and in some places it is 150 yards in breadth; from the bridge to the South gate, it is decorated by a handsome range of buildings, amongst which the Assembly-house makes an elegant appearance; add to this, that active spirit of industry so eminently conspicuous amongst all ranks, but especially the mercantile people of Yarmouth upon the quay, and its being almost the only agreeable walk in or near the place, render it infinitely the pleasantest part of the town, and the best situation for trade.

The market-place is a handsome area, and if the houses situated upon the East side were improved, it would be inferior to few in the kingdom; there also wants a convenient fish market, and it is shocking to see butchers daily slaughtering calves, sheep, &c. in the centre of such an opulent town, resorted to by crowds of genteel company from almost every part of England.

The Theatre erected in 1778 at an expence of 1500l. is a neat building, well adapted to the intended purpose; it stands on the scite of a chapel formerly belonging to the Dutch congregation. The Norwich company of comedians perform here for the space of six weeks in the winter season, and a short time in the summer.

The Bowling-green is pleasantly situated upon the East bank of the river, and the assembly-room being open two nights in every week during the bathing season, agreeable entertainment can seldom be wanting.

The Bath-house was built in 1759, and cost near 2000l. It stands upon the beach, at about three furlongs distance from St. George's Chapel. You enter a neat room 18 feet by 20 having two windows fronting the town and three next the sea, upon the right of the entrance are four closets, having each a door into the bath-room. The Bath is 15 feet in length by 8 feet wide; this is the gentlemens apartment, and that appropriated to the use of the ladies is so much like it, that a particular description is unnecessary. The sea water is raised every tide by the assistance of a horse-mill into a reservoir, at about 50 yards distance from Baths, into which it is conveyed by separate pipes. In short here is every conveniency to be desired by the Valetudinarian; good accommodation, neatness and civility, without being, " *Too civil by half.*" The Angel and Wrestlers are good inns, and for those who prefer private lodgings, there are plenty in the town, neat, and to be had on reasonable terms, but in point of of pleafantnefs, thofe in the market-place have a decided preference.

A handfome public-room was built adjoining to the north end of the bath-houfe in 1788; it is 45 feet long, 27 wide, and 15 high, having 5 large windows in a femicircular form fronting the Sea; here the company are accommodated with tea and coffee every morning, and afternoon, a public breakfafting every Tuefday and Friday, and occafional concerts during the bathing feafon: the London and Country Newfpapers are provided; and, there being no Coffee-room in the town, it is an excellent lounging place, well calculated agreeably to fill up that tedious vacuity, which too often obtrudes upon a ftate of mere amufement, at a watering-place. The Subfcription is 5s. for each Gentleman, and 2s. 6d. for a Lady, during the feafon, to go to the room whenever they pleafe; and 9d. for tea, 1s. tea and coffee, and 2s. 6d. each concert, to occafional vifitors.

The Jetty clofe to the bath-houfe is 110 paces in length and 24 feet broad at the head, (where there is a crane) gradually decreafing to 7 feet on the land fide; the fea breezes keep it cool, and the lively fcene of fhips almoft perpetually under fail, in various directions, render it a moft defirable walk after bathing.

St. Nicholas Church was founded by Herbert de Lozinga the firft Bifhop of Norwich, about the year 1113, greatly enlarged in 1250, and the following year dedicated to St. Nicholas, the patron of fifhermen.

men. It confifts of three ailes; the middle remarkably the leaft both in height and breadth, but in length it extends further towards the Eaft than the other two, being 250 feet from Eaft to Weft. The breadth of the three ailes together is 108 feet. It is a fpacious but not very neat church. The fpire appears crooked in every direction, and with the tower is 186 feet high, ferving for a very good fea-mark. At the Eaft end of the middle aile ftands the communion table, where before the Reformation ftood the great or high altar, and over it, a loft or perch called the Rood-loft, which fupported a large crucifix, behind which was a veftry. The Rood-loft, was erected by Roger de Haddefco, prior of St. Olave's in 1370, and ornamented with curious decorations and devices, at his own expence; it was called, "*Opus pretiofum circa magnum altare,*" i. e. "the precious or costly work about the great altar," and when lighted by lamps and candles, (according to ancient cuftom) muft have appeared exceedingly fplendid and folemn. Our pious anceftors fhewed great zeal in fupporting the expences incurred by thefe lights, which were kept continually burning before the fhrines of the crucifixes, or thofe of their favourite faints; for befides certain annual rents collected by the wardens, whofe bufinefs it was to take care of fuch decorations, legacies were frequently bequeathed to churches for the fame purpofes.

There formerly was a chronological table of remarkable events relating to Yarmouth, hanging in the South aile of this Church, with the following whimfical

and

and singular observation. *"There never was in it (Yarmouth) an Ecclesiastic publickly detected of the crime of carnality."*

There is an excellent *Organ in this church, esteemed to be inferior only to one at Haerlem in Holland. To this church there once belonged 6000 persons of an age able to communicate, i. e. of 16 years and upwards.

In the North West corner of the North aile is a chamber vestry, containing a library of ancient books of about 200 volumes, mostly folios, but of little value. In this room there is a desk of singular construction, in which are seven shelves so constructed as to revolve and present the books on either to your hand, without deranging those on the other shelves.

St. Nicholas is a curacy in the gift of the Dean and Chapter of Norwich, and was the only place of worship, for those of the established religion, in this populous place, till the year 1716, when a beautiful chapel was built nearer the centre of the town, and dedicated to St. George.

In

---

* The first mention of an Organ which we find, (in our Northern Histories at least) is in the annals of 757, when Constantine Cupronimus, Emperor of the East, sent to Pepin K. of France, among other rich presents, a musical machine, which the French writers describe to have been composed of pipes and large tubes of tin, and to have imitated sometimes the roaring of thunder, and sometimes the warbling of a flute.

In reading monumental inscriptions, we cannot but regret that we become acquainted with many virtues only when it is too late to enjoy them, and are introduced to excellent parents, husbands, children and friends but to lament their departure, and to bewail their loss. We insert the following Epitaph, upon a Sailor, which is in the Church-yard, for its singularity.

 Tho' *Boreas* blow, and Neptune's waves
  Have tost me to and fro,
 By God's decree, you plainly see,
 I'm harbour'd here below:
 Where I must at anchor lye
  With many of our fleet;
 But once again we must set sail,
  Our Admiral CHRIST to meet.

The Inhabitants of Yarmouth have experienced infinite trouble, and been at great expence in maintaining the Haven. The present cost 4,273l. 6s. 8d. and is the seventh which has been made; it was begun in the year 1578, and is in or near the place where it had been about 30 years before; it met with several obstructions, sometimes from the difference of opinion, as to the place most proper for the purpose, but principally from the great expence attending the enterprize, and nothing very material was effected before 1559, since which it has been annually supported at so great an expence, that in the year 1667 the town was 9,400l. in debt, had sold lands and tenements to the yearly value of 400l. besides having had various supplies from government, and other aids on this distressing occasion. It appears by Swinden's history, that the expences incurred on this account from 1567 to 1770, that is 204 years, amounted to 241,578l. 9s. 11d. and by dividing this into two periods of 102 years each, we observe, that the first 102 years, from 1567 to 1668, cost 65,296l. 18s. 2d. or little more than 640l. per annum, whilst the second 102 years, from 1669 to 1770 amounted to 176,281l. 11s. 9d. or 1,728l. per annum. The annual expences now are about 2000l.

There have been eleven different acts of parliament, the last being obtained in the year 1785, by which it is enacted, that all ships unlading in the haven of Yarmouth or in Yarmouth road, extending from the South part of the town of Scratby in Norfolk, to the N. part of the town of Corton in Suffolk, shall pay for every Chaldron of coals (Winchester measure) last of wheat, rye, barley, malt, or other grain, and for every weigh of salt and every ton of any other goods or merchandize whatsoever, (fish only excepted) a sum not exceeding one shilling, to the Collector, to be appointed by the town of Yarmouth; the money so raised to be applied towards the repair of the piers of Yarmouth and depthening Brayden; the river running by Norwich from the New-mills to Hardley Cross, &c. depthening the river Waveney, Yare and Bure, and repairing the Bridge and public Quays at Yarmouth.

Thirteen ships are employed in the carrying trade, between London and Yarmouth, six from Dice Quay and seven from Symond's Wharf, one from each Wharf sailing every Saturday. The expence of freight is about 20s. per ton, except hogsheads of sugar, and other heavy articles for the grocers, which are

are brought at a much cheaper rate. The keel freight and other expences upon goods configned to Norwich, is about half as much as the fhip freight.

Four fhips are employed in the Hull trade, which go and come alternately.

A Stage coach paffes three times a week between Yarmouth and London. The Mail coach once every day, and a machine from Yarmouth to Norwich twice every day, during the fummer feafon, and once every day in the winter. The Barge comes from Norwich every Monday and Thurfday, and returns the next days, in which there are good accommodations for paffengers, who may by this means take a moft agreeable trip in fine weather, at a fmall expence.

In 1340 John Perebourne, a Burgefs of this town, was made Admiral of the King's northern fleet, and meeting with a French fquadron of 400 fail off Sluys, Nafhe fays, " he fo flafhed and fliced them, and bat-
" tered them, with his ftone darting engines, no ord-
" nance being then invented, that their beft mercy
" was fire and water, which hath no mercy."

In 1337 the Yarmouth navy confifting of 20 men of war, conveyed King Edward the Third's plenipotentiaries to the court of Hainault, from Dort to Yarmouth. In 1342 the King embarked on board their fleet, on his expedition in to Brittany, but while he lay entrenched before Vannes, Prince Lewis of Spain difperfed the Yarmouth fleet, by which Edward was driven to great ftreights for want of provifions. Edward returning to England in March 1343, fummoned the Captains

to

to appear at Westminster, to account for their behaviour, but the issue of this inquiry is not known.

In 1346 at the taking of Calais, Yarmouth assisted the King with 43 ships, on board of which were 1075 mariners. It appears by the Roll of the high fleet of Edward III. before Calais, that there were 706 ships and 14,151 mariners employed upon that memorable occasion, and that Great Yarmouth then supplied the King with more sailors than any sea-port in England, London not excepted.

Tho' a little extraneous to the intention of this publication, we hope it may amuse some of our readers to be informed, that the Navy of England was at this time, and for more than two centuries after, fitted out something in the manner that the militia is now; every sea-port, and other confiderable town, being obliged to furnish its quota. On K. Edward's invasion of Brittany, there were eighty-two towns thus assessed in proportion to their trading importance. The King on the part of government furnishing 25 ships. The scale of importance of the different towns of that day, (445 years ago) when compared with what they are now, affords a most striking proof of the vicissitudes to which commercial places are liable. Fowey, in Cornwall then sent near twice as many ships as London did; and the names of many towns which stood pretty high on the list, are now nearly forgotten.

The following is part of the List:
Fowey, 47; Yarmouth, 43; Dartmouth, 31; Plymouth, 26; Shoreham, 26; London, 25; Bristol, 24; Sandwich, 22; Dover, 21; Southampton, 21; Winchelsea,

Chelsea, 21; Weymouth, 20; Looe, 20; Newcastle, 17; Boston, 17; Hull, 16. The ships carried from 16 to 30 men, and the average might be about 25 to 50 each. *MS. in the Cottonian Library.*

The above mode of raising a naval force was first practised in 1007, when an invasion was expected from the Danes, with this difference, the assessment was then laid upon lands in general. To oppose the Spanish Armada, in 1578, which pride, vanity and folly had christened Invincible, a similar assessment took place upon the principal towns. But this illegal and arbitrary tax, under the name of ship-money, was destined to be opposed by Sir Edmund Hambden,* in the reign of the ill-advised and unfortunate Charles I. The issue of Hambden's trial, and the consequences resulting from it, are sufficiently known — No man can ascertain the secret motives of another's actions—but every Englishman ought to rejoice that his country has at all times produced those bold spirits, who have resolutely and successfully opposed the depression of its *real* liberties.

In 1352 the Corporation of Great Yarmouth gave to the College of Windsor, a last of red herrings, to be delivered yearly for ever, at Yarmouth: One of the reasons assigned for this gift was, because King Edward III. had been baptized at that College. The grant was further confirmed till the 17th of Henry VI. 1439 The herrings were sometimes delivered in kind, and at others a composition in money
was

---

* Hambden had been assessed 20s. for an Estate which he possessed in the county of Buckingham.

was paid. In the 12th of Henry VII. the Chamberlains were allowed in their accounts 4l. by them paid to the Deacon of Windſor, according to ancient cuſtom; this allowance continued till the 13th of Elizabeth, when they were again delivered in kind. Many diſputes aroſe about the delivery of theſe herrings, which were often ſaid to be of the worſt quality, and as ſuch had been refuſed by the deputies of Windſor. In 1661 the town was three years in arrear on this account, which they then unwillingly ſettled. In 1718 the cauſe of the diſpute was removed by the town agreeing to pay 9l. for that year and 8l. for the future, which is ſtill continued to be paid to the Dean and Canons of Windſor in lieu of the laſt of herrings.

There was an ancient cuſtom in this town for the Prior and Monks, and afterwards the Dean and Chapter, or their farmer of the parſonage, to provide a breakfaſt for the inhabitants on Chriſtmas day in every year, which continued till the 21ſt of Elizabeth, (1579) when a dreadful peſtilence carrying of 2000 of the inhabitants, the cuſtom ceaſed for ſome time, and 5l. was paid yearly to the Churchwardens inſtead of the entertainment, but it was again revived, and continued till the reign of King James, when by an agreement between the farmer, Mr. Goſling, and the Bailiffs, it was ſettled to pay them 10l. in lieu of the breakfaſt.

A ſand-bank of near a mile ſquare, was thrown up oppoſite to Scratby, four miles to the North of Yarmouth, which becoming dry and firm land about the year 1578 was so much elevated above high water mark that grass grew there, and sea fowls built their nests upon it. To this place many of the inhabitants of Yarmouth frequently went in the summer season for recreation, and on the 2d of August 1580 an elegant entertainment was given by the Bailiffs of Yarmouth to a select company of gentlemen, and imagining that it would accumulate and become of importance to the town, formal possession of it was taken by the name of Yarmouth Island, but they were opposed by Sir Edward Clere, of Ormesby, Knt. who claimed it as a parcel of the manor of Scratby, and erected a frame of timber upon it, as a testimony of his right. It was the more eagerly contended for on account of the many valuable goods cast ashore upon it from the ships lost on the coast, particularly in the year 1582, when several parcels of silk and other valuable articles were found there and carried to Yarmouth, as had been usual, and applied to the use of the town. The contest however between Yarmouth and Sir Edward Clere was of short duration, for what neither law or equity had been able to accomplish, or perhaps would have settled for many years, the elements easily and expeditiously determined, for in the very same year, a strong easterly wind and a boisterous sea, in a single day swept away the Island, " leaving not a wreck " behind."

In the year 1549 a body of the Insurgents belonging to the Rebel Kett, being denied admittance into Yarmouth, by the town's-people, who also refusing to supply his camp with beer, or pay any respect to his orders,

orders, Kett determined to storm the place; for this purpose a large body of his people, having made themselves masters of Lothingland, procured six pieces of ordnance from Lowestoft, and brought them to a close at the North end of Gorleston, intending to batter the town from thence; which being perceived, a party of town's-men were detached to set fire to a large stack of hay, on the West side of the Haven, and the wind being Northerly, it drove the smoke directly upon the face of the enemy, and prevented their seeing the approach of the Yarmouth-men, who by this stratagem surprized the Rebels, killing several, and taking 30 prisoners, with the six pieces of cannon, all which were safely conveyed into the town. The rebels exceedingly irritated by this disaster, approached the walls, and destroyed great part of the materials provided for the Haven, they then marched across the Denes to the South gate, but being repulsed by the fire of the cannon from the walls and mounts, they fled and never more returned.

In 1348—Seven thousand and fifty people died here of the Plague.——In 1579 it carried off about 2000: and in 1664, 2,500 died of the like pestilence.

Though Yarmouth Roads, on the East-side of the town, are very safe, and the chief rendezvous of the colliers between Newcastle and London, and other merchantmen, which are constantly passing and repassing, still the coast is particularly noted for being one of the most dangerous and most fatal to sailors in all Britain, a melancholy instance of which happened

about

about the year 1692, when a fleet of 200 sail of light colliers went out of Yarmouth Roads, with a fair wind, to pursue their voyage, and were taken short with a storm of wind at North-east. After they passed Wintertonness a few leagues, some of them, whose masters were more experienced seamen, or who were not so far out as the rest, tacked and put back in time, and got safe into the Roads; but the rest pushing on, in hopes to keep out to sea and weather it, were by the violence of the storm driven back, when they were too far embayed to weather Wintertonness, and so were forced to run West, all shifting for themselves as well as they could: some ran away for Lynn-Deeps, but few of them (the night being dark) could find their way thither; some, but very few, rid it out at a distance; the rest being above 140 sail, were all driven on shore and dashed to pieces, and very few of the people on board were saved. At the very same unhappy juncture, a fleet of loaded ships coming from the North and just crossing the same bay, were forcibly driven into it, not able to weather the Ness, and were involved in the same ruin that the light fleet was; also some coasting vessels laden with corn from Lynn and Wells, and bound for Holland, were, with the same unhappy luck, just come out to begin their voyage, and some of them lay at anchor: these also met with the same misfortune; so that in the whole above 200 sail of ships and above 1000 people, were lost in the disaster of that one miserable night. A misfortune somewhat similar, happened in 1790.

In this town was born Arthur Wilson, Efq. who wrote the life and reign of King James I. [printed 1653] with fo much freedom, that inftead of a hiftory, he is faid to have written a pafquinade. He was an attendant for many years upon Robert D'Evereux, Earl of Effex, and afterwards fteward to Robert Earl of Warwick, who are much favoured in his hiftory, now almoft forgotten. He died at Felftead in Effex, 1652.

Dr. Thomas Soame was born in Yarmouth: He was the fon of a fifherman, but defcended of an eminent family of that name; his coufin, John Soame, being a man of fo great an eftate, that in 1648 he paid a compofition of 1430l. for it, and was then dwelling at Burnham, in this county. After paffing through his fchool education, he was bred up in academic learning in Peter-houfe, Cambridge, where his uncle, Robert Soame, was Mafter, and being admitted into holy orders, became Minifter of Staines, in Middlefex, and Prebendary of Windfor. He was, in the times of rebellion, a firm loyalift, and fo much compaffionated his Majefty's wade in his war with the Parliament, that he was not mindful of his own; for he fent all he had to the King; fo that when the Rebels came to plunder him, they found nothing to take but himfelf; which they accordingly did, and imprifoned him firft in Ely-houfe, and then in Newgate and in the Fleet. He died not long before the reftoration of Charles II.

A Mrs. Cromwel lived many years in this town, and died here at an advanced age, about the year 1750, unmarried:—She boasted of being lineally descended from Oliver Cromwel, whom she is said not less to have resembled, in the hard forbidding, and shrewd cast of her features, than in that daring and resolute promptness of spirit which subdues the greatest difficulties. She conducted the Salt-works, as might be expected from such a character, with vigor and proportionate success. Henry Cromwel, no relation to Oliver, being High Steward of this place, in 1659, it is very probable she was descended from him, but such innocent vanity, if vanity it be, is very excusable, and it may be doubted which of the two Gentlemen it was the greater honor to claim affinity to—an honest High Steward of Yarmouth, or a successful Usurper of the government of England—and the terror of all surrounding nations.

In the reign of King Charles II. Sir Robert Paston, of Paston, in this county, was from this place created Viscount, and afterwards Earl of Yarmouth; this title becoming extinct, Amelia Sophia de Walmoden, who came into England in 1739, was advanced to the dignity of Baroness and Countess of Yarmouth, by King George II.

During the civil war in the reign of King Charles I. Yarmouth, as well as the whole county of Norfolk, was in the possession of the parliament. Oliver Cromwel died September 3, 1658, and at an assembly of the Corporation of this Borough in November following, a committee was ordered to draw up an address to Richard Cromwel, who it was expected would succeed to the protectorship of the kingdom. In this address Oliver was called the *" Good"* and the *" Great man,"* it lamented that *" The Captain of " the Lord's Host was fallen in Israel,"* and the oppressed loyalists were stigmatized by the names of *" Sons of " Belial,"* and *" children of darkness,"* who had endeavored to cut off this *" Captain of the Lord's Host."* before his time, that he might not go down to his grave in peace. But this fulsome fanatical cant, and the flattering expectations entertained by those who drew up the address, were but of short duration, for upon the restoration in 1660, the town (having no doubt chosen another committee) thought proper to send a congratulatory address to Charles II. to return the Fee-farm purchased of the parliament, with the arrears due; and further to ingratiate themselves with the King, they presented him with 500l. as a mark of their loyalty. And on the 3d of January following it was ordered that the name of Henry Cromwel, as High Steward of Yarmouth, should be defaced and erased out of the Records of the town; that the address to Richard Cromwel, the late *pretended Protector*, be utterly disclaimed, obliterated and made void, and the ordinance made for the presenting thereof, be defaced to all intents and purposes. By these means the addressers to Richard Cromwel, seem to have purchased the favors of Charles II. for in 1663 he granted the Corporation a new Charter, with more extensive privileges than formerly.

An Account of the Plants growing on the Beach at YARMOUTH.

THE Study of Botany offers no speculation more curious than the attachment of plants, and the vegetable societies, as they may be called, formed by the means of this connection.

The sea-coast of Yarmouth, for about two miles each way, is nearly a level common, elevated between two and three yards above high-water mark. From the verdant edge of this common to the sea is a gentle slope, composed of a deep fine sand, intermixed with great quantities of loose pebbles called *shingle*. As the tides are here uncommonly low, the highest not rising six feet, the distance from high to low water-mark is but a few yards. From high water to the turf of the common is somewhat further; and it is this apparently desart slip of ground to which the present botanical observations are confined. The beach to the Southward of the town is principally our field, as being the most regular formed.

BUNIAS CAKILE, *Sea Rocket*, in many places approaches nearest to the water, striking its fibrous roots into the loose sand, and harbouring between the stones. Its purplish flowers, resembling those of the small kind of stock, enliven the bare spot on which it grows.

SALSOLA KALI, *Prickly Glasswort*, is here but sparingly found, accompanying the former. It grows

more

more plentifully on the banks of the river Yare, near its mouth.

ARUNDO ARENARIA, *Sea Reed-Grass* or *Marrum*, grows somewhat higher, in scattered tufts, forming little hillocks of sand. It is this property of binding the sand by its deep matted roots, which renders it so valuable on the coasts of England and Holland, which are protected from the ocean by ranges of sand-hills. At Caister, two miles North of Yarmouth, begins a line of these hills, of considerable height, on which this grass grows abundantly.

ARENARIA PEPLOIDES, *Sea Chick-weed*, remarkable for the depth and length to which it runs its roots, is found first sparingly, but afterwards in such plenty, that its broad stiff leaves make their chief verdure of the sandy beach near its junction with the turf of the common.

ERYNGIUM MARITIMUM, *Eryngo*, or *Sea Holly*. This singular and beautiful plant grows in an irregular scattered manner on the beach, and also strays higher on the common, where it is most naked and sandy.

CAREX ARENARIA, *Sea-Carex*. This where it begins forms a regular line at an equal distance from the sea, first thinly covering the sand, but growing thicker and thicker as one proceeds higher. Its horizontal creeping roots, and frequent shoots, bind the sand in the manner of the Reed-grass.

CONVOLVULUS SOLDANELLA, *Sea Bindweed* or *Scottish Scurvy-grass*, grows most plentifully at the edge

edge of the junction of the beach with the common, or upon the bareft fpots of the latter, laying its large and beautiful flowers upon the naked fand. It is really furprifing to fee fo fine a flower growing abundantly upon fo expofed and barren a foil.

ONONIS REPENS, *Creeping Reftharrow.* This grows thinly on the beach, but copioufly on the fandy parts of the common, running its ftrong roots very far into the loofe foil.

GALIUM VERUM, *Ladies Bed-ftraw.* This appears thin and fcattered about the junction of the beach with the common, but afterwards becomes fo plentiful as to form the chief covering of the fandieft fide of the common, fcenting the air with its ftrong perfume when it flower.

Thefe are plants which may be confidered as properly belonging to the fandy flope of land, from highwater mark to the level of the verdant common, here called the *Denes.* Some others occafionally ftray into it, among which have been found the *Hypochæris radicata, Long-rooted Hawkweed,* and *Cerafium arvenfe, Corn Moufe-ear Chickweed;* but thefe are to be confidered as cafual guefts. It is obfervable, that of thofe above enumerated, only the two firft are annuals; the reft are all furnifhed with very ftrong running roots, peculiarly adapted to the fituation, and ferving a moft ufeful purpofe in confining the loofe foil, which would elfe be torn away by the violence of the wind and waves.

Obfervations

Observations on the Annual Passage of Herrings.

THE herrings are found on the East side of the Atlantic, or rather in the North sea, in the favourable month of June, about the Islands of Shetland, whence they proceed down the Orkneys, and then dividing, they surround the British Islands, and unite again off the land's end in September; the united shoal then steers in a south west direction across the Atlantic. They arrive off Georgia and Carolina about the latter end of January, and in Virginia about February; coasting thence, Eastward to New England, they divide, and go into all the bays, rivers, creeks and even small streams of water, in amazing quantities, and continue spawning in the fresh water until the latter end of April, when the old fish return into the sea where they steer northward, and arrive at Newfoundland in May, whence they proceed in a north-west direction, again across the Atlantic, and re-visit the Shetland Islands in June—It has been observed, that their going sooner or later up the American Rivers depends upon the warmth or coolness of the season; that if a few warm days invite them up, and cool weather succeeds, it totally checks their passage, until more warm weather returns. From all these circumstances, it is thought, that a certain degree of warmth is peculiarly agreeable to them, which they endeavour to enjoy by changing their latitude according to the distance of the Sun. Thus they are found in the

British

British Channel in the moderately warm month of September, but leave it when the Sun is at too great a distance, and push forward to a more agreeable climate: When the weather in America becomes too warm in May, they steer a course to the cooler northern seas, and by a prudent change of place, perpetually enjoy that temperature of climate which is best adapted to their nature.

American Philosophical Society.—vol. 2. 1786.

The manner of fishing for and curing Herrings, at Yarmouth.

THE Merchants fit out pretty large decked boats or vessels, usually from 40 to 50 tons burden, each of which has a master, mate, hawseman, waleman, netropeman, and netstowerman, besides 5 or 6 labourers, called capsternmen, who all engage to serve the whole fishing Season, viz. from about the 20th of September to the 22d of November, at certain wages, besides a reward of so much per last, to the master, mate, hawseman, and waleman for every last of Herrings caught during the season; and the boat being victualled and having several tons of salt on board, proceeds, sometimes a few, at other times 10 or 12 leagues from the shore, and about the close of day they strike or take down two of her masts, and put out the nets, which are all fastened to ropes called warropes, near the thickness of a man's wrist, joined one at the end of another, to the length of about 700

fathoms,

fathoms, or 1400 yards, and faftened to the boat's bow or head, which (while the nets are out) is always againft the wind, and the veffel being gently driven by the wind and tide aftern, or backwards, the war-ropes, with the nets thereto fixed, are kept ftraight out the full length of the war-ropes, and hindered from entangling or driving together, and the weight of the nets and ropes in the water keep the veffel's head to windward, and while fhe thus flowly drives aftern, the war-ropes and nets, fo faftened to her bow, are very flowly drawn after her, and the herrings getting their heads through the mefhes of the nets, ftick by the gills, and can neither thruft their bodies through, or get their heads back (1); after the nets have laid in the fea the greater part of the night, they are hauled in, and when a confiderable quantity is caught, the boat returns to Yarmouth Roads and delivers them at the Beach, and taking in a further fupply of provifions goes to fea again, and fo continues during the whole fifhing feafon.

If the boatmafter has not an opportunity of returning to Yarmouth the following day, to deliver his herrings, they are falted on board, and perhaps kept a week or ten days before they are landed, when they are taken to the fifh-houfes and again flightly falted, (2) and after lying about 24 hours upon the fifh-houfe

(1) The Mackrel are caught in a fimilar manner, tho' a fleet of Mackrel nets extends much more than twice the length of a fleet of Herring nets.

(2) A ton of falt cures about 4 lafts of Herrings.

house floor they are well washed, by the Towers, (3) in large vatts filled with fresh water; they are then spitted through the head upon spits about four feet long, and the size of a man's thumb, by the Rivers, and hung up by the Towers, in the fishhouse, generally a large lofty building from 40 to 50 feet high, fitted up with baulks and splines (called loves) at proper distances from each other to receive the ends of the spits, which are placed across the same in regular order, one above another, from the very top of the building down to within about seven feet of the floor. As soon as this is completed, many wood fires are made under them, and continued day and night, with some little intermissions, for about a month, by which time the herrings are properly smoaked and dried for foreign markets, when they are taken down and packed in barrels, of 10,000 each, for exportation or home consumption.

This branch of trade is of great importance to the nation, for when in a flourishing state it employed more than 200 fishing vessels, and in some successful years 70,000 barrels have been exported, exclusive of the home consumption, which may be averaged at 15,000 yearly. This fishery gives bread to some for the whole, to others for a great part of the year, to about 2,000 Fishermen and 4,000 Braiders, Beetsters, (4) Towers, Rivers, Ferry-men, Carpenters, Caulkers, Spinners, &c. including Seamen to transport the

(3) Towers. Men employed in the Fish-house to cure and hang them.

(4) Beetsters, Women employed to mend the nets:

THE NORFOLK TOUR.

the herrings chiefly to Italy, and produces in a succefsful year, at a moderate computation (exclufive of a very large fum paid for freights at foreign ports to our fhips) a clear gain to the nation of upwards of 70,000l. befides, the 15,000 barrels confumed at home, are fo much gain to the nation, as they add to the ftock of provifions.

A letter from Aberdeen dated June 10, 1788 fays; ' Laft week was caught by the Fifhermen near Don ' mouth, a herring of a moft uncommon fize, it mea- ' fured from the fnout to the tip point of the tail two ' feet, round the thickeft part of the body 15 inches, ' immediately above the tail 4 inches 1-half, and ' weighed 5 pounds 4 ounces.'—Thofe of the largeft fize caught near Yarmouth, do not meafure more than 12 inches in length, 6 inches 1-half round, and weigh 9 ounces: But Mr. Herriot a celebrated Mathematician, affures us, that in the months of February, March, April and May, Herrings on the coafts of Virginia, are caught 18, 20 and even 24 inches long.

The Dutch fix their entering on the Herring Fifhery upon their own coafts to A. D. 1163. In the old Chronicle of John Francis le Petit, there is a very diftinct account of this matter. It is there faid, that the inhabitants of Ziriczee, in the Ifle of Zealand, were the firft who barrelled Herring, and that afterwards the people of Biervliet found the method of preferving them more effectually, by taking fome fmall bones out of their heads, which operation they call *Kaken*, i. e. gilling, or jawing the Herring.

William

William Beackels John, a Swede, who died in 1397 has been suppofed to have invented the art of pickling herrings. But profeffor Springel has shewn that herrings were caught at *Gernemve*, i. e. Yarmouth, fo early as the year 1283; nay, in Leland's Collect. vol. 3. p. 173, we meet with a proof, that pickled herrings were fold in 1273; and there are extant German Records which fpeak of them in 1236.

Nafhe, a cotemporary writer with, and an imitator of the more celebrated Tom Coriat of peregrinating memory, in enumerating the excellencies of Herrings fays, a red herring is wholefome in a frofty morning; it is moft precious fifh merchandife, becaufe it can be carried through all Europe; no where are they fo well cured as at Yarmouth. The poorer fort make it three parts of their fuftenance. It is every man's money from the King to the Peafant. The fifhery is a great nurfery for feamen. The round or cob dried and beaten to powder is a cure for the ftone. Rub a quart pot or any meafure round about the mouth with a red herring, the beer fhall never foam or froth in it. A herring drawn on the ground, will lead hounds a falfe fcent. A broiled herring is good for the rheumatifm. The fifhery brings more fhips to Yarmouth than affembled at Troy to fetch back Helen. He adds, Wife men of Greece, in the mean while to fwagger fo about a W- - - e! At the end of what he calls his play in Praife of Red Herrings, he boafts of being the firft author who had wrote in the praife of fifh or fifhermen. Of the latter he wittily and farcaftically fays, " For " your feeing wonders in the deep, you may be the
" fons

"sons and heirs of the Prophet Jonas;— you are all
"Cavaliers and Gentlemen, since the King of fishes
"chose you for his subjects;—for your selling smoke
"you may be Courtiers;—for your keeping fasting
"days Friar Observants; and lastly,—look in what
"town there is the sign of the three Mariners, the
"huff-capped drink in that house you shall be sure of
"always."

This very scarce Pamphlet is re-printed in the 6th vol. of the Harleian Miscellany.

CAISTER, next YARMOUTH.

IN the celebrated Notitia Imperii, or survey of the Roman Empire, published by Pancirollus in 1593, it appears that the commander of the Stablesian Horse, under the * Count of the Saxon shore in Britain, was stationed at a place called *Garianonum*, (that is the Mouth of the Garienis or Yare) but where that ancient Fortress was situated, authors are not agreed. The venerable Camden places it at Burgh-Castle, in Suffolk, and says that Yarmouth rose out of its ruins, but

* The Count of the Saxon shore, had in all under his command 2,200 foot and 200 horse, stationed at different places on the coasts of Norfolk, Suffolk, Essex and Kent. The Roman troops in Brittain consisted of 5 legions, which with their auxiliaries, amounted to about 14,000 horse, and 72,000 foot; these were distributed into near 150 fortresses.- This great military establishment seems to indicate, either that the Romans esteemed England to be a very valuable part of their unwieldy Empire, or the natives did not patiently bear the Roman yoke.

but Sir Henry Spelman contends for its having been at Caister. Where Camden and Spelman differ in opinion on a topographical subject, who shall decide?—There can be no doubt of the Romans having occupied both stations, though very probably at different times, as each haven became more or less navigable. Those who contend for the greater antiquity of Burgh-Castle remark, that parts of anchors and other pieces of iron, which could have been in use for maritime purposes only, have at various times been found in the marshes adjoining, and even in the walls of the Castle, but surely such evidences by no means warrant this conclusion, as they tend but to strengthen an opinion generally admitted, that an arm of the sea which formerly overflowed the marshes between Yarmouth and Norwich, must nearly have reached Burgh-Castle: and as the coins frequently dug up at Caister, in a place called the East-field Bloody furlong, are acknowledged to be of more ancient date, than those found at Burgh-Castle, it may be inferred, so far as the evidence of coins are admitted, that Caister was really the *ancient Garianonum*. It is the generally received opinion, that the Yare formerly had two channels by which it entered the British ocean, one to the North, at Cockle-water or Grubb's-haven by Caister, the other to the South near Gorleston. The channel by Caister was in the infancy of Yarmouth, esteemed to be the best harbour, and the inhabitants accordingly built the town further to the North than it now stands; but the North-east winds prevailing upon this part of the coast, formed a sand-bank, which choaking

ing up the channel at Caifter, reached along the fhore nearly to Gorlefton, and in procefs of time becoming firm land, the inhabitants deferted the ruined channel at Caifter, and removed to the Southern one near Gorlefton, at which time it is moft probable that Burgh-Caftle was built and became the *new Gariano-num* of the Romans. Thefe two ftations were extremely well fituated on each fide of the river, upon fine eminences in the fight of each other, and admirably well calculated to defend the fhore againft the predatory defcents of the Saxons, who upon the decline of the Roman Empire, became very bold and dexterous pirates, paying frequent and moft unwelcome vifits to the inhabitants of Norfolk, Suffolk, Effex and Kent; the the coafts of which were called the Saxon-fhore, from being oppofite to the people of Germany called Saxons.

Caifter was the ancient feat of the family of Faftolff, Captain Grofe took a view of this place in 1771 and obferves, that from the materials, which are Englifh brick, it cannot be older than the beginning of the reign of Henry VI. [1449] when that manor belonged to Sir John Faftolff a General and Knight of the Garter. The Manor of Caifter had been in the family ever fince the 9th of Edward II. [1305] and it is more than probable, fome houfe or caftle might then be ftanding. Tanner mentions one as early as Edward I. [1274].

William de Botoner, alias de Worcefter, in his Itinerary relates, that this caftle was befieged twice in the

the reign of Edward IV. (between 1469 and 1483) the firſt time (1469) by Thomas Mowbray, Duke of Norfolk, and the ſecond by Lord Scales. In the account of theſe tranſactions, the foundation of the preſent Caſtle is mentioned as being directed by the laſt will of Sir John Faſtolff. During the time of theſe ſieges, it belonged to John Paſton, Eſq. who was one of the executors by the will of Sir John Faſtolff.

In the collection of letters publiſhed by Sir John Fenn, of tranſactions during this dark period of Engliſh Hiſtory, he has preſerved one dated Sept. 1469, relating to the firſt of theſe ſieges; it is from John Paſton, Eſq. to Sir John Paſton, Knight, and is thus expreſſed, "We were ſore lack of victuals (and) " gunpowder, men's hearts lack of ſurety of reſ- " cue, (were) driven thereto to take appoint- " ment!"

The caſtellated manſion of Caiſter, tradition ſays was finiſhed by Sir John Faſtolff with a part of the money which he received for the ranſom of John II. Duke of Alençon, whom he took priſoner at the battle of *Verneuil, in 1429, called the battle of Herrings, becauſe, it being the time of Lent, great part of the convoy which Sir John was conducting to the army, then beſieging Orleans, conſiſted of Herrings. In this battle Sir John with about 2,500 Engliſh, defeated

* The French forces at this battle have been variouſly repreſented by, the French writers, ſome calling them 4,000, and others between nine and ten thouſand.

feated near ten thoufand French and Scots, of whom 2,500 were killed, and many perfons of diftinction, with others, taken prifoners, without the lofs of one Englifhman of eminence. Tradition fays, that after the battle the Englifh marched twice round the walls of Orleans, infultingly crying, *frefh herrings to fell*, which provoked the French to make two defperate fallies, and proving fuccefsful, they were infpired with fuch a new fpirit of confidence and refolution, as afterwards turned the fortune of war in their favor. But the enthufiafm and military exploits, of the famous Joan of Arc, who at this time made her appearance, had undoubtedly a more powerful effect upon the lively minds of Frenchmen, than any filly taunt that could be ufed by the Englifh foldiery.

The ruins of Caifter fhew it to have been both capacious and ftrong. It was moated round, but the moat is now filled up, except on the Weft, which was the grand entrance. The houfe formed a rectangled parallelogram, the South and North fides longer than the Eaft and Weft, the ftables in the front, the beft rooms on the right hand of the fquare, under which was a noble vault, and over it probably the great hall. The embattled brick tower at the North Weft corner is ftanding above 100 feet high, and on an arch over a bow window in the infide of the ruins, was the *Arms of Sir J. Faftolff furrounded with the garter,

neatly

---

* They were taken down a few years ago, and depofited in the Library of his Excellency the late Earl of Buckinghamfhire, at Blickling.

neatly carved in ſtone. To the tower adjoins a dining parlour 59 feet long and 28 broad. The great fire-place of which is ſtill to be ſeen. At preſent only the Weſt and North walls are remaining, together with the tower. The South and Eaſt ſides are nearly levelled with the ground.

Eaſt from the Caſtle ſtood the *College, forming three ſides of a ſquare larger than the former, with two round towers; the whole now converted into barns and ſtables. The Caſtle moat is ſaid to have communicated with a creek which was navigable to the ocean; and, adjoining to the farm-houſe is a ſmall building, called the barge-hóuſe, now uſed as a ſtable, in which is ſhewn the crown of a large arch of about 8 feet diameter, which muſt have been capable of receiving a boat of conſiderable burden.

FASTOLFF (John) Knight and Knight Banneret, a valiant and renowned General, Governor and Nobleman in France, during our conqueſts in that kingdom, under King Henry IV. V. and VI. of England, and Knight Companion of the moſt noble order of the Garter, was the ſon of John Faſtolff Eſq. and Mary the daughter of Nicholas Park, Eſq. his wife. He was deſcended of an ancient and famous Engliſh family in the county of Norfolk; which had flouriſhed there, and in other parts of the kingdom, in very honourable diſtinction before the conqueſt: and from a train of illuſtrious anceſtors, many of them dignified with

---

* This College is ſaid to have been founded by John Paſton, ſen. Eſq. in 1464.

with the honour of knighthood, invested with very eminent employments, and possessed of extensive patrimonies. Sir John the subject of this account was born in the year 1377, either at Caister, or in Yarmouth, at the former of which he died Nov. 6, 1459, aged 82, and was buried at the Abbey church of St. Bennet in the Holme.

The first honourable public employment in which Sir John seems to have been engaged, was his attendance upon Thomas of Lancaster, afterwards Duke of Clarence, and second son of King Henry IV. when he wa Lord Lieutenant of Ireland, in 1401, at which time Sir Jo n was in the 25th year of his age. In '408 he was marr..d in ..eland to a rich young widow of quality, named Melicent, Lady Castlecomb, daughter of Robert Lord Tibitot, and relict of Sir Stephen Scrope, Knight. This connection we may reasonably believe engaged his settlement in that kingdom, or upon his estate in Norfolk, till his appointment to a command of some forces, or to a place of trust under the Regency in France, where he continued, according to the testimony of Caxton, the first English Printer, ' to signalize his military abilities for forty years,' great part of the time under John Plantagenet, the Great Duke of Bedford, and Regent in France, during which he was made Knight Banneret in the field of battle, Baron of France, Knight of the Garter in England, Steward or Marshall of the Regent's household, the King's Lieutenant of Normandy for one year, and after Governor of Anjou and Maine, for many years, Captain of the city of Mans, and the towns of Alençon, Mayn, Fresney, in Vicont, for 14 years, likewise Caen, Verneuil and Harfleur, some years, the last of which places he valiantly and successfully defended when besieged by the French: And when finally settled at home, he was constantly exercised in acts of hospitality, munificence and charity, a founder of religious buildings and other stately edifices, a generous patron of worthy and learned men, and a public benefactor to the pious and the poor.

Mr. Hume observes, that there is no part of the English History since the Conquest so obscure, so uncertain, so little authentic, or consistent, as that of the wars between the two Roses, and it is remarkable that this profound darkness falls upon us just on the eve of the restoration of Letters, and when the art of printing was already known in Europe (but not in England). It was in these turbulent and unenlightened times that Sir John Fastolff lived, and it cannot be a matter of much surprise, that his real character has been misunderstood or misrepresented, when we know so little of our general history.

At the time when Prince Henry is said to have commited many excesses unbecoming his high station, our hero was honourably employed in France. In the play, Sir John Falstaff is a man of mean, necessitous, shifting circumstances throughout, Fastolff in record was richly possessed of lands and estates in several places, from his youth, Falstaff in the poet's account was near three-score before the battle of Shrewsbury,

Fastolff

Faſtolff in hiſtory, not above twenty-ſix. The theatrical Falſtaff ends his life ſoon after his princely companion aſcends the throne, and before he goes into France; but the hiſtorical Faſtolff demoſtratively ſurvived King Henry V. no leſs than thirty-ſeven years.

Drayton in his Poly-Olbion, on comparing Sir John Faſtolff with Sir Philip Hall, ſays

Strong Faſtolff with this man compare we may;
By Sals'bury who, oft being ſeriouſly employ'd,
In many a brave attempt the gen'ral foe annoy'd;
With excellent ſucceſs in Maine, and Anjou fought,
And many a Bulwark there into our keeping brought;
And choſen to go forth with Vaudemont in war,
Moſt reſolutely took proud *Renate Duke of Barre.

In one of Mr. Aſhmole's choice old volumes of MSS. there is a conciſe character of our hero, written in the reign of King Henry VII. by Sir Thomas Wriotheſley, then King of Arms, wherein he is called, ' a rich knight and a grete bilder; having bilded ' Caſter-hall in Norfolk, a royal palace in Southwork, ' and another in Yermouth; and a ſpeciall goode ' maiſter to the officers of armes.'

There is not a character throughout Shakſpeare's Plays that has afforded ſo much ſatisfaction and delight,

---

* Renate, after the ſiege of Orleans brought ſuccours to Charles VII. the young King of France.

light, both on the stage and in the closet, as that of *Sir John Falstaff*, nor one that has occasioned so much controversy to identify the real person of this dramatic hero: Whether it was originally drawn for Sir John Oldcastle, Lord Cobham, (the first Martyr to the Protestant cause in England) or not, seems foreign to the present inquiry, which attempts only to prove, from the best authorities extant, that in no one circumstance do the poetical character of Falstaff, as drawn by Shakspeare, and the historical character of Sir John Fastolff, of Caister, agree, or that would lead an ignorant reader to confound them. but a little quibble which makes some conformity in their names.

Every one has seen upon the stage *Sir John Falstaff* exhibited in the various characters of an old humorous, vapouring, cowardly, lewd, lying, drunken and necessitous debauchee about Prince Henry's court. But history informs us, from the various *legacies which Sir John Fastolff left by his last will, that he died immensely rich; to enumerate them would too much extend this article, and we shall observe only, that he left 4000l. in the hands of Thomas Howes, his confessor, to lay out in repairs of churches and collegiate houses, and his executors sold 3033 ounces of silver—— That he lived in great splendor and magnificence, is evident from the many houses he built and occupied— that he was sincerely pious and benevolent, may be admitted from his donations to religious institutions, and his attention to the poor, during his life and at his death — that he was valiant is demonstrative

from

* At this time money was seven times its present value.

THE NORFOLK TOUR.

from the whole tenor of his military conduct for forty years, and the testimony of the best judges, his cotemporaries — and that his character and abilities as an accomplished Gentleman were held in high estimation, need no other evidence than the certainty of his possessing a great share of confidence and favor from three succeeding Kings. If these inferences are fairly drawn from the history of the life of John Fastolff, it will no longer be believed that Shakspeare's character of his fat Knight, had any reference or bore any resemblance to Sir John Fastolff, of Norfolk. But as light ridicule frequently sticks closer to character than the most honourable truths, it has been the fate of our Knight to be remembered for imputed follies and crimes which he never committed, and forgotten for those meritorious actions which history has truly recorded of him.

The theatrical character of *Falstaff*, has been thus elegantly and forcibly drawn by Dr. Johnson. Falstaff unimitated, unimitable Falstaff, how shall I describe thee? thou compound of sense and vice; of sense which may be admired, but not esteemed; of vice which may be despised, but hardly detested: Falstaff is a character loaded with faults, and with those faults which naturally produce contempt. He is a thief and a glutton, a coward and a boaster, always ready to cheat the weak, and prey upon the poor, to terrify the timerous, and insult the defenceless. At once obsequious and malignant, he satirizes in their absence those whom he lives by flattering. He is familiar with the

Prince only as an agent of vice, but of this familiarity he is so proud, as not only to be supercilious and haughty with common men, but to think his interest of importance to the Duke of Lancaster. Yet the man thus corrupt, thus despicable, makes himself necessary to the Prince that despises him, by the most pleasing of all qualities, perpetual gaiety; by an unfailing power of exciting laughter, which is the more freely indulged, as his wit is not of the splendid or ambitious kind, but consists in easy scapes and sallies of levity, which make sport but raise no envy. It must be observed, that he is stained with no enormous or sanguinary crimes, so that his licentiousness is not so offensive but that it may be borne for his mirth.

Of the Comedy of the Merry Wives of Windsor, Mr. Rowe has preserved a tradition, that it was written at the command of Queen Elizabeth, who was so delighted with the character of Falstaff, that she wished it to be diffused through more plays; but suspecting that it might pall by continued uniformity, directed the poet to diversify his manner, by shewing him in love. No task is harder than that of writing to the ideas of another. Shakspeare knew what the Queen, if the story be true, seems not to have known, that by any real passion of tenderness, the selfish craft, the careless jollity, and the lazy luxury of Falstaff must have suffered so much abatement, that little of his former cast could have remained. Falstaff could not love, but by ceasing to be Falstaff. He could only *counterfeit* love, and his professions could

be

be prompted, not by the hope of pleasure but of money.

This Comedy is remarkable for the variety and number of the personages, who exhibit more characters appropriated and discriminated, than can be found in any other play, and its general power, by which all works of genius shall finally be tried, is such, that perhaps it never yet had reader or spectator who did not think it too soon at an end.

BURGH-CASTLE

IS in the county of Suffolk, at the distance of three miles S. West of Yarmouth, and stands upon a hill adjoining the South bank of the *Waveney, near the junction of that river with the Thyrn and Weasum. Its elevated situation commands an extensive view of the hundreds of East and West Flegg, as far as Acle on the West; an extent of coast of about twelve miles from North to South, and seems to have been admirably chosen to alarm and defend this part of the country, from the sudden invasions of the pirates of ancient times, as well as against the warlike Iceni, who reluctantly submitted to the dominion of the Romans, and often by force of arms attempted in vain to expel

* Its standing upon the South bank of the Waveney, not the Yare, spoils the Etymology, and thence leads us to imagine, that it never could have been the ancient Garianonum of the Romans, though there is no doubt of its having been a Roman fortress.

expel them. It is a four-sided oblong pitched camp, crowned with a wall inclosing an area of 4 acres, 2 roods, and, including the walls, 6 A. 2 R. 20 P. The walls, composed of rows of brick and flint alternately, are nine feet in thickness and fourteen feet high: The East side is the most perfect, and has four flanking towers, now in part standing, the two nearest each end, being 55 yards from each other, and the two intermediate ones 110 yards asunder. The North and South sides are each 107 yards.

The country from Caister to Burgh-castle, is one continued plain for three miles in length; within this space lies Breydon-water (Breydon is a Saxon word signifying broad-water) and the whole level carries evident marks of having been covered by the ocean, the mouth of the Yare, at that time being an Æstuary, or arm of the sea. This is the traditional account, in support of which, Mr. Ives published a history of Burgh-castle, with an ancient map of the country as it is *supposed* to have appeared in the year one thousand. And a manuscript copied by him, says, that about the time of Edward the Confessor [1040] the sea retreated from the sand, at the mouth of the Æstuary, on which Yarmouth now stands, and the whole level of the fens from Yarmouth to Norwich, was then an arm of the sea, entering by the mouth of the Hierus.

CASTOR at present an inconsiderable village, situated about four miles South west of Norwich, upon the little river Tesse; according to Camden and other respectable

respectable historians, was formerly the *Venta Ice-norum*, the moſt flouriſhing city, or principal ſtation of the Romans in the country of the Iceni, called afterwards Eaſt Anglia. We need not wonder ſays Camden, that of the three Venta in Britain, this ſhould have loſt its name, when it has loſt its very being, for now, ſetting aſide the broken walls, the remains of four gates and two towers, which were viſible in the year 1749, and the Roman coins, which are at this day frequently dug up, there are not any traces of its ancient magnificence left: The deſcription of this place agrees exactly with thoſe given by Polybius, Vegetius and others, concerning the ancient way of encampment among the Romans; the places alſo for the four gates, are ſtill manifeſtly to be ſeen. The Porta Pretoria looked towards the Eaſt, oppoſite to which (without the Porta Decumana, and cloſe by the river ſide) there ſtill remains ſome ruins of a tower. The walls incloſing the camp were of flint and very large brick.

Skinner ſays in his Etymologicon: "*Caſtor in Com.* " *Norf. olim.* VENTA ICENORUM: *ex cujus Ruinis* " *orta eſt Norwich civitas*:" however, except ſome few ruins of the camp, there is not now (1794) the leaſt trace of any thing remarkable remaining. The camp lies near a furlong S. W. from the town of Caſtor, and leads you by a gentle deſcent down to the little river Teſſe, which at the time of the eſtabliſhment of the Roman Camp here, and when the ſea, it is thought, overflowed all the level land now between Yarmouth and Norwich, was very probably a river of

---

* Blomefield was of opinion that the Venta Icenorum was at North Elmham.

confiderable breadth, and that it was not called the Teffe until it approached the Roman Camp at Tafeburgh, three or four miles higher.

The figure of the Camp is a parallelogram, whofe two longeft fides are each 440 yards, and its ends, or two fhorter fides, 360 yards each, without-fide the rampart and ditch, on the infide of which it is but 392 yards in length, and the breadth 264. The breadth of the foffe and rampart is in fome places 48 yards, and in others not above 30. The whole ground taken up including the foffe and rampart being 32 acres, 2 rood and 36 poles. The area within the ditch and rampart is 21 acres, 1 rood and 21 poles. The ruins of the two old towers, one on the North fide, and the other at the weft end, were remaining in 1749. They were built in a manner perhaps peculiar to the Romans *at that time*. They began firft with a layer of bricks laid flat as in pavements: on that they placed a layer of clay and marle mixed together, and of the fame thicknefs as the bricks; then a layer of bricks, afterwards of clay and marle, then of bricks again, making in the whole three layers of bricks and two of clay: over this were placed bricks and lime 29 inches, the outfide being faced with bricks cut in fquares, then bricks and clay again, *ftratum fuper ftratum*, as high as the old ruins now remain ftanding.

The mortar is ftill extremely hard: It is a compofition of lime, fand and afhes. The Roman bricks were made of two different forts of clay mixt; when burnt one appeared red the other white, and when Mr. Arderon

Arderon examined them in 1749 were exceedingly hard and folid, and he fays, very little worfe than when they were laid down. They meafured 18 inches by 12, and 2 inches thick. Philos. Tranfactions, 1749, No. 493.

The Emperor Claudius Cæfar, in the 46th year of the chriftian æra, gained confiderable footing in this part of Britain, and his Lieutenant Oftorius having fubdued the Iceni, the invaders fettled here, raifed camps, appointed colonies, and fixed ftations, principally upon the banks of rivers, to defend their conquefts againft foreign invafion, and the attempts of the natives to regain their freedom. Thus landing at the mouth of the river Yare, they built a ftrong caftle upon the firft elevated fituation, on the South fide, placed a garrifon of Stablefian horfe there, and named it *Garianonum*, (from its fituation on the Garienis or Yare) fome remains of which are ftill very perfect: the town that belonged to it affuming the Saxon name Burgh, from this fortification, and is at this day called Burgh Caftle. Oppofite to this, on the Northern fide of the Garienis, they erected another fortification, and called it Caifter: And following the courfe of the river till it divided into two ftreams, they turned with that on the Southern fide, and at the firft ftreight, where the paffage could eafily be defended, fixed this camp, which for its dimenfions and ftrength was named Caftrum, or *The Camp*, by way of eminence.

It was about the year 418 after Chrift, that the Romans in general quitted Britain; but having afterwards

wards sent some small detachments of troops to assist in repelling the incursions of the Picts, and the predatory invasions of the Northern pirates, they cannot be said to have finally withdrawn themselves till the year 446,* when, those who remained, and the natives joining together, became one people; Castor being then in a great measure deserted, fell rapidly into decay, and the inhabitants fixing upon the place where Norwich now stands, on account of its being higher ground, on a better stream, and more convenient for fishing, it suddenly rose to great maturity, out of the ruins of Castor, then no longer regarded but as a place of defence, and as such was afterwards held by the Saxon, English and Danish Kings, till Edward the Confessor gave it to the Monastery of St. Edmund's Bury, where it continued with little variation till the Conquest.

The CITY of NORWICH.

THE rise of great towns is owing to such a variety of causes, that it is often difficult satisfactorily to point out the principal one, but with respect to Norwich, there is every reason for believing that the foundation of its present magnitude and opulence is in a great measure to be ascribed to its affording an asylum

---

* In General Roy's military antiquities, it is said, that the FINAL departure of the Romans from Britain was in the year 420, and tho arrival of the Saxons, A. D. 449.

lum to the (a) Dutch and Flemings, who, from the bad policy of the Spanish Court, and the cruelty of the Duke of Alva, were obliged to forsake their native country about the year 1565. These unhappy people, persecuted at home for their religious opinions, found in a foreign country, that to be peaceable citizens is the only test of fidelity required for protection amongst an enlightened people, and in return they introduced the manufacture of bombazines and a variety of worsted stuffs, by which so many families in Norwich have since been enriched, and the population increased, from about (b) 14,840, to 41,051.

It has been said that the city in ancient times was much more populous than it is at present, and that in the year 1348, more than fifty-seven thousand persons died here of the Plague; but, as the walls of Norwich then prescribed its extent, there seems to be sufficient reason for believing this account to be much exaggerated; perhaps it might be true if applied to the city and county of Norfolk. There having been 58 or 60 churches in Norwich, and now only 35, has also been urged as a proof of its former great population,

(a) The number of these People at first permitted to settle here was 330, but in a very short time they amounted to 3925.

(b) In 1377 the inhabitants of several great towns in England were enumerated, when Norwich was found to contain 5,300 people. The muster-roll delivered to government, of men capable of bearing arms in Norwich in 1575, contains 2,120 names. The usual calculation is, that one person in every six, or at least in every seven, in any kingdom or district, is so qualified: whence we are inclined to believe that Norwich at that time did not contain above 14,840 people;

tion, but the decay of churches does not prove the people of former times to have been more numerous, but to have been more devout, or that the inhabitants have changed the modes of their religious worship.

Mr. Hearne says, he believes the city of Norwich was either repaired after some devastation, or else some additions were made to it by Alfred the Great, (i. e. between the years 872 and 899) for, on one of his coins, published by Sir Andrew Fountaine, there is a Monogram, which Mr. Ed. Thevaites, in his notes upon these coins, has ingeniously guessed to be *Civitas Northvicum*.—The inscription is ÆLFRED RE: This reading is certainly *ingenious*, but they who have an opportunity of examining the plate of the coin will find it very difficult to make out, *Civitas Northvicum*, in the Monogram.

An old vulgar distich, handed down to us by tradition, says,

Castor was a City when Norwich was none,
And Norwich was built with Castor stone.

PASSING by those accounts of the origin of this city, which seem calculated rather to amuse the credulous than satisfy candid and rational investigation, we shall quote Camden's opinion on this subject, who observes, that, " so far is the city of Norwich from " having been built either by Cæsar, or Guiteline " the Briton, as some fabulous authors assert, that " the word Norwich is not any where to be found be- " fore the Danish wars."

The

The city was burnt and deſtroyed in 1004 by * Swain, the Dane, who returned a ſecond time in 1010, when many of his followers ſettled here, and it increaſed ſo rapidly, that from the Domeſday-book of Edward the Confeſſor, it appears to have contained 1,320 Burgeſſes, and *it is ſaid*, 25 parochial churches. It continued to increaſe till 1075, when Ralph de Waiet, Earl of Norfolk, rebelling againſt William the Conqueror, the caſtle was beſieged and taken, and great part of the city deſtroyed; but ſoon recovering from theſe misfortunes, it again began to flouriſh, and at the time of making the Domeſday-book of the Conqueror in 1086, only eighty-two years after its having been deſtroyed by the Danes, it contained 738 houſes, which at the rate of five perſons to a family, makes 3,690 inhabitants. Upon the Conqueror's death, Roger Bigod held the caſtle for Robert Curthoſe, Duke of Normandy, elder brother of Rufus; waſting the city and county, and plundering all thoſe who refuſed to join with him. This diſpute was compromiſed, and Roger Bigod remained in poſſeſſion of the caſtle, and held it peaceably

---

* Swain, with his whole fleet, is ſaid to have ſailed quite up to the caſtle, the marſhes between it and the ground on which Yarmouth now ſtands, being then covered with water, forming a large arm of the ſea. When the ſmall ſize of the ſhips of thoſe days is conſidered, there is nothing improbable in this relation; which ſeems to acquire conſiderable ſtrength by its being well known, that in the reign of Canute, Norwich was a Fiſhing Town, and it was not likely that Fiſhermen ſhould fix upon a place for their reſidence, which was thirty miles diſtant from the ocean.

ably during this King's reign. The city being once more freed from the evils attending the factious contentions of the Nobles, Herbert de Lofinga, then Bifhop of Thetford, removed the See hither, after having made many unfuccefsful attempts to fix it at the rich abbey at Bury. This event took place April 9, 1094, from which time the city has been daily increafing in wealth, trade, and buildings: And to encourage its growing greatnefs, King Henry I. granted to the citizens the fame liberties and privileges as the citizens of London enjoyed.

In the reign of King Stephen (1172) it was made a corporation, to be governed by bailiffs, in the room of a port-reeve, under which government it had been from the Saxon time; and in the year 1403, the citizens obtained a charter from King Henry IV. for the election of a Mayor, and two Sheriffs yearly, inftead of the bailiffs.

The cities appear by Domefday-book, to have been at the Conqueft, little better than the midling market towns of the prefent time; York itfelf, though it was always the fecond, at leaft the third city in England, and the capital of a great province, which was never thoroughly united with the reft, contained then but 1,418 families. Norwich 738, Exeter 315, Ipfwich 538, Northampton 60, Hertford 146, Canterbury 262, Bath 64, Southampton 84, Warwick 113. Thefe were amongft the moft confiderable in England, and hence it appears, that Norwich was next to York in fize.

The

THE NORFOLK TOUR.

The first predatory incursions of the Danes into Britain were in 789, but their invasion of the kingdom of the East Angles, of which Norfolk was a part, did not take place till 886; when the natives being more anxious for their present interest than for the common safety, entered into a separate treaty with the enemy; and furnished them with horses, which enabled them to make an irruption by land into the kingdom of Northumberland, where they seized the city of York. Hume's Hist. vol. 1.

From this time the Danes were firmly established in Norfolk, particularly the Eastern part of it, and very probably built a Castle, or repaired one, which had been built by the Saxons, when the Roman station at Castor was deserted soon after the year 446. Several reasons are assigned for the Danish invasion,—to revenge themselves for some pretended injuries, or national affronts; though the true motive probably was; England, divided against itself; situated in a happier climate; much richer and in every respect preferable to their own dreary and inhospitable country, presented an inviting prospect to the lawless desires of uncivilized plunderers—When a rich nation loses the power of protecting itself against both internal and external enemies, it will not be long before the former promote its downfall by intestine divisions, and the latter profit by their ingratitude.—It is idle to expect, and most dangerous to depend upon the honour and the law of nations, without the means of inforcing the observance of them.

G Were

Were we not assured that the ancient Danes were more numerous upon the sea than on land, we could not read the history of the eighth, ninth and tenth centuries without observing with surprise, the sea covered with their numerous fleets, (sometimes of 700 sail) and from one end of Europe to the other, the coasts of those countries, now the most powerful, a prey to their depredations. During two hundred years they almost incessantly ravaged England, and at length subdued it. Alfred the Great, about the year 900 having expelled or subjugated the Danes who had invaded England, with some of the more peaceable of them colonized Norfolk, then forming a part of East Anglia, which though their countrymen had made desert, they by peace and industry soon restored to a flourishing condition. The ancient inhabitants had been extirpated, and this Danish colony may be looked up to as the original people, or parent stock, of the present race of Norfolk-men. At the time when the Danes desolated England, the profession of piracy was so far from appearing dishonourable to them, that it was in their eyes the certain, and perhaps the only road, to honours and fortune; for it was wisely contrived, that the word honour, to which so many different ideas are annexed, was among them solely confined to a disregard of danger; and to be the most renowned Pirate of the North was synonymous with being the greatest man in Europe.

The Saxons gave the name to the Castle of Norwich by which the city has ever since been called: They wrote it Nordwic, or, their *d* being pronounced like our *th*,

Northwic,

THE NORFOLK TOUR.

Northwic, fignifying a Northern Caftle, as the Caftle of Norwich is with refpect to the Roman ftation at Caftor. After all the refearches of the moft eminent Antiquarians on this fubject, it muft be acknowledged the evidence amounts to this only, that as the city derives its name from the Caftle, it certainly muft be of lefs antiquity, but as the time when the *firft* Caftle was built cannot be afcertained, it is in vain to attempt fixing the age of the city.

Norwich on account of its trade, wealth, beauty, extent, populoufnefs, the falubrity of the air, the goodnefs of its markets, and the induftry of its inhabitants, is defervedly ranked amongft the moft confiderable cities in Britain. Its Latitude, according to Sir Henry Spelman is 52 degrees 45 minutes, North. Longitude 1. 19 Eaft of the royal obfervatory at Greenwich. It is pleafantly fituated on the fide of a hill, ftretching from North to South, on the banks of the river Wenfum. It is 108 miles from London by Newmarket, 110 by Colchefter, 114 by Bury St. Edmund's; and it is fomewhat remarkable, that Norwich, Bury and Lynn form an equilateral triangle, each fide meafuring 42 miles. It is alfo 43 miles from Ipfwich; and 22 from Yarmouth by land, and 30 by water. It ftands upon more ground than any other city in England, being rather more than one mile and a half in length, from King-ftreet gate to Magdalen-gate, and one mile and a quarter broad from Bifhop-gate to St. Benedict's-gate: towards the South it gradually contracts like a cone, containing little more than King-ftreet and Ber-ftreet, both of them being very long aud populous. It has thirty four churches besides the cathedral, and is encompassed by a ditch and the remains of a flint-stone (a) wall, which was flanked with forty towers, in the ancient method of fortification, and had twelve gates for entrance on all sides, except the East, which is defended by the river Wensum, after running through the city from East to West, and over which there are five stone bridges, Coslany, Black-friars, Fye-bridge, White-friars, and Bishopgate.—Such walls towers and gates as enclosed Norwich, being built before the invention of (b) gunpowder, they have long ceased to be useful in a defensive view, or perhaps to be at all useful; and becoming burdensome to the people to keep in repair, have been suffered to decay, eight of the gates, in the years 1792, 1793 and 1794 were taken down, and two considerable openings made in the walls, one between Ber-street gate and Brazen-doors, the other close to Chapel-field. These additional avenues have undoubtedly their use. And to gentlemen disposed to venerate whatever is antique, let it be hinted, that however obnoxious to their feelings modern improvements may be, nothing on earth is calculated to stand for ever: And that which is now modern, will like the ancients whom they have displaced, in time themselves become antiques. The city is plentifully supplied with

(a) Begun in 1294 and finished in 1310.

(b) The discovery of gunpowder is generally attributed to Schwartz, a Monk of Cologne, but the English Friar, Roger Bacon, was the real discoverer of it some years before, but his humane philosophy prevented him from making the process public.

with fresh water, conveyed through pipes to all parts of it, from the water works at the New-Mills, first erected in 1430, improved in 1695, but not brought to their present perfection before 1720.

'Norwich is governed by a mayor, recorder, steward, two sheriffs, twenty-four aldermen, (of which the mayor is one) and sixty common council-men, a town-clerk, chamberlain, and sword-bearer, attended by officers suitable to the dignity of the city: 'The mayor is elected by the freemen, on the first day of May, and sworn into his office on the guild-day, which is always the Tuesday before midsummer-day, except when midsummer-day falls on a Wednesday, and then the guild is kept on the Tuesday se'nnight before midsummer-day; he is chosen from among the aldermen, is justice of the quorum during his mayoralty, and afterwards justice of the peace during life, unless he is lawfully removed from his office of Alderman.

One of the sheriffs is chosen by a letter from the court of Aldermen, sent out about the 7th of July, and returnable, if a full assembly can be made, within fourteen days, upon paying a fine of eighty pounds to the corporation, till the 10th of August; on which day, whoever holds it must serve the office: The other sheriff is elected by the freemen on the last Tuesday in August, and they are sworn into office on Michaelmas-day. No dissenter from the established church, no attorney, or professional man, nor any other person who will take an oath of not being worth three thousand pounds, can be *compelled* to serve,

It

It is said that a person worth 2,000l. is liable to serve, or to pay 50l. but there is no instance of enforcing such a law.

The common council-men are elected by the freemen, dwelling in each of the four great wards separately, for Conisford great ward on the Monday, Mancroft on the Tuesday, Wymer on the Wednesday, and the Ward beyond the water, (or Northern ward) on the Thursday before Passion week.

The mayor, with the sheriffs, hold courts every Wednesday and Saturday, to hear complaints, and to do every other act tending to the peaceable government of the city.

The recorder, who must be a barrister, assists in the mayor's court as chief judge, is always justice of the quorum, and one of the council for the city. The steward who must also be a barrister, assists in the sheriffs' court as chief judge, is likewise justice of the quorum, and the other council for the city.

The twenty-four aldermen are chosen for the twelve smaller wards, two for each ward, whose office it is to keep the peace in their several divisions, and upon the death or resignation of any one of them, the freemen of the great ward, in which the smaller ward is included, must elect another in his room, within five days of the death or resignation of his predecessor.

The quarterly assemblies are held on February 24, May 3, the day before the Guild-day, and September 21.

The city is divided into four great wards, and these are again sub-divided into twelve smaller wards, choosing two aldermen each.

I. Conisford ward, contains South-Conisford, North-Conisford, Ber-street, and takes in the Hamlets of Lakenham, Trowse - Milgate, Bracondale, and Carrowe, and elects twelve common council-men.

II. Mancroft ward, contains St. Stephen's St. Peter of Mancroft, St. Giles, and the Hamlet of Eaton, and chooses sixteen common council-men.

III. Wymer ward, contains East Wymer, Middle-Wymer, West-Wymer, with the Hamlets of Heigham and Earlham, and chooses twenty common council-men.

IV. The Northern ward, or the long ward, contains Coslany, Colgate, Fyebridge, with the Hamlet of Pockthorpe, and chooses twelve common councilmen.

The arms are Gules, a Castle tripple towered, Argent; in base a Lion of England, passant gardent.

The city sends two members to parliament chosen by the freeholders and others being free by inheritance, purchase or servitude, in number about 3000, and the returning officers are the sheriffs. The freemen must have been admitted to their freedom twelve months before they are enabled to vote. The first Summons was in the 25th year of the reign of Edward I. (1296) but it is not known who were then returned.

By

By an act obtained by the city in the year 1726, called the Tonage Act, a duty of 4d. per ton is laid upon all goods brought up the river higher than Thorpe-hall: the duties to be applied towards rebuilding and repairing the walls, bridges, gates, wastes, staithes, and streets. The increased expences of such works having of late years made the income very inadequate to all these purposes, the gates have been taken down, and the walls suffered to decay, by which the tonage revenue will better be enabled to fulfil the remaining objects of its original designation.

The Markets are on Wednesdays and Saturdays; the latter is remarkable for every good quality belonging to a market; plenty, variety, goodness, cheapness and neatness. There are four fairs, on the day before Good Friday; St. Faith's, October 21; The Tuesday after St. Michael; And Maudlin, or St. Mary Magdalen.

The liberties of the city and county of Norwich, as confirmed by Mary I. in the third year of her reign (1556) comprehends a circuit of about fourteen miles, containing nearly six thousand six hundred and thirty acres.

From the Guild-hall, in the Market-place,

	M.	F.
To Mile-crofs on the north, is	1	6
Thorpe, east	1	4
Harford bridges, south	2	2
Earlham bounds, west	2	4

By Charter, dated the 5th year of Henry IV. (1403) the citizens of Norwich were empowered to choose a

Mayor, together with twenty-three other Aldermen, as part of the body corporate, from which time until the prefent æra there has never been a period at which all the twenty-four then living had been elected into the office of Chief Magiftrate.

Before the year 1786, various methods had been adopted for numbering the inhabitants of Norwich, but being founded on principles of calculation, generally admitted on fuch occafions, without an exact enumeration, they had tended rather to perplex than fatisfy candid inquiry; and whilft fome contended for their being 48,000 people, others eftimated them at but 36,000: To clear up fuch doubts, and for other and more material reafons, an exact account from houfe to houfe was taken in May 1786; and may be feen in the firft column of the Parochial Lift in the next page. It is to be obferved, that the inhabitants within the precinct of the Cathedral, and the foldiers quartered in the city are not included in the prefent lift, and we think it cannot be any exaggeration to eftimate them at one thoufand, making the total 41,051, which, fuppofing the account taken in 1752 to have been tolerably correct, we find to be an increafe of near 5000 people; and, when it is confidered, that Norwich furnifhed the army and navy with 4000 recruits during the late war, not many of whom returned, it muft be admitted, that if the ftrength of a nation, or the confequence of a town, is to be eftimated by the number of its inhabitants, Norwich has fomething to boaft of, and nothing to fear.

THE

THE PAROCHIAL LIST.

	No. Souls in 1786.	Houses in 1752.	No. Souls in 1752.	No. Souls in 1693.
St. Peter Southgate	507	72	425	470
St. Etheldred	254	57	247	243
St. Julian	846	126	595	593
St. Peter Permountergate	1362	327	1408	1376
St. John Sepulchre	1114	158	1004	781
St. Michael at Thorn	1442	273	1127	865
St. John Timberhill	975	200	890	668
All Saints	825	106	578	425
St. Stephen	2360	402	2314	1769
St. Peter Mancroft	2299	420	2288	1953
St. Giles	1117	195	961	910
St. Benedict	900	127	715	652
St. Swithin	643	141	751	496
St. Margaret	859	223	856	664
St. Lawrence	1018	176	952	668
St. Gregory	1113	248	1002	772
St. John Maddermarket	1571	235	1107	657
St. Andrew	1773	236	1334	935
St. Michael at Plea	502	119	482	479
St. Peter Hungate	394	90	341	267
St. Simon and Jude	443	84	420	362
St. George of Tombland	720	161	737	722
St. Martin at Palace	1109	267	1083	819
St. Helen	446	80	386	338
St. Michael Coslany	1185	244	1046	1026
St. Mary	1202	236	1178	949
St. Martin at Oak	2153	351	1698	1243
St. Augustin	1899	266	1226	850
St. George of Colgate	1272	259	1295	1154
St. Clement	800	123	816	593
St. Edmund	531	108	520	370
St. Saviour	593	162	810	701
St. Paul	1681	292	1461	983
St. James	608	166	696	416
Precinct of the Close		129	700	650
Pockthorpe fub.	1272	197	1116	732
Heigham fub.	923	164	653	544
HAMLETS.				
Lakenham	486	35	165	221
Eaton	260	59	226	153
Earlham	66	9	68	50
Hellefden	103	12	70	65
Thorpe	82	5	36	69
Trowfe, Carrowe, Bracondale.	348	85	386	258
	40,051	7,131	36,169	28,881

THE NORFOLK TOUR.

A Table of Baptisms and Burials in Norwich for 23 years.

Year.	Baptized.	Buried.
1719	993	1266
20	814	1260
21	827	1026
22	889	728
23	949	1004
24	988	1078
25	921	932
26	931	823
27	865	1165
28	774	1417
29	843	1731
30	877	1136
31	938	854
32	933	1011
33	937	981
34	955	1104
35	807	885
36	896	896
37	889	1405
38	996	1078
39	949	974
40	916	1173
41	851	1456
	20,738	25,383

The number of people in Norwich in 1693, 1752, and 1786, being *known* by the Parochial list & page 72, the average annual increase between each period is easily ascertained, and if added to the survey, will nearly give the number living in any particular year. Many other observations present themselves to an inquisitive mind, but we will finish this article by inferring from what has been stated, that *Norwich* is not inferiour to any place of the same size in England, in point of healthiness; and we hope to be pardoned for adding, pleasantness, plenty, and whatever else (if we are well disposed) contributes toward rendering life comfortable.

By this Table the annual average number of Births, is 901, 2-thirds, and Burials, 1,103, 2-thirds.

A Table of Baptisms and Burials in Norwich for 11 years:

Year.	Baptized.	Buried.	Buried under 10 years old.
1784	1164	1180	568
85	1227	1041	459
86	1185	1368	650
87	1151	1063	461
88	1154	1192	461
89	1050	1138	425
90	1055	1219	656
91	1096	1112	518
92	1166	973	328
93	1094	1161	573
94	963	1064	508
	12,305	12,511	5,607

In 1786 the inhabitants were found by a survey to amount to 41,050. It is evident from the second Table, that the annual average number of burials in Norwich for the last eleven years, is 1,137, 4-elevenths, or rather less than one, thirty-sixth of its inhabitants, for 1,137 4-elevenths multiplied by 36 is 40,936. This table exhibits a very singular fact: In *great* towns where the burials considerably exceed the births, it has been stated by the most respectable political arithmeticians, that the number of deaths for any ten years being ascertained, and the annual average multiplied by 27, or at the utmost, by 28, the product will be the number of inhabitants it contains. The deaths in Norwich being not full 1-thirty-sixth of the number of inhabitants, proves, either some error in the computations of those who have written on the subject, or that the place is at this time singularly favourable to longevity. Dr. Price has informed us, that half the number of children born in Norwich, die under *six* years of age, and of 1,185 persons dying here within the year, 664 are children below the age of *ten:* But by the third and fourth columns of this table it appears, that out of 1,137 who died annually in the last 11 years, 509 only, have been under 10 years old. Within the same period, 6,372 males, and 5,933 females were born, which is in the proportion of 20 to 19.

' The males born have exceeded the females by 40 on an annual average.

A particular of the Inhabitants in 1786.

Belonging to the city	29,200
Aliens	10,851
Precinct of the Cathedral, and Soldiers	1,000
Total	41,051

It appears that the number of houses in 1752 was 7,139, and the inhabitants 36,169, that is 5 1-fifteenth-persons to each house; since that time a great many of the smaller houses within the gates have been pulled down, and larger ones erected upon their site; the city by this means has been rendered more healthy and beautiful, and to make up for the deficiency of houses within the walls, a great many have been built without the gates, and the whole may now be reckoned at 7,500; which, allowing 5 1-half people to each house, makes 41,250, a number sufficiently near to warrant the conclusion of there being 7,500 houses.

It may further be observed, that from the year 1693 in which the first enumeration that we know of was taken, to 1752, a period of 59 years, the inhabitants of Norwich had increased 7,288, or rather more than 123 annually. From 1752 to 1786, that is 34 years, the increase was 4,882, or rather more than 143, communibus annis. Again: From 1693 to 1786, a space of 93 years, the increase was 12,170, or near 131 annually.

If

If we suppose one person at man's estate to dwell in each house, Norwich will be able, on any emergency, to furnish 7,500 men able to bear arms.

Finally, admitting the usual computation to be right, that, at a medium, the proportion of males to females, is as 14 to 13, Norwich has at this time 22,047 males, and 19,004 females.

The combers employ spinners all the country round; and the manufacturers use many thousand packs of yarn spun in other counties, even as far as Yorkshire and Westmoreland, as well as considerable quantities of Irish yarn, which is imported from Dublin and Cork, by way of Yarmouth.

From the most accurate calculation lately made it appears, that 12,000 looms are employed in the manufacture, and allowing six persons in the whole to each loom, there are consequently 72,000 people employed; but this is to be understood as a calculation for the whole county, and not for Norwich alone, where it is acknowledged there are little better than half of the people said to be employed. It is a common idea in Norwich, to suppose each loom, with its attendants, to work 100l. per annum; this makes the total amount 1,200,000l. a very large sum for one manufacture to produce in a year, and what some intelligent gentlemen engaged in the manufactory have controverted, whilst others no less exact, and from their extensive business, acknowledged to be competent judges, are still of opinion, that this calculation comes very near the truth.

The general amount of the Norwich manufacture, has also been calculated thus:

To Rotterdam by shipping every six weeks, goods to the value of per ann.	150,000l.
Ten tons by broad wheel'd waggons, weekly to London at 60l. per ton on an average,	312,000l.
By occasional ships to Ostend, Hamburg, the Baltic, Spain and Italy,	738,000l.
	1,200,000l.

Other modes of calculation have been adopted, but the two preceding so exactly agree in the sum total, and differ so little from the rest, that it is unnecessary to add any more on the subject here. Nor, concise as we wish to be on this occasion, ought we to omit observing, that in the seventy years last past, the manufacture has increased as from four to twelve.

The staple manufactures are crapes, *bombazeens, and camblets; besides which they make in great abundance damasks, sattins, alopeens, &c. &c. &c. They work up the Leicestershire and Lincolnshire wool chiefly, which is brought here for combing and spinning, whilst the Norfolk wool goes to Yorkshire for carding and cloths. And within a few years it has been discovered, that the Norfolk sheep yield

---
* Bombazeens were invented in 1575, by the Dutch settled here, to whom the Corporation granted an exclusive privilege for manufacturing them.

yield a wool about their necks and shoulders, equal to the best from Spain; and is in price to the rest as 20 to 7. The earnings of the manufacturers are various, dyers and hot-pressers about 15s. a week, combers about 12s; some of the best weavers from 14s. to a guinea, weavers in general, on an average, not more than six shillings, but then many women can earn as much, and children by spinning pipe-filling and tyre-drawing, earn from 9d. to 2s. 6d. a week each. It is a well ascertained fact, that where the industrious man with his family earn from 10 to 12s. a week, they live happy and comfortable, and seldom want employment, whilst, they who can earn from 14s. to a guinea a week, too often spend that in idleness which can be procured with so much ease, and work two or three days only instead of six.

If 72,000 people as has been stated do work to the value of 1,200,000l. annually, it is between 16 and 17l. for each person's wages. The materials are said to cost one tenth of the total manufacture, or 120,000l. This leaves the amount of labour 1,080,000l. in which is included the profit of the master manufacturer, and if that is stated at 14 per cent. and deducted accordingly, it reduces the earnings to about 11l. 11s. a year for every person employed. And it may be stated as no contemptible fact, that the same number of people employed in any manufacture, will earn one million a year; for the variations of earnings in any general given number of people is not very great, let the *manufacture be what it may*, few of them work more than to live.

To

To the principal Manufacture of that variety of stuffs, which for some centuries has been carried on with great success in Norwich, both for foreign markets and home consumption, we have the satisfaction to announce the late introduction of the Cotton Manufacture to an extensive degree, and of shawls and a variety of fancy goods of the same kind, for dress and furniture, which in taste and elegancy surpass any thing of the kind hitherto made in England. The Woollen Cloth Manufacture is also carried on to a considerable extent, and the Iron Foundry finds employment for a number of hands.

In the year 1738, when Norwich did not in all probability contain more than 33,00 people, it was said, in wealth, trade, buildings and population, not to be exceeded by any city or town in England, except London and Bristol; but such are the rapid changes which commerce effects, that in some of these particulars it is now far surpassed by Liverpool, Manchester, Birmingham, Sheffield, Newcastle and Bath; and from being the third place of importance in the kingdom, is become the eighth, as Norfolk, in magnitude, is about the eighth county. It is not hence to be inferred that the general trade of the city has declined, for whatever vicissitude the principal manufactures for foreign markets may have experienced, the home-trade, there is reason for believing, has continued to flourish: In evidence of which it seems sufficient to state, that in the year 1738 there were but thirty-seven common carriers who came weekly to the city;

in 1794 they amount to one hundred and twenty-four; and the stage coaches have increased in a still greater proportion.

Norwich adds much to the trade of Yarmouth, by the importation of coals, Irish-yarn, wine, fish, oil, and all other heavy goods, which come to it from thence by the river Yare, and the exportation of its manufactures to Russia, Germany, Holland, Norway, Spain, Portugal, Italy, Flanders, &c. The goods thus now exported, went formerly through the medium of the London merchants, but since the introduction of *foreign riders, the manufacturer is also the merchant.

During the last and the present war, Norwich has supplied the army and navy with above six thousand recruits, without feeling any inconvenience from so large a drain of its active inhabitants; but the really industrious seldom enlist.

A LIST of the MEMBERS of PARLIAMENT for the CITY of NORWICH, from the year 1700 to the present time, with the STATE of the POLL at each CONTESTED ELECTION.

November 19, 1701.
EDWARD Clarke Esq;   1142
Peter Thacker, Alderman 1041
Rt. Davy, Esq; Recorder 1042
Thomas Blofield Esq;   759
    N. B. Mr. Sheriff Nall alone returned Mr. Clarke and Mr. Davy, (the other Sheriff, Mr. Havers, dissenting) and, after an Hearing and Scrutiny before the Committee of Elections, the House of Commons declared them duly elected.

1702

---

* Persons employed by the Manufacturers to procure orders abroad.

THE NORFOLK TOUR. 79

1702.

Robert Davy, Efq;	1318
Thomas Blofield, Efq;	1260
Edward Claik, Efq;	953
Charles Lord Pafton	933

1703.

Capt. Thomas Palgrave, VICE
Mr. Davy, DECEASED

1705.

Waller Bacon, Efq;	1281
John Chambers, Efq;	1267
Thomas Blofield, Efq;	1136
Captain Thomas Palgrave	1074

N. B. Mr. Bacon and Mr. Chambers not being Freemen, but only Freeholders, the Sheriffs made a double Return ; bnt on the fitting of the Parliament, the two firft were declared duly elected.

May 19, 1708.

Waller Bacon, Efq;	1521
John Chambers, Efq;	1412
Thomas Blofield, Efq;	1139
James Brogden, Efq;	239

October 18, 1710.

Robert Bene, Efq; Mayor	1315
Rd. Berney, Efq; Steward	1298
Waller Bacon, Efq;	1107
S. Gardiner.Efq; Reeorder	1078

Aug. or Sept. 1713.

Robert Bene, Efq;	1282
Richard Berney, Efq;	1272
Waller Bacon, Efq;	1141
Robert Britiffe, Efq;	1107

Feb. 2, 1715.

Waller Bacon, Efq;	1662
Robert Britiffe, Efq;	1652
Robert Bene, Efq;	1326
Richard Berney, Efq;	1319

1722.

Waller Bacon, Efq;
Robert Britiffe, Efq;

Aug. 30, 1727.

Rohert Britiffe, Efq;	1626
Waller Bacon, Efq;	1542
Miles Branthwayte, Efq;	1265
Richard Berney, Efq;	1188

May 15, 1734.

Horatio Walpole, Efq;	1785
Waller Bacon, Efq;	1749
Sir Edward Ward, Bart.	1621
Miles Branthwayte, Efq;	1567

Feb. 19, 1735.

Thomas Vere, Efq ; VICE W. Bacon, DECEASED	1820
Miles Branthwayte, Efq;	1486

May 6, 1741.

Horatio Walpole, Efq;	1772
Thomas Vere, Efq;	1621
William Clarke, Efq;	829

1747.

Rt. Hon. Horatio Walpole
Rt. Hon. John Lord Hobart

April 15, 1754.

Rt. Hon. Horatio Walpole
Rt. Hon. John Lord Hobart

June

June 25, 1756.

Edward Bacon, Efq; vice H. Walpole, created a Peer

Dec. 8, 1756.

Harbord Harbord, Efq; now Ld. Suffield, vice Ld. Hobart. who fucceeded his Father as Earl of Buckinghamfhire, Sept. 22

Jan. 2, 1760.

Edward Bacon, Efq; having accepted the office of one of the Commiffioners of Trade, RE-ELECTED.

March 27, 1761.

Harbord Harbord, Efq; 1729
Edward Bacon, Efq; 1507
Nockold Tompfon, Efq; 718
Robert Harvey, Efq; 499

March 18, 1768.

Harbord Harbord, Efq; 1812
Edward Bacon, Efq; 1596
Thomas Beevor, Efq; 1136

Oct. 1774.

Sir Harbord Harbord, Bart.
Edward Bacon, Efq.

Sept. 11, 1780.

Sir Harbord, Harbord, Bt. 1382
Edward Bacon, Efq; 1199
William Windham, Efq; 1069
John Thurlow, Efq; 1103

April 5, 1784.

Sir Harbord Harbord, Bt. 2305
Wm. Windham, Efq; 1297
The Hon. Henry Hobart 1233

Sir Harbord Harbord, Bart. called up to the Houfe of Peers, by the title of Lord Suffield.

Sept. 15 & 16, 1786.

The Hon. Henry Hobart 1450
Sir Thomas Beevor Bart. 1383
Robert John Buxton, Efq; 10

A felect Committee of the Houfe of Commons, determined this to be a void election, March 9, 1787.

March 15, 1787.

The Hon. Henry Hobart 1393
Sir Thomas Beevor, Bart. 1313

June 18, 1790.

The Hon. Henry Hobart 1492
William Windham, Efq; 1371
Sir Thomas Beevor, Bart. 656

Mr. Windham having vacated his feat by accepting the office of Secretary at War, an Election took place,

July 12, 1794.

The Hon. Wm. Windham 1236
James Mingay, Efq; 770

By a private act of parliament paſſed the 3d. of Geo. II. for regulating Elections for members of parliament to repreſent the city of Norwich, it is ordered, that every freeman before he polls, " ſhall ſwear, he " has been admitted a freeman of the city for twelve " calendar months laſt paſt, and has not before polled " at that election."—The right of election is in the Freeholders, and ſuch Freemen only of the city as are entered in the books, *and do not receive alms or charity*. The latter part of this clauſe is ſufficiently plain, but it is evaded, or has never been enforced.

THE CASTLE

NEVER belonged to the city, but always was, and now is, a part of the county of Norfolk. It is ſuppoſed to have been *firſt* built by Uffa King of the Eaſt Angles, about the year 575. In 642 it became a royal caſtle, and one of the ſeats of King Anna. In the Daniſh wars it often changed maſters, and after Alfred the Great had overcome that people, he is ſuppoſed to have erected *the firſt building of brick or ſtone*, about the year 872, which was deſtroyed by Swain the Dane 1004, and re-built by his ſon Canute 1018. Roger Bigod, Earl of Norfolk, is ſuppoſed to have pulled this down, and to have erected the preſent building on its ſite, which was afterwards repaired and beautified by Thomas Brotherton, in the reign of Edward II. Before the year 1135, it was appointed a place of confinement for the King's priſoners. In 1189 Richard I.

made

made Roger, fon of Hugh Bigod, conftable of this caftle, but he having joined the rebellious Barons, was difpoffeffed of it in 1212, but reinftated on his fubmitting to the King, and died conftable in 1220. In 1240 the cuftody of the caftle was committed to the fheriff of the county. In 1312 Thomas de Brotherton was appointed conftable, who adorned and crowned it with battlements as it now appears. In 1325 the general quarter feffions of the peace for the county of Norfolk, were ordered to be held in the Shire-houfe, erected within the limits of the caftle, in the parifh of St. John Timberhill, a little on the left of the grand entrance. In 1339 it was granted to the fheriff for a public gaol for the county, as it ftill remains. In 1381, the cuftody of the caftle or king's gaol, was granted to John de Grey for life, with the annual ftipend of twenty pounds payable at the Exchequer, being the allowance formerly made to the conftable of the faid caftle, and afterward to the fheriff of Norfolk.

The Caftle, was originally defended by a wall furrounding it on the brow of the hill on which it ftands, and by three ditches, over which there were as many bridges: The firft has been immemorially deftroyed, the ruins of the fecond remained till the ditches were levelled in 1738; the third now ftanding, is a handfome bridge of but one arch, of 41 feet diameter. The outermoft ditch extended on the Weft to the edge of the prefent market-place, on the North it encompaffed London Lane, on the Eaft it nearly reached King's Street, and on the South to the Golden Ball Lane. The poftern or back entrance into the caftle, was on

the

the North-eaft, having a communication with the Earl's palace, then occupying the whole fpace between the outer ditch and Tombland. The grand entrance was, as it now is, on the South. The caftle is fquare, and has within its court a Chapel dedicated to St. Nicholas, which being a royal free chapel, is exempt from all epifcopal jurifdiction. The chaplain is appointed by the juftices of peace for the county, with a falary of thirty pounds a year. From the fummit of the hill, which appears to have been raifed by art, with incredible labour, and ftands almoft in the middle of the city, there is a moft agreeable view of the furrounding buildings, interfperfed with gardens which, together with the adjacent country and river, compofe a moft delightful landfcape. From this intermixture of buildings with gardens, Norwich has been compared to "A City in an Orchard."

The SHIRE-HOUSE, adjoining to the caftle on the North fide, in which the Summer Affizes and Quarter Seffions are held, and other county bufinefs tranfacted, was built by Mr. Brettingham on the fite of that burnt down, on the 30th of September 1746. It has two courts of juftice, a large grand jury chamber, and other convenient apartments; particularly a large room on the Weft fide, erected in the year 1784, having a communication with each court, by which means the Judges are relieved from the difagreeable apprehenfion of fqueezing through thofe elbowing crowds which too often block up the avenues to our courts of juftice.

The

The Castle-hill was repaired and the ditch and sides of the hill planted with shrubs and a variety of trees, and a bank thrown up within the boundary, at a considerable expence to the county in the year 1774; but there being none to guard, what was intended both for use and ornament, the bank soon fell into decay, and it appeared that the money had been expended to very little purpose; this probably suggested the idea of dividing the ditch between the bank and the bottom of the hill, into various allotments, which were given to such persons as chose to accept of them, and keep up the fences. By this means the hill is kept in good repair, the plantations upon the sides are in a flourishing state, and the bottom is laid out into gardens according to the fancy of each possessor.—Stangers have acknowledged the view from the summit to be superior to any thing of the kind in Europe.

As whatever regards the castle may be esteemed of consequence by the antiquarian, we have taken some pains to abridge the ingenious account given of it by Edw. King, Esq. in his observations on ancient castles, published in 1782.

Mr. King observes, that an high artificial mount, with a *round* keep at the top covering nearly the *whole* surface, are the characteristic marks of Norman Castles, whereas such prior Saxon castles as were built, like Norwich castle, on great mounts, or ancient barrows of still earlier date, cover but a *small part* of the respective hills on which they were built.

There

There is indeed a tradition, of the caftle's having been built in its prefent form (a fquare) by Roger Bigod, about the time of William Rufus; and finally compleated by Thomas de Brotherton, even fo late as the time of Edward II. but this feems to be a miftake, for though it may be true, of the portal, (a) ftaircafe, outworks, and the many great buildings formerly inclofed within it's limits and outward walls; yet, as the Keep or mafter tower (the only confiderable part now remaining) in the ftile of its (b) architecture is in many refpects fo different from that of the towers erected in the reigns of William Rufus and Henry I. and II. and the ornaments vary fo much from thofe ufed in the reign of Edward II. that Mr. King thinks this building of much greater antiquity, and compleatly Saxon; for though King Canute was himfelf a Dane, he undoubtedly made ufe of many Saxon architects; as the far greater number of his fubjects were Saxons: nor is there any *authentic* account whatever of the deftruction of the caftle built in his time, either by war or by accident; or of its being

(a) The arms of Thomas de Brotherton are ftill to be feen in part of the wall of the ftair-cafe.

(b) The refemblance which the devifes, and the mode of fortification, both in this Saxon caftle, and in that at Colchefter, have to thofe built even in the more improved Norman times, feem to indicate, that the general plan was taken from ftructures of ftill earlier date than either. Efpecially as the defcription given by Jofephus of the tower of Antonia at Jerufalem, may lead us to fufpect this mode of building to be very ancient indeed, and to have been known, and introduced even before the age in which he lived.

being taken down, in order to erect the present structure: certain it is, that all it's *ornaments are in the true Saxon stile; so that it is to be considered as one of the most compleat Saxon remains in England: as the bridge leading to it is unquestionably one of the noblest and most perfect Saxon arches now extant.

The inside of the castle, instead of containing an open yard, as it now does, was filled up with floors of most magnificent and spacious apartments. And although the timbers are at present removed, yet traces of the original disposition of the whole may plainly be observed by any person accustomed to examine these kinds of buildings: and there are still visible the marks of the strong partition-wall, running across from East to West.

It appears also, that the apartments on the ground-floor of this castle were vaulted over with stone; for a great part of the old vault still remains, and also the great stone arches of the buttresses, and a stone vaulting where the present chapel is. The ancient chapel, mentioned in old records, was, most probably, on a level with the principal floor, and state apartments; and not here, where there was neither light nor a convenient approach.

At the extremity of the remaining part of the partition wall on the West side, may be seen a part rounded

---

* That the Saxons ornamented many of their buildings very richly, is manifest from the church at Barfriston, in Kent; from the well-known tower at St. Edmund's Bury; and from two church towers at Dover and Sandwich, which are both richly adorned with pilasters, and small round arches, as this castle is.

ed off, and now cafed with brick, having the appearance of a round tower: and in the middle of this a deep, circular cavity of ftone work, like the pipe of a well, which has been filled up in the memory of perfons now living. Here therefore was in all probability, the original well in the wall of the caftle; as at Rochefter and Canterbury. And it appears that there was alfo a paffage to it from one of the galleries, through the wall, the entrance to which is now bricked up, but ftill vifible.

As to the galleries themfelves, a part of them ftill remains, and it is manifeft, that there were two; one nearly level with the ftate apartments, and another ftill higher up in the building.

Although it appears upon record, that this caftle was ufed as a prifon fo early as the reign of Henry I. yet we muft by no means conceive from thence that it was ufed for that purpofe *only*; and that the whole building was from the firft, a mere prifon, as it now is. The fact feems to have been; that the vaults or dungeons of this, and other caftles, fo faid to have been prifons, were appointed *by royal authority*, to be *public* and privileged prifons at *all times*; whereas the dungeons of other caftles, were permitted to be ufed as fuch only in the times of war, and it was unlawful at other times to confine any perfons therein; whilft the upper apartments of all thefe towers, in both cafes were conftantly ufed as ftate apartments, for the refidence of great officers and their attendants, notwithftanding standing the prisons underneath. And hence perhaps arose the practice, in early times, of committing *state* prisoners to the custody of different lords, at pleasure, which was continued down to the time of Henry VIII.

The front of the castle is not precisely facing the East, but rather inclines a little towards the South. Its length is 92 feet 10 inches, and the length of the North and South fronts is 98 feet each: the height of the walls is about 50 feet.

A vast pile of building, somewhat resembling the architecture of the old castle, was added to it on the East side in the year 1793. The walls are built with the stone called Scotch Granite, of a competent thickness to defy escape, and resist the injuries of time for many centuries to come. Within the square are the Gaoler's house, and separate places of confinement for Debtors and Felons, well adapted to those purposes. THE COVNTY GAOL, over the great arch at the entrance, is sufficiently conspicuous: perhaps the ingenious Stone-mason, delighted with viewing this ponderous building, and master-piece of *his* art, was apprehensive of its intention being mistaken. But if the letters were meant to resemble those of the same import in the Saxon Alphabet, he surely has not chiseled out a *striking likeness*; and if the Roman character was his model, he seems to have been almost equally unfortunate, unless he hoped to impose upon the credulity of some future Antiquarian, by closely imitating the uncouth formation of the latter, as used

in

in monumental infcriptions fourteen hundred years ago.

St. ANDREW's HALL.

FORMERLY the monaftery church of the (a) Black Friars, or Benedictine Monks, is a beautiful ftructure, about 50 yards in length and 30 wide; confifting of a nave and two ailes, each half the breadth of the nave, covered with lead, and fupported by twelve neat and very flender pillars, and was new paved in 1646. The (b) Mayor's guild-feafts, are always held here; and in different apartments about it are the courts of Confcience, the Guardians for the poor, &c. This noble fabric was built by Sir Thomas Erpingham, Knight, who died in 1428, before it was completely finifhed, which was effected by Sir Robert Erpingham, his fon, rector of Bracon, a friar in this houfe. The windows were originally of very fine painted glafs, but now entirely demolifhed. The St. George's company ufually held their feafts and meetings at the *Stone* lately removed, which covered the grave of Robert Barnard, Efq. of this city, buried here in 1511. The company or fraternity took its rife in 1385, and were a fociety of brethren and fifters, affociated in honour of the martyr St. George.

In

(a) There is a Print of this in Stevens's Supplement to Dugdale's Monafticon, 1718.

(b) The firft Mayor's feaft held here was in the year 1544.

In 1704, the company prefented the mayor with the fword of ftate now ufed, in a fcabbard of crimfon velvet, with gilt lockets and a mourning fcabbard of black velvet with gilt lockets; two new ftaves with filver heads, having the city arms, viz. the caftle and lion, on pedeftals of filver, to be borne before the mayor by the two marfhal-men, and two new filver badges with the city arms, likewife to be worn by marfhal-men when in waiting: at the fame time they had a new ftaff made, with a filver head, reprefenting St. George and the Dragon, the arms of the company, on a pedeftal, to be borne by their beadle before the aldermen of the faid company.

In 1731, February 24, the committee appointed for that purpofe, reported at an affembly held that day, that they had treated with the St. George's company, who had agreed to deliver up their charters, books and records, into the hands of the corporation, provided they would pay their debts, amounting to 236l. 15s. 1d. which being agreed to, they were accordingly delivered up, and are now depofited with the city records in the Guildhall.

In the centre of the Eaft end is a clock, over which is carved the effigies of Juftice, and underneath, the royal arms of England. On each fide hang the pictures of Queen Anne, George Prince of Denmark, Robert Earl of Orford, John Lord Hobart, afterwards Earl of Buckinghamfhire, Horatio Walpole, Efq. Lord Suffield, and two Hiftorical Paintings by Mr. W. Martin, of Edward and Eleanora, and the

the

the death of Lady Jane Gray, with feveral Aldermen and benefactors to the city. The figure of St. George killing the Dragon, neatly carved, was placed here in 1686, by order of the St. George's Company.

On the walls in the North and South ailes, are placed elegant paintings at full length, fuperbly framed, of thofe gentlemen who have gone through the public offices of the Corporation with dignity and honour. Thefe paintings ferve at once as a public teftimony of the great efteem the gentlemen reprefented are held in, and are no contemptible proofs of the abilities of fome of the moft ingenious painters who have refided in, or occafionally vifited the city.

The fteeple was very neat, and of an hexagonal form at top; it ftood between the nave and the choir, and fell down in 1712. The yard on the South fide, was called the green yard, where fermons were preached on thofe Sundays and holidays, when there were none at the cathedral crofs: it was alfo ufed as a burial place for thofe who died of the plague in the parifh of St. Andrew; and in the grand rebellion, the artillery company exercifed here, and depofited their arms in the low rooms adjoining to the porch.

A handfome room for the city Library was re-built in the Gothic tafte in 1774, under the direction of the late Mr. Rawlins.

The earls of Northumberland and Huntingdon, the lords Thomas Howard, and Willoughby, with many other nobles and knights, being on a vifit to the duke

THE NORFOLK TOUR.

of Norfolk, were entertained with their retinue at the Duke's Palace in 1561. The guild happening at this time, William Mingay, Esq. the Bishop's register, then mayor, invited them and their ladies to the feast; who all expressed the greatest satisfaction at their generous reception. The mayor's share of the expence and his bill of fare were as follows. The feast-makers, four in number, paying the rest.

At the time this feast was made money was six times its present value.

	£.	s.	d.
Eight stone of beef, at 8d. a stone, and a sirloin by	0	5	8
Two collars of brawn	0	1	0
Four cheeses at 4d. a cheese	0	1	4
Eight pints of butter	0	1	6
A hinder quarter of veal	0	0	10
A leg of mutton	0	0	5
A fore quarter of veal	0	0	5
Loin of mutton and shoulder of veal	0	0	9
Breast and coat of mutton	0	0	7
Six pullets	0	1	0
Four couple of rabbits	0	1	8
Four brace of partridges	0	2	0
Two Guinea cocks	0	1	6
Two couple of mallard	0	1	0
Thirty-four eggs	0	0	6
Bushel of flower	0	0	6
Peck of oatmeal	0	0	2
Sixteen white bread loaves	0	0	4
Eighteen loaves of white wheat bread	0	0	9
Three loaves of meslin bread	0	0	3

Nutmegs,

Nutmegs, mace, cinnamon and cloves	0	0	3
4lb. Barbary sugar	0	1	0
Sixteen oranges	0	0	2
A barrel of double strong beer	0	2	6
A barrel of table beer	0	1	0
A quarter of wood	0	2	2
Two gallons of white wine and Canary	0	2	0
Fruit, almonds, sweet water, perfumes	0	0	4
The cook's wages	0	1	2
Total	1	12	9

After dinner, Mr. John Martyn, a wealthy and honest man of Norwich, made the following speech,

' Maister Mayor of Norwich, and it please your wor-
' ship, you have feasted us like a King. God bless
' the Queen's grace. We have fed (1) plentifully,
' and now whilom I can speak plain English, I hear-
' tily thank you maister Mayor; and so do we all.
' Answer, boys, answer; your beer is pleasant and
' potent, and will soon catch us by the caput, and
' stop our manners. And so huzza for the Queen's
' Majesty's grace, and all her (2) bonny brow'd dames
' of honour. Huzza for maister Mayor, and our good
' dame Mayoress. (3) His noble Grace, there he is,.
' God

(1) He is supposed to have been a common council-man, or perhaps a sheriff.

(2) This is familiar enough, and looks as if the fumes of the potent beverage had begun to attack the honest orator's CAPUT.

(3) The Duke of Northumberland, and his suite.

'God bless him and all this jolly company: To all our friends round county, who have a penny in their purse, and an English heart in their bodies, to keep out Spanish Dons, and Papists with their faggots to burn our whiskers.—Shove it about, twirl your cap-cases, handle your jugs, and huzza for maister Mayor, and his brethren their worships.'

The honesty, freedom, loyalty and good humour of this speech would at any time intitle the orator to a patient hearing and an approving smile.

THE GUILDHALL.

ORIGINALLY a small thatched building, erected on Carrowe fee for collecting the toll of the maket. In the time of Edward III. it was called the toll-booth, and in the latter part of his reign a single room was added to it, of stud-work, and thatched, from which addition it acquired the name of the Guildhall. In this state it continued till the reign of Henry IV. when that prince granting the city a charter for electing a mayor, instead of bailiffs, it was resolved to build a new Guildhall, Prisons, &c. the old one being so very small and mean as to have room only to erect a seat for the mayor and six others to sit. In consequence of this resolution at an assembly held 1407, John Danyel, Robert Brasyer, and twenty-two others, were elected to compose a set of laws for the government of the city agreeable to the charter, and to consult proper means to raise money for building a Guildhall: This matter

matter was purfued fo vigoroufly, that within the courfe of the year the work was got fo forward that the arches under it, defigned for prifons, were compleated. In 1409 the roof was raifed, and in 1412 the prifons were made ufe of, but the whole building was not perfected till 1413, when the windows of the council-chamber were glazed, and the chequer table was placed in it. In 1435, the porch and tower called the treafury, the lower part of which being the prifon called little eafe, were built, and in 1440, all the city records, which till that time had lain difperfed in the monaftery of the White Friars, the chapel in the fields, &c. were collected together and depofited here. The ftalls joining to the hall, now covered with lead, were the ancient fcriptories, or places where the writers fat at elections. In 1511, the roof of the council-chamber at the Eaft end of the guildhall, and the treafury fell down: the council-chamber was repaired in 1523 and 1524, but the treafury tower was never rebuilt. The windows contained many ftories on painted or ftained glafs, relating to the adminiftration of juftice. The glafs has been fo much broke and mifplaced that little of the original defigns can be collected: but one large and two fmall windows remain perfect at the eaft end, to perpetuate the remembrance of this beautiful art. The room is adorned with the pictures of King William and Queen Mary, many eminent men of the county, mayors of the city and other benefactors.

In

In 1597, an order was made that "the rooms on the East end of the guyld-hall, heretofore used for a common gayle, shall cease to be used for a prison after 20 October next: and that the common gaol for the county of this cittie, shall be kept in the house called the Lamb," where it still continues. The sheriff's office continued to be kept on the North side of the Guildhall till 1625, when it was removed into the old chapel opposite to it on the South side, but that running into decay was pulled down, and the present sheriff's office built on its site.

In this Hall the assizes and quarter sessions for the city are held. Here is also the mayor's office, for the daily administration of justice; the town-clerk's and chamberlain's offices; and all elections for Mayor, Aldermen, Sheriffs and Common-councilmen are here determined.

The ASSEMBLY HOUSE. The vestibule projects about 26 feet from the principal building, and is 15 feet wide; ascending four steps, upon the right is a card room 22 feet square, and a proportionate height, and on the left another 22 feet by 28; above the card rooms are two other rooms of the same dimensions, and over the vestibule a store room. The long room is 66 feet by 23, the ceiling very neatly stucco'd, from whence hang five elegant glass lustres, that in the centre having 24 branches, the two next 8 each, and the two end ones 14 each; it has five windows on the South side, and a Venetian one at the West end; is wainscotted round, about nine feet high,

high, and above are stucco pannels, ornamented with festoons. The small room is 50 feet by 27, the ceiling the same as the long room, from whence there are four brass chandeliers suspended by gilt links; in other respects, the ornaments are nearly the same as in the long room. The orchestras are over the doors at the entrance of each room, supported by two neat fluted pillars, The tea room is between the two rooms appropriated to dancing, and is 27 feet square: an elegant chandelier of 24 branches is suspended in the centre of the ceiling by a gilt link. On the South side of this room is a recefs of about ten feet, in the form of a half decagon; in this place tea and other refreshments are delivered out to the company.

The communication is by two doors with arched casings, ten feet high and five feet wide, so constructed as to be easily removed, and then the eye commands at once a suit of rooms of 143 feet, illuminated by ten branches holding 150 candles; and the company forming into one row, may dance the whole length of the building.

The THEATRE, built by the late Mr. Thomas Ivory, after the model of old Drury Lane house, will conveniently hold about 70l. and like all others intended for the same purpose, appears much to advantage when moderately filled with company, and properly lighted; 'tis then that any traveller having a taste for theatrical amusements, neatness and elegancy, cannot fail of being agreeably entertained

with

with the appearance of the audience, the performers and the house.

BLACK FRIAR's - BRIDGE, formerly called New-bridge, was built of timber about the time of Henry V. re-built in the reign of Edward IV. and in 1586 again re-built with stone, this also becoming ruinous, and it being thought that the three arches of which it was composed, too much impeded the passage of the water, when a flood was to be apprehended, it was taken down in the year 1784, and a new one of Portland stone with but one arch, built in the same place, from a plan given by Mr. Soane; and, as great weights would be constantly passing over, it was necessary to have the new bridge as flat as possible without injuring the navigation. The chord line of the arch is forty-two feet. The foundations of the abutments are piled and planked. The voussoirs of the arch have their joints worked perfectly smooth, and are set dry in milled lead, and in the middle of the joint of each voussoir are inserted two cubes of iron of three pounds weight, let equally into each stone, and channels are sunk from the tails of the voussoirs to the cavities of the iron joggles, and the whole of the cavities and channels are run full with lead; the superstructure is finished with iron railing, and it is much the handsomest bridge in the city.

The whole expence of pulling down the old bridge, and building the new one, was one thousand two hundred and ninety pounds. The steps next to St. George's bridge-street, which were in Mr. Soane's plan,

plan, are not executed, the houfes being too clofe to the bridge.

The DUKE's PALACE

ANCIENTLY confifted of many tenements, purchafed by Alan Percy, clerk, brother to the old Duke of Northumberland: He fold it to the Duke of Norfolk, in the time of Henry VIII. who converted it into a palace, and made it his principal place of refidence.

In 1602, the old palace was demolifhed, and a noble one begun by Henry Duke of Norfolk, but fcarcely finifhed before it was pulled down by his grandfon Thomas, on account of the ill-behaviour of the mayor, in not permitting his comedians to enter the city with trumpets, &c. From that time it has been entirely neglected: The fmall remaining part of the building is hired of the Duke for one of the city workhoufes.

Dr. Fuller remarks, that this palace was the greateft he had ever feen out of London. It had a covered *Bowling-alley*, (the firft of the kind in England) and, when Duke Thomas was taxed in 1596 for afpiring to the Crown of Scotland, by marriage with the unfortunate Queen Mary, he protefted to Queen Elizabeth, that when he was in his *Bowling-alley* at Norwich, he counted himfelf as great as a King in Scotland.

The BISHOPRICK.

THIS Diocefe was once divided into two Bifhopricks, the one of Suffolk, at Dunwich, then on the fea coast, now under the water, and generally called Southwold Bay; the other of Norfolk, at North-Elmham. Sigebert, King of the East Angles, returning out of France, after the death of Gerpenwald, where he had been banished, and there converted to christianity, and being placed on the throne, had brought over with him Felix, a Burgundian, made him Bishop of the East Angles, and placed his See at Dunwich, in the Eastern part of Suffolk. In 636 his third successor, Bifus, being old, divided this Diocese into two parts, appointing Bedwin the first Bishop of that part which is now called Norfolk, placing his See at North-Elmham in 673. After the death of St. Humbert, the tenth and last Bishop of Elmham, both Sees laid vacant upwards of 100 years, by reason of the devastations of the Danes. In the year 955 both Sees were joined in one at Elmham, and continued there till 1075, when Herfast, or Arfastus the 22d Bishop removed the seat of the See to Thetford, in Norfolk, where it continued till 1088; there being only three Bishops of Thetford; the last, Herbert Lesing, or de Losinga, the 24th Bp. translated the See to Norwich, in the reign of Wm. Rufus, 1088, where it has continued ever since. The value of the Bishoprick is greatly diminished since the Reformation, as King Henry VIII. seized all the lands belonging to it, and gave only in exchange the lands belonging to the monastery of St. Bennet in the Holme.—This See has given to the church of Rome two Saints; and to the nation five (1) Lord Chancellors, one (2) Lord

(1)---1073 Arfastu:-- Galfagus---1088 H. Losinga---1299 John Salmon---and again 1320.

(2) Lord Treasurer, one (3) Lord Chief Justice, one Bishop Almoner, and one (4) principal Secretary of State.

The Bishoprick possessed revenues of very considerable value from the earliest times; and it now stands charged in the King's books at 834l. 11s. 7d. halfpenny, and pays first fruits but no tenths, they having been remitted by Queen Elizabeth, in lieu of the two manors of Swanton in Norfolk, and Sudbone in Suffolk, which she severed from the See, during a vacancy, on the death of Bishop Hopton.

The Bishops of Norwich, by immemorial custom, always have, and still do enjoy a power of union, or uniting any two cures with institution, any where within the limits of the diocese, and of any value; and that either by *perpetual* or *personal* union. The perpetual union was always made with the consent and approbation of the Bishop, patrons of the churches, and incumbents, and answers to a consolidation: The personal union lasts only during the life of the incumbent; it answers to an Archbishop's dispensation, and requires in this diocese, only the Bishop's consent: This right was never disputed by either King, Pope, or Archbishop.

The Diocese, besides four peculiars, contains the whole counties of *Norfolk and Suffolk, in which there

(2). 1332---William Ayrmin-----(3) 1200 John Gray.----
(4) 1426 Wm. Alnewick.

* Except Emneth, in Norfolk, which belongs to the Diocese of Ely: and four parishes in Suffolk.

are 1314 parifhes, 800 in Norfolk, 527 in Suffolk and 16 in Cambridgfhire, and of thefe, 385 are impropriate. It is valued in the King's books at 899l. 18s. 7½d. and is computed to be worth near 3000l. annually. The clergy's tenth, amounts to 1117l. 13s. 0d. ¾.

There are fix Prebends in the church, five whereof are in the gift of the King, but prefented to by the Lord Chancellor, or Lord Keeper; and one is annexed to the Mafterfhip of Catherine Hall, Cambridge, and prefented to upon a vacancy by the Fellows of that College with the Mafterfhip. None of the Prebends are charged with the payment of Firft Fruits or Tenths; but they pay with the Deanry in lieu thereof, 89l. 11s. 5d.

The four Archdeaconries, viz. of Norwich, Norfolk, Sudbury and Suffolk, are in the gift of the Bifhop, who appoints alfo the chancellor, principal regifter, and the commiffaries to the archdeacons and their regifters, an high fteward, and fteward of courts, a general receiver of rents, &c. an auditor, bailiffs of the feveral manors, the general apparitor, and the porter to the principal gate of the palace, leading to St. Martin's Plain.

The CATHEDRAL.

THE Cathedral was founded by Bifhop Herbert in 1096, when Roger Bigot with moft of the nobility and Barons of the diocefe affifted at the ceremony, and by pecuniary

niary donations contributed largely to the undertaking: this firſt building was chiefly compriſed of wood, which by various accidents, and the turbulence of the times, was often greatly damaged by fire. The preſent Cathedral is a fine Gothic free-ſtone building, brought to the magnificent ſtate in which it now appears by the bounty and induſtry of its numerous and worthy benefactors at various times, and completed by Wm. Middleton the 36th Biſhop about the year 1284. The roof is adorned with various little images, well carved, repreſenting the hiſtorical paſſages of Scripture, from the creation of the world to the aſcenſion of Jeſus Chriſt, and the deſcent of the Holy Ghoſt. The length of the whole building, from the Weſt door to the entrance of the chapel of St. Mary the Great, (which ſtood at the Eaſt end, but is now in ruins) is 400 feet; and the extent of the tranſept or croſs ailes, from the North to South, 180.

 The ſhaft or ſpire, is very handſome and well proportioned, and the higheſt in England except Saliſbury. In 1629 the upper part of it was blown down, and re-built in 1633. It is 105 yards and 2 feet from the pavement of the choir to the top of the pinnacle; ſtrongly built with free-ſtone on the outſide and brick within. The upper window is the higheſt aſcent inward. The top ſtone of the ſpire conſiſt of half a globe, one yard two inches broad, with a channel round it; from whence extend eight leaves of ſtone, ſpreading outward, under which begin the eight rows of crockets, continued down the ſpire, at five feet diſtance from each other. The weather cock, placed
here

here at the Restoration, is three quarters of a yard high, and one yard two inches broad, as is also the cross bar.

The original church, as left by Bishop Herbert, consisted of the whole choir, tower, and the two transepts, with the North and South ailes of the choir beyond the transepts, and extended to the division between the nave and the anti-choir, and no further; the lower part of which, now remaining, is the original building; but some of the ornaments between the arches, and the entire roofs and upper parts, are of a later date. After the building was completed, it was dedicated to the honor of the Holy Trinity, on the 24th of September, on which day the dedication feast was annually celebrated. Bishop Eborard, who succeeded Herbert, built the whole nave, or body of the church, and its two ailes from the anti-choir or rood-loft door, to the West end; and the present building, except the roof of the nave and Western end, is of his foundation.

This was the state of the church till 1171, when it received considerable damage by an accidental fire; which was fully repaired by John of Oxford, the fourth Bishop, about the year 1197, who completely fitted up and oanamented the church, and presented it with a new set of vestments.

The next addition to this pile was the noble chapel of the Virgin Mary, or St. Mary the Great, built by Walter de Suffield, the tenth Bishop; a person so remarkable for sanctity and goodness, that his shrine was visited by pilgrims from various parts, and numerous miracles were said to be wrought at his tomb.

This

This wonder-working power received a full confirmation from the miraculous escape, as they termed it, of this chapel from the rage and fury of the citizens in 1272; when the whole church, tower, and adjacent buildings, were totally defaced by fire, in an insurrection of the citizens, occasioned by a violent dispute they were then engaged in with the monks. This affair cost the city three thousand marks, which, with the liberal donations of the King, Queen, Bishop and Nobility, so fully repaired and completed the church, that on Advent Sunday, 1278, King Edward I. and Eleanor his Queen, the Bishops of London, Hereford, and Waterford, and several of the Nobility, were present at its re-dedication by Wm. de Middleton, then enthroned Bishop of the See. At the same time, John de Chisil, Bishop of London, dedicated the altar where the body of St. William was buried, to the honour of our Saviour and all Saints; Thomas de Canteloupe, Bishop of Hereford, dedicated the opposite altar, by the choir door, to the honour of the blessed Virgin, St. John the Baptist, St. Giles the Abbot, and all holy Virgins; and Stephen Bishop of Waterford in Ireland, dedicated the altar, at the sacrist's chamber-door, to St. Peter and Paul, and all the Saints. But it soon after appearing that the old tower was much weakened by its being set on fire in the late insurrection, a new one was erected by Bishop Ralph de Walpole, and entirely finished at his sole expence.

In 1361, on the 15th of January, the steeple of the cathedral was blown down, by which accident the choir received considerable damage; to repair which, Bishop

Bishop Percy gave 400l. and obtained an aid of 9d. in the pound from his clergy for the same purpose: and from these funds the present tower was built, and the spire erected. In 1629, the upper part of the spire was blown down and re-built in 1633.

In 1463 the church was considerably damaged with lightening, which was the means of its receiving very large improvements and additions: For it was at this time, that the noble roof covering the nave of the church, and carved with most of the principal stories of the Old Testament, and the upper part of the nave itself, were begun and finished at the expence of Bishop Lyhert and his friends: Who also paved the Cathedral, built the stone rood-loft now remaining, and erected a tomb over the founder, which was destroyed in the grand Rebellion: And that the memorial of such worthy benefactors, might be transmitted to posterity, the windows of the nave were adorned with the arms of England, Edward the Confessor, Charles Earl of Richmond, and many other eminent persons.

After Lyhert's death, Bishop Goldwell, his successor, beautified the tower and the roof of the choir, with the same kind of work as his predecessor had ornamented the nave; fitted up the choir itself and chapels adjoining, in the form they remained in till the late alterations, by Bishop Younge; and covered the vaulted or arched stone roof with lead.

In 1509 Bishop Nix repaired the the transept ailes which had been much damaged by a late fire, and covered them with a stone roof. Thus the church remained till the dissolution, when the crucifixes, images

ges and pictures, were removed, and the arches where the images stood filled up, and whitened over. In 1601 part of the spire was struck down by lightning, but the damage was soon repaired; and the church continued in this state, till the outrageous devastations committed in it in the year 1643, by order of the then ruling powers, who demolished the organ, broke the painted glass in the windows, defaced the monuments, destroyed the vestments, and committed every kind of sacrilege, under the pious mask of pure religion, and necessary reformation.

At the Restoration, the church was fitted up again in its former manner; and in the same place where the organ had stood, the present one was erected by Dean Crofts and the Chapter. and afterwards beautified by Dean Astley. At the same time the present cope was given by Sir Philip Harbord, then high sheriff of Norfolk: And the city gave 100l to purchase plate for the altar.

From that time till about the year 1740, very little had been done, when Dean Bullock and the Chapter caused it to be thoroughly cleaned and repaired. It was again completely repaired and beautified by the Dean and Chapter in Bishop Younge's time, 1763. In the windows at the East end of the choir is a representation of the transfiguration, and the twelve apostles, painted on glass, by Dean Lloyd's Lady: It is allowed to be a very curious piece of workmanship, and the choir is now one of the most complete and beautiful in the kingdom.

The

The best general view of the Cathedral, is from the North side, in the Bishop's garden.

The CLOISTER, situated on the South side of the church, is the largest quadrangle of the kind in England, each side measuring about 58 yards in length, is near 14 feet broad, and 16 feet six inches high; the stone roof being ornamented with elegant carvings, representing the visions of the Revelation, our Saviour's Crucifixion and Resurrection, the Legends of St. Christopher, St. Lawrence, &c. At the grand entrance at the South-west corner, the Espousals, or Sacrament of Marriage, are carved in stone; and as soon as you enter the Cloister from hence, on the left hand, are the two lavatories, where the monks used to wash their hands. Over one of them is carved a fox in a pulpit, in the habit of a secular priest, holding up a goose to his auditory: Intended as a reflection on the secular clergy, or parish priests, to whom the monks bore an inveterate hatred.

In 1297, Robert de Walpole, Bishop of Norwich, undertook the building of that part of the cloister lying on the South side of the church, and the old chapter-house; which he finished, together with so much of the cloister as extends from the grand entrance into the church, called the prior's entrance, with all its curious work, to the passage leading to the chapter-house, now to Life's Green, near to which he caused a stone to be placed, with this inscription:

"Dominus Radulfus Walpole Norwicensis episcopus me posuit."

Richard

Richard de Uppehall, whom the Bishop employed in directing these works, added three more of the arches on that side of the cloister; the other five arches, and the South side of the cloister reaching to the arch over which the espousals, or sacrament of marriage, are carved, were built by Bishop Salmon and his friends; and by the profits arising from the office of pittancer, which the convent expended on this work. The North side adjoining to the church, was erected by Henry de Well, who expended thereupon the sum of two hundred and ten marks, over and above 20l. given by John de Hancock, and a portion of the pittance money alloted for that purpose. The West side, beginning at the espousals aforesaid, together with the sumptuous carved entrance near the refectory or common eating hall, the lavatories, and the door entering into the strangers hall, were built by Jeffrey Simonds, Rector of St. Mary in the Marsh, at the expence of 100l. and the part ranging from the strangers hall-door, to the entrance into the church, together with that entrance, by the executors of Bishop Wakeryng.

In 1382, Walter de Berney, citizen of Norwich, gave 100l. towards the iron work and glazing of the cloister windows; which work was perfected at the charge of the several families of Morley, Shelton, Scales, Erpingham, Gourney, Mowbray, Thorpe, Savage, &c. whose arms were to be seen in the windows of the cloister, above the bars, before the glazing was demolished. This famous and elegant cloister was finished in 1430, in the hundred and thirty-third year from its being first undertaken.

The

The BISHOP's PALACE stands on the North side of the church: It was built by Bishop Salmon, about the year 1320, and within half a century has been considerably improved, and the gardens elegantly laid out.

The gate, called Erpingham's or Lower Gate, built by Sir Thomas Erpingham, leads to the West entrance of the cathedral; upon the outside of the gate, are the Escutcheons and arms of Erpingham, and of Clopton and Butler, being an Orle of Martlets; or such families who married with the Erpingham's. The word *Pœna*, which is several times repeated upon the gate, shews it to have been built by way of pennance.—On the left hand through the gate, is the Free Grammar School, formerly a chapel dedicated to St. John the Evangelist.

The Deanry was formerly the prior's lodge, and with the long inclosed gallery, where the sick monks used to walk, still remain entire.

In digging for gravel in the burial ground inclosed by the cloisters of Norwich Cathedral, in 1788, when part of the lower close was inclosed, and a handsome garden made, some few bones and abundance of hair was found belonging to bodies, that by the gravestones were ascertained to have been buried from 160 to 180 years. Some of the hair was four feet in length, and of a beautiful brown colour. The reason of hair living so long in the earth, has by many been attributed to the low damp situation of the cathedral.

St. PETER

St. PETER of MANCROFT.

THIS is the principal parish in the city, and with the parishes of St. Giles and St. Stephen, constitutes the great ward of Mancroft. At the commencement of the Confessor's reign it was an open field; that part of it now the market-place, being the great croft, or close, of the castle, upon the outward West ditch of which it abutted. From its situation, the church, built on the South-west part, was distinguished by the name of Magna Crofta, or Mancroft. Towards the end of the Confessor's reign (1066) it began to be inhabited; and at the Conqueror's survey, the whole field was owned and held by de Waiet, or Gauder, Earl of Norfolk, in right of his castle, who granted it to the King in common, to make a new burgh between them, which contained the entire parishes of St. Peter of Mancroft and St. Giles. This Robert founded the old church of St Peter and Paul at Mancroft.

St. PETER's CHURCH, standing in an elevated situation, near the West or upper side of the market-place, was begun in 1430 and finished in 1455. It has a fine square tower steeple, 98 feet high, though designed at first to have been much higher, as appears both from the double buttresses reaching to the top, and the thickness of the walls: In this tower there is an excellent peal of twelve bells, cast by Messrs. Pack and Chapman, of London, in 1775, the Tenor weighing 41 cwt. The money paid for exchanging the old ten bells for this new peal of twelve, amounting to

L more

more than 800l. was raised by voluntary subscription. The whole building is of free-stone, extending 212 feet, the breadth from the North to South 66 feet, the ailes are 20 feet broad, the nave 30 and 90 feet long, The height from the pavement of the nave to the summit of the roof is 60 feet, the whole being covered with lead, and supported by two rows of pillars, remarkably neat and slender, forming eliptic arches at their top.

The chancel is sixty feet long, and the same, breadth with the nave. At the East end of the chancel is the old vestry, and under it a room called the treasury, supported by an arch: The present vestry is in the South-east corner of the church. The high altar, which is very advantageously raised above the rest of the church, stands upon another arch, through which there formerly laid a common passage, now stopped up. The altar-piece representing the story of St. Peter being delivered out of prison, was painted by that ingenious artist, Mr. Catton, and presented to the parish by Alderman Starling, in 1768. The furniture of the altar is crimson velvet, and the plate exceedingly grand, all but one cup being double gilt: One piece of it is remarkably curious, being an elegant standing cup and cover, of silver, double gilt, weighing 46 oz. 1 gr. 1 pt. given by Sir Peter Gleane, Knight, whereon is beautifully chafed the story of Abigail bringing presents to David.

In the vestry hangs a neat old painted carving in alabaster, of nine female saints, probably designed for some altar of St. Margaret, who is the principal figure,

figure, and here represented as holding down a dragon; amongst the rest is St. Hilda, holding a book and pastoral staff, and St. Barbara, a tower and palm-branch. There are also paintings of our Saviour's Resurrection, and St. Paul in prayer, and a few books, the most curious of which, is an octavo manuscript bible upon vellum, written in 1340, and a folio manuscript much more ancient, containing all St. Paul's epistles with a comment; it is beautifully illuminated and formerly belonged to Robert de Nowell.

St. LAURENCE's CHURCH

STANDS upon the spot, which before the retreat of the sea, and whilst this continued a considerable fishing town, was the quay or landing-place for all herrings and other fish brought into this city. The tithes of this fishery were so considerable, whilst in the hands of the Bishop of the East Angles, that about the year 1038 on Bishop Alfric's granting the quay, staithe, hagh (or close inclosed with hedges) together with the adjoining mansion, to Bury-abbey, and the abbot's undertaking to build the church, he reserved to his monastery a yearly payment of a last of herrings. On this hagh, in the time of the Confessor, the parish began to be built, the abbey having parted with it; though they reserved the quay or staithe, on which they founded the old church, which was a rectory in two medieties: The abbey had the house and one mediety, and the rectory the other. In William Rufus's time the medieties were joined, and ever since it hath continued one entire rectory. The last of herrings, payable by the rector of the abbey, was converted into a yearly payment of 40s. some time in the reign of Henry III. which continued to be paid till that of Henry VII. when it was remitted on account of the smallness of the profits. The rectory being valued at five marks was taxed at half a mark. and paid 3d. synodals. It remains in the King's books at 4l. 13s. 9d. and being sworn of the clear yearly value of 16l. 5s. 11d. $\frac{1}{2}$ is discharged of first fruits and tenths, and capable of augmentation.

The old church was pulled down about the year 1460, and the present beautiful and regular pile finished in 1472, at the expence of the abbot and monastery of Bury, the parishioners, and many private benefactors. It consists of a noble square tower, one hundred and twelve feet high, having a door at the West end; over it on the North part is carved a representation of the martyrdom of St. Laurence in stone; the saint is seen broiling on a grid-iron, and the soldiers are busied in tending the fire. On one part is figured a King crowned, designed to represent the FATHER, with a sword in his hand, striking at the Emperor Decian, at whose command this cruelty was exercised on the saint, who is falling under the stroke. On the other side is another piece of carving, representing Edmund the King tied to a tree, and the Danes shooting arrows in his body; near them lies his head among some bushes, alluding to the part of the legend, which says, that when they could not kill him with arrows, Hinguar the Danish General ordered them to smite off his head, and throw it amongst the thickest thorns in an adjacent wood,

THE NORFOLK TOUR.   115

wood, where a wolf finding it, preserved it from being devoured by any bird or beast of prey, till it was discovered by the Christians, and buried with the body.

The CHAPEL in St. George's of Colgate, is an elegant octangular structure, built in the year 1756 by the late Mr. Thomas Ivory.

The NORFOLK and NORWICH HOSPITAL without St. Stephen's gate, is a very neat building in the form of an H; it cost 9,295l. was erected and is still supported by voluntary contributions, and was first opened for the reception of in-patients November 7, 1772.

The physicians and surgeons attend in turn to take in-patients, every Saturday, at eleven o'clock in the forenoon; and every Tuesday, at the same hour, to prescribe to the out-patients.

The Governors meet every Saturday at eleven o'clock, to transact the business of the hospital.

STATE OF THE PATIENTS
From JULY 11, 1792, *to* JULY 17, 1793.

	In.	Out.	Tot.
Patients remaining on the books last year	62	140	202
Patients admitted from July 11, 1792, to July 17, 1793. - - - -	454	387	841
	516	527	1043
Discharged { Cured - - -	287	221	508
Relieved - -	52	80	132
Not likely to receive benefit -	19	2	31
Incurable - -	1	0	1
For non-attendance -	0	68	68
At their own request -	19	7	26
Went away without leave -	11	0	11
For irregularity - -	3	0	3
Deaths - - - -	20	5	25
Remaining on the books - -	78	160	238
	490	553	1043

' N. B. There appear to have been twenty six in-patients less and twenty-six out-patients more discharged than were admitted because twenty-six who were admitted as in-patients were afterwards made out-patients.

One hundred and sixty-one patients have this year been admitted as casualties, and cases that would not admit of delay, of whom one hundred and thirty-one have been discharged cured, two greatly relieved, one by request, eight have died, and nineteen remain on the books; sixty of them were fractures—to which the doors of this House are open at all hours, without any particular recommendation; six have undergone the operation for the stone, and were cured.

A GENERAL ACCOUNT of the PATIENTS admitted and discharged from the first opening of the Hospital for Out-Patients, July 11th, 1772, and for In-Patients, Nov. 7th, 1772, to July 7th, 1793.

		In.	Out.	Tot.
Patients admitted		8170	5966	14136
Discharged	Cured	5319	3268	8587
	Relieved	1204	1125	2329
	Not likely to receive benefit	88	39	127
	Incurable	176	108	284
	For non-attendance	0	1204	1204
	At their own request	368	214	582
	Went away without leave	154	0	154
	For irregularity	44	8	52
Deaths		405	174	579
Remaining on the books		78	160	238
		7836	6300	14136

N. B. There appear to be three hundred and thirty-four in-patients less, and three hundred and thirty-four out-patients more discharged than were admitted, because three hundred and thirty-four who were admitted as in-patients were afterwards made out-patients.

BETHEL

BETHEL or BEDLAM.

FOUNDED by the third daughter of John Man, Esq. and widow of the Rev. Mr. Samuel Chapman, rector of Thorpe by Norwich, in the year 1713, "for the convenient reception and habitation of lunaticks, and not for natural-born fools or ideots." According to the desire and advice of her late husband, by her will, dated Dec. 4 1717, she settled all her estates in Norfolk and Norwich on trustees, giving to them, and the majority of them, the sole power and management of the house, ordering them to choose, and place, or displace the master (who is to dwell therein and take care of the lunaticks) and to appoint physicians, apothecaries, &c. Those only who are destitute of friends or relations to be kept there gratis: and according to the directions of the will there are as many poor destitute lunaticks kept as the revenues will afford, (which are greatly increased through the good management of the trustees and by numerous benefactions) the inhabitants of the city of Norwich being always to be preferred: and whenever it shall happen that the trustees be enabled to maintain more than the city offers for relief, they are then impowered to receive such objects from any parish in the county of Norfolk or elsewhere: but the physician must first certify that they are proper objects, and the master have an appointment under the hands of a majortiy of the seven trustees before he can receive any one into the house. The trustees may also admit lunaticks whose friends or parishes agree to pay

pay them the moderate allowance of 4s. or 4s. 6d. a week.

A very elegant committee room has been lately built, which is adorned with the portraits of the foundress and several of the trustees.

The master's salary, besides his dwelling and two chaldrons of coals yearly, is forty pounds; ten pounds of that sum are in lieu of the money given by those who visit the house, now put into a box, the keys of which are in the trustees hands, and applied by them to the increase of the foundation.

The PUBLIC LIBRARY. In October 1794, the Public Library was removed from the city Library room, adjoining to St. Andrew's Hall, to the building formerly the Roman Catholic chapel, in Wymer-street, where books are delivered by the Librarian to the subscribers every day between the hours of eleven and two, Sundays and the following days excepted, 29th of May, 4th of June, the Guild-day, and the day preceding; 25th of October and 5th of November.

Several churches and other buildings in the city are encrusted with cut flints. The North wall of * Bridewell, thus built, is seventy-six feet in length, by about twenty-five feet high, and esteemed to be one of the greatest curiosities of the kind in England.

The

---

* Bridewell was built by Bartholomew Appleyard about the year 1370. Wm. Appleyard his son, the first Mayor of Norwich, served his Mayoralty here in 1403. The building was burnt down Oct. 22, 1751, and again much damaged by fire July 28, 1753.

The * flints are squared to such a nicety that the edge of a knife can scarcely be insinuated between the joints: most of them are about three inches square, the surface is very smooth, and no brick-work can appear more regular.

A gentleman desirous of spending a few days in Norwich, and of being acquainted with every thing in it worth observation, will not omit of seeing the various employments of its extensive manufactories, in stuffs, cottons, Shawls, and other ornamental furniture, the first and last of which are here carried to a perfection no where else to be met with in England.—Of the public buildings, we recommend to his particular notice, the Cathedral, with the adjoining cloisters; the Castle; the Barracks; St. Andrew's Hall; the Guild Hall in the market-place; St. Peter of Mancroft Church; the Theatre, and the Assembly House. The Buildings in St. Giles's-street and Surrey-street, and Mrs. Chambers's House on St. Catherine's-hill, will well repay the trouble of a transient view. There are two good general prospects of the city; one on the South east, from the meadows leading toward Thorpe; the other on the North east, from the shooting ground: The view from the lower part of Bracondale-hill will amply gratify any gentleman hav-

* Mr. Talman says that the Jews introduced the art of squaring flints: and Dr. Cromwell Mortimer, Secretary to the Royal Society, in a note on a paper of Mr. Arderon's on this very wall, observes, that the gate of the Austin Friars, at Canterbury, that of St. John's Abbey, at Colchester, and the gate near Whitehall, Westminster, are in the same taste. But the platform on the top of the Royal Observatory at Paris, which, instead of being covered with lead, is paved with flint after this manner, is an instance that the French have in some measure recovered this art. Phil. Transf. abr. vol. 10, p. 1304.

ing a taste for beautiful landscape; and the public Gardens or Chapel field, may administer some consolation to a half weary traveller after perambulating our ill-paved streets.

AMES says the *Art of Printing* was first invented about 1457, but by whom, or at what place it was first practised, typographical historians are not agreed. Hollingshed gives the honor of the invention to John Guthenberg, and fixes the place to Mentz, in Germany, about 1440. Fox and others contend, that John Fust, or Faustus, a goldsmith of Strasburg, and afterwards citizen of Mentz, was the inventor, about the year 1450, and that Guthenberg learnt it of him. The people of Harlem in Holland, confer the same honor upon Laurence Coster, their fellow citizen. From such a contrariety of evidence it is now impossible to determine who was the inventor of this noble art, which soon spread over the greater part of Europe, rapidly diffusing knowledge and learning among mankind.—Though the art is said to have been introduced into England about 1457, we do not know of any book printed in this kingdom of so early a date, and if it was then at all known amongst us, it must have been confined to some few of the Religious, who are accused of having sold the books so printed for *Manuscripts*—A deception which had been practised by Fust, when he carried several copies of the first great work in printing (the Bible in Latin) to Paris. Be this as it may, William Caxton, a mercer of London, certainly learnt this art in Flanders or Germany about 1457, after he was more than 50 years old, and there printed an English translation of *Recuyel* or the history of Troy in 1471, soon after which he returned into his native country, and the firſt book known to be printed in England by him, is a tranſlation from the French of THE GAME OF CHESS, 1474, which if not the *firſt book printed in England*, is certainly the firſt that was printed in this country with *fuſil metal types*: For though Frediric Corſelli, a Dutchman or German, is ſaid to have printed at Oxford, in 1468, *Sancti Hieronymi expoſitio in Symbolum Apoſtolorum*, it has been doubted, whether there ever was a Printer of that name in England, and if there was, the book here noticed is printed with ſeparate *wooden types*.

Thomas Bouchier, elected Archbiſhop of Canterbury in 1554, deſerved highly of the learned world, for being the principal inſtrument in introducing the noble art of printing into England. This diſcovery being ſo beneficial to learning, and its introduction among us reflecting ſo much honour on this Prelate's name, a ſhort account of it may not be unacceptable in this place. The Archbiſhop being informed that the inventor John Guthenberg, had ſet up a Preſs at Harlem, was extremely deſirous that the Engliſh might be made maſters of ſo beneficial an art. To this purpoſe he perſuaded King Henry VI. to diſpatch one Robert Tournour, belonging to the wardrobe, privately to Harlem. This man, furniſhed with a thouſand marks, of which the Archbiſhop ſupplied three hundred, embarked for Holland, and, to diſguiſe the matter, went in company with one Caxton, a merchant of London, pretending himſelf to be of the ſame profeſſion. Thus concealing his name and his buſineſs,

ness, he went first to Amsterdam, then to Leyden, and at last settled at Harlem; where having spent a great deal of time and money, he sent to the King for a fresh supply, giving his Highness to understand, that he had almost compassed the enterprize. In short, he persuaded Frederic Corselli, one of the Compositors to carry off a Set of Letters, and embark with them in the night for London. When they arrived, the Archbishop thinking Oxford a more convenient place for printing than London, sent Corselli down thither. And lest he should slip away before he had discovered the whole secret, a guard was set upon the Press. And thus the Mystery of Printing appeared ten years sooner in the university of Oxford than at any other place in Europe, Harlem and Mentz excepted. Not long after there were presses set up at Westminster, St, Alban's, Worcester, and other monasteries of note. After this manner Printing was introduced into England, by the care of Archbishop Bouchier, in the year of Christ 1464, and the third of King Edward IV.

After the introduction of Printing into England by Caxton, near a hundred years elapsed before it was practised in Norwich, and then it was introduced by Anthony Solmpne one of the strangers, for which he was presented with his freedom. The only piece which he is known to have printed, is intitled, "Cer-
" tain verses, written by Thomas Brooke, Gentleman,
" of Rolsbie, concerned with Throgmorton and others,
" in a conspiracy in Norfolk, in the time of his
" imprisonment, the day before his death, who suf-
" fered at Norwich the 30th of August 1570." These

are

are contained in thirty-two verses and at the end, " *Finis quod*, Thomas Brooke, imprinted at Norwich, " in the parish of Saynt Andrewe, 1570.

Were it not known that the art of printing in England, was almost exclusively confined to London, and the Universities of Oxford and Cambridge, till the beginning of the present century, it would be difficult to believe, that after its having been practised in Norwich in 1570, it ceased there for 130 years, and we hear no more of it till 1701, when a Mr. Francis Burges carried on the business upon a very small scale, in a house near the Red-well, and there published a pamphlet of 17 pages, in 1701, entitled some Observations on the use and original of the noble Art and Mystery of Printing; which I believe was the first Essay in the Art made here, that had any pretensions to be called book-work.

Mr. Burges meeting with but little encouragement in his business at Norwich, published this pamphlet by way of apolgy for the attempt, in which he endeavoured to prove, what has been generally admitted, that the Art of Printing is of considerable use in a trading place, a great means of promoting piety, and a certain method of doing good to other trades. He next gives a short history of the invention of the Art, and quotes some passages from Junius, and other ancient writers, tending to shew, that Laurentius Coster, of Harlem, in Holland, was the first who practised it in Europe, about the year 1440. Printing is said to have been known in China, above two thousand years, but having no letters to make words, their method is so different from what is practised in Europe, that it scarcely

scarcely deserves the name of printing. They have as many boards, as there are pages in the book, on which their characters are carved, one representing a man, another a house, &c. and of these characters they have such a multitude, that few of them know the one half.

The origin of Printing has been ascribed to the less important invention of cards, by which, it was at least, certainly preceded. Cards have been known ever since the year 1388, and the discovery of them attributed to Jaquemin Gringonneur, who made them for the purpose of amusing Charles VI. King of France. The names engraved in wood under the figures, are the first known impressions of letters. By degrees a greater quantity of text was added.

The art of making paper from linen rags, was brought into Spain by the Arabs, and first practised in Valencia and Catalonia; thence it passed into France in 1260, Germany 1312, England 1320, and 1342. The first book printed upon paper made in England, is *Bartholomeus de Proprietatibus Rerum*, by W. de Worde, without a date, but supposed in the year 1493 or 1494.

The KEELS and WHERRIES which navigate between Norwich and Yarmouth, are acknowledged to be superior to the small craft on any other stream in England, for carrying a larger burden, and being worked at a smaller expence. They are from 15 to 50 tons, have but one mast, which lets down by a windlas placed at the stern, carry one large square sail, are covered close by hatches, and have a cabin superior to
many

many coasting vessels, in which it is not unfrequent for the keelman and his family to live. They are navigated by never more than two men, often by a man and his wife, or one man and a boy. The usual passage for a loaded keel, is from twelve to sixteen hours, when light they sometimes perform it in five hours. The river is sufficiently broad in all places to admit two keels easily to pass each other, and in some parts it is twice that breadth. In the whole distance, 32 miles, there is neither lock, bridge, or other impediment to navigation. By these craft, grain of every kind that is grown in the county, flour, part of the goods manufactured in Norwich, for foreign markets, and other heavy articles are sent to Yarmouth; and they bring from thence, coals, grocery, iromongery, fir timber, deals, wine, spirits, &c. The freight for grocery, and other heavy goods imported, does not exceed one shilling and six-pence per ton, but smaller articles pay about four-pence half-penny the hundred weight.

In the beginning of the civil war in the reign of Charles I. Norwich sent a party of 50 dragoons to join Colonel Cromwel's regiment at Cambridge, and immediately after raised 100 more, and mounted them upon horses, taken from the loyalists in the city, whom they called *malignants*. The parliament laid a weekly assessment upon the whole kingdom of 33,518l. of which the county of Norfolk raised 1,250l. in the following proportions: The county 1,129l. Norwich 53l. Lynn 27l. 11s. 10d. Yarmouth 34l. 16s. 5d. and Thetford 5l. 11s. 9d.

As the following verses contain a handsome compliment to our fair citizens, serve to convey some idea of the city itself near 200 years ago, and were not thought unworthy of a place in the venerable Camden's excellent Britannia, we hope they will be acceptable to the readers of the Norfolk Tour. They were written in Latin by Arthur Johnston, principal of the Marischeal College in Aberdeen, and next to the elegant Buchanan, the best Latin poet of modern times. Johnston was born in 1580, at Caskiebean, in Scotland, which town he celebrates. He mentions a curious fact, viz. that the shadow of the high mountain of Benochie, distant about six English miles, extends to the house of Caskiebean at the Equinox. He was physician to King Charles I. and published an elegant version of the psalms in Latin verse, in 1637, which has been reprinted several times; he was the author of Musæ Anglicanæ, or commendatory verses upon persons of rank in church and state at that time, also of some Epigrams and other smaller works, and died at Oxford in 1641.

 A town, whose stately piles and happy seat
 Her citizens and strangers both delight.
 Whose tedious siege and plunder made her bear ⎫
 In Norman troubles an unhappy share,   ⎬
 And feel the sad effect of dreadful war.   ⎭
 These storms o'er blown, now bless'd with constant
  peace,
 She saw her riches and her trade increase.
 State here by wealth, by beauty wealth's outdone;
 How blest, if vain excess be yet unknown!
 So fully is she from herself supply'd,
 That England, while she stands, can never want an
  head.   Dr.

Dr. Fuller in the history of the Worthies of England, published in 1662, observes, that he had been in Norwich about forty years before, "when many of the houses were covered with thatch; he wishes that the city may long flourish in its full lustre, and then quaintly adds, yea may their STRAW in due time advance into TYLE, and thereby their houses be better secured against the merciless element of fire, whose furious raging is seldom bounded unless by the want of fewel to feed on." Could the same author have visited Norwich in the year 1794, there had been little occasion for his remark on thatched houses, and he would have seen his wish fully accomplished in the beauty and present improved state of the city.

KETT's REBELLION.

THE emptiness of the treasury on the demise of Henry VIII. the factious disposition of ambitious courtiers during a minority, the alterations then carrying on in the established religion of the country, and the war with the Scots and French, might be fully sufficient to excite discontent and rebellion, without having recourse to the petty domestic grievance of the Inclosure of Commons and Waste Lands, and that after the evil, if it were one, had been ordered to be removed.

Kett's Rebellion made its first appearance at Attleburgh the 20th of June 1549, in the second year of the reign

---

* Perhaps STRAW and TYLE may be taken as one of Fuller's pleasant puns, from Jack Straw and Watt Tyler.

reign of Edward VI. when that King was but nine years old, and by the 7th of the following month it had made such progress, that the insurgents assembled at Wymondham in great numbers; and having chosen Robert Kett, a tanner of that place, for their leader, their first exploit was levelling the fences of one Flowerdew of Hetherset, against whom Kett is said to have entertained some personal animosity. The inclosures which Kett had made underwent the same fate; and their next determinaton was open and undisguised rebellion.—Popular tumult is the dangerous engine of malignant faction! and the pleasure arising from the hope of levelling all distinctions in society, one of the highest gratifications to a vulgar mind. Whatever the leaders of the insurgents at first held out to beguile the unwary, they undoubtedly entertained a wish, and had some faint expectations, of being able to overturn the Government both in church and state, which they sufficiently manifested when their numbers became formidable, by demanding the suppression of the gentry, the placing of new counsellors about the King, and the re-establishment of ancient Rites. Of this disposition Kett knew how to avail himself, and within less than a month from the commencement of the insurrection, he had collected a body of more than twenty thousand men round his standard, and encamping upon Moushold-hill, besieged Norwich, and committed every kind of excess, such as burning a great part of the city, plundering the adjacent country, and wantonly destroying many of the principal inhabitants, and that for no other reason, but that of their being Gentlemen. To so high a

pitch

pitch of irregularity and extravagance had they arrived, that three thousand bullocks, and twenty thousand sheep, besides all kinds of poultry in abundance, were devoured in their camp in a few days. Government at first used every possible means to persuade these deluded people to disperse and quietly return home, and follow their various occupations, but their own folly, or the knavery of their leaders, construing that into fear, which alone originated in motives of mercy and humanity, they obstinately refused all the offers of peace which were made. This obliged Government to pursue the more efficient measures, which the safety of the country had placed in their hands, and the Marquis of Northampton, with fifteen hundred horse, was sent to relieve the city: He was accompanied by the Lords Sheffield and Wentworth, and many other eminent persons: He entered Norwich the last day of July, and was attacked the same night by the rebels, whom he repulsed after killing three hundred of them, but they renewed the attack the next day, when a furious engagement took place on St. Martin's Plain, in which the Lord Sheffield with about fifty soldiers were unfortunately killed, and the King's forces obliged to retire out of the city. John Dudley, Earl of Warwick, with part of the forces raised for the Scottish war, was next sent against this lawless banditti; he was accompanied by the Marquis of Northampton and other persons of distinction, and many of the principal citizens, who had joined him at Cambridge. On the 23d of August he encamped with his troops between Norwich and Eaton,

whence

whence he sent a summons to the city (then in possession of the rebels) and afterwards a herald to Kett's camp on Moushold, offering a general pardon to all who would lay down their arms and quietly return home; which proving ineffectual, the Earl's troops the next day forced their way into the city by Brazen-door, St. Stephen's-gate, and the breaches made between that and St. Giles's. The main body under the command of the Earl himself, entering by St. Bennet's-gate, proceeded directly to the market-place, where he fixed his head quarters. Some ammunition waggons, belonging to the army, for want of proper orders, having been driven through the city as far as Bishop-gate, were seized by a party of the rebels, who when conveying them to their camp, were overtaken and defeated by a party of the Earl's forces, under Captain Drury, and most of the waggons recovered. The rebels still remaining in the city, had frequent skirmishes with the King's troops; intelligence of which being carried to the Earl, he immediately marched and attacked their principal body then posted in St. Andrew's street, near the church, in which 130 rebels were killed on the spot, many taken prisoners, and the rest entirely driven out of the city. On the 26th the Earl was reinforced by a body of 1400 Swiss, but the rebels still confident of success from the great superiority of their numbers, aided by the wrong application of some equivocating vulgar prophecies which they had got by heart, such as

  The Country Gnoffes, Hob, Dick and Hick,
   With clubbes, and clouted shoone,
  Shall fill up Dussyn dale,
   With slaughter'd bodies soone.

And

> The heedlefs men within the dale,
> Shall there be flain both great and fmall.

refufed to hearken to all overtures of peace which the Earl made, and inconfiderately quitting the advantageous poft they occupied upon Moufhold-hill, which had rendered the Earl's horfe of but little fervice, and enabled them to do fo much mifchief to the city, they marched to the adjacent valley called Duffyn dale, where ftrongly intrenching themfelves, they imprudently determined to hazard a general engagement. Fuller fays, " The Englifh are accufed of always " having a prophecy for every occafion, and the re- " bels fancied that Duffyn dale might be interpreted " as meaning a foft pillow or bed for death to reft " upon, they fancied themfelves upholfterers to make, " whereas they proved the ftuffing to fill the fame." The Earl marched out of the city on the 27th of Auguft to attack them, but before he proceeded to extremeties, Sir Edmund Knevet and Sir Thomas Palmer, knights, were fent to acquaint them, that if even then they would repent and lay down their arms, they fhould be pardoned, one or two only excepted. By which the two Ketts were undoubtedly meant This being unanimoufly refufed, an order for the attack was given, which commencing by a general difcharge of the artillery, they were fo far difconcerted as to become an eafy conqueft, for the Earl's light horfe, and the infantry under Captain Drury, coming up at the fame time, broke in amongft them before they could recover themfelves, or clofe their ranks, and made a terrible carnage; however they once more faced about

about, and fought more desperately than might have been expected from such a rabble. The main body of their army being thus entirely broken, a general flight ensued, in which Robert Kett, their principal commander took the lead. In the battle and pursuit more than three thousand five hundred of them were killed, a great number wounded and taken prisoners; with very little loss to the King's forces. Thus rage was conquered by courage, number by valour, and rebellion by loyalty.

There still remained a party of reserve unattacked; who having strongly barricaded themselves with the carriages belonging to the army, seemed determined to stand it out to the last extremity. The Earl therefore to avoid further effusion of blood, once more offered them pardon, upon the same conditions as before; but suspecting this to be a stratagem, they hesitated to comply, till the Earl taking Norroy with him, proclaimed their pardon, on which the whole company crying out God save King Edward, thankfully accepted it. After the battle the whole plunder was given to the soldiers, who openly sold it in the marketplace. The next day, on intelligence being received that Robert Kett was apprehended in a barn at Swannington, the Earl sent twenty horsemen to conduct him to Norwich; and the same day nine of the principal ringleaders (the two Ketts excepted) were sentenced to be drawn, hanged and quartered at the Oak of Reformation, as they themselves had christened it; thirty were executed at the gallows without Magdalengate; and forty-nine at those by the cross in the market; in the whole about three hundred suffered. Some

THE NORFOLK TOUR. 123

Some gentlemen who had been cruelly treated by the infurgents, urged the Earl to further acts of feverity, which he fteadily refufed to comply with, declaring, that none fhonld fuffer who had accepted the offer of pardon.

The two Ketts were committed prifoners to the tower of London, tried and convicted of high treafon, and on the twenty-ninth of November in the fame year, were delivered to Sir Edmund Windham, high fheriff of Norfolk and Suffolk, who conducted them to the places of execution; Robert was hanged in chains upon a gibbet on the top of Norwich Caftle, and William upon Wymondham fteeple.

Robert Kett, was a tanner in Wymondham, of confiderable property, and efteemed to be a moft daring and refolute fellow.—Fuller remarks, that " he was " more wealthy then men of his condition ufually " are, that he had more wit (a word in Fuller's time " ufed to exprefs knavery) than wealth, and more " confidence, now called impudence, than either." And Stow obferves, " that he poffeffed 50 l. a year in " land, and was worth above one thoufand marks in " goods." William Kett, his brother and partner in iniquity, was a butcher in the fame town, and remarkable for defperate hardinefs: His family was one of the moft ancient and flo rifhing in Wymondham, for in the twenty-fecond of Edward the Fourth, John Knyght, alias Kett, was a principal owner there. After his conviction it was prefented at a court holden for the King's manor there, that Robert Knyght, alias Kett, who wa hanged upon Norwich caftle for treafon, died feized of thirty acres of land held of the faid

manor,

manor, which efcheated to the King, who of his great clemency regranted them to William, fon and heir of the faid Robert, and his heirs for ever.

In all civil commotions the Wife and Prudent are oppreffed by anxiety, the thoughtlefs are elevated by hope, and thofe who are bankrupt in fortune and reputation, exult in the general diftruction; and in a civil war expect to retrieve their credit and conceal their infamy.

LIVES OF EMINENT MEN
BORN AT NORWICH,
OR, WHO HAVE PRINCIPALLY RESIDED THERE.

HERBERT LOSINGA, the firft Bifhop of Norwich; Bale fays that he was born at Orford, in Suffolk. He was fome time abbot of Ramfey in Huntingdon, afterwards prior of the monaftery, of Fifcaud in Normandy, whence in 1088 he returned with King William Rufus, of whom he obtained various preferments; was made Lord Chancellor, and in three years was grown fo rich as to be able to purchafe the abbey of Winchefter for his Father Robert; and the Bifhoprick of Thetford for himfelf, at the price of 1,900l. Hence the verfe was made, *Filius eft pater abbas, Simon uterque.* Meaning that both of them were guilty of Simony; for this Simoniacal act he was fummoned to Rome by Pope Pafcal II. and by way of penance commanded to build feveral churches and monafteries, all which he actually, and 'tis faid, religioufly performed. Camden fays that the word

Leafing

Leasing in Saxon signifies a *Lye* or *Trick*, and for this reason Bishop Herbert had the surname of *Losinga*, as being made up of lying and flattery, by which he raised himself to great honors and preferments. From the works of charity and munificence, which he left as witnesses of his immense riches, he was called by William of Malmsbury, *Vir pecuniosus*. Fuller asserts that Bishop Herbert was born at Oxford, but adds, that he might well serve for two counties, being so different from himself, and two persons in effect. When young loose and wild, deeply guilty of the sin of Simony: When old nothing of Herbert was in Herbert, using commonly the words of St. Hierom, *Erravimus juvenus emendemus senes*. When young we went astray, now old we will amend. He was an excellent scholar for those times, comely of personage, and wrote many learned treatises mentioned by Pitsæus. In the latter part of his life he was mild, affable, blameless in his carriage, pure, innocent, and of exemplary virtue; sincerely repenting of his former Simoniacal practices, and to atone for them built the Cathedral at Norwich, and a palace for himself and successors, on the North side; a monastery for 60 monks on the South, St. Leonard's church (now called Kett's castle) upon Moushold-hill, another in the Bishop's court, now the close, St. Margaret at Lynn, St. Nicholas at Yarmouth, St. Mary at Elmham, and the Cluniac monastery at Thetford.—In reviewing this list, we cannot help expressing our astonishment, that they should (as we may say) have been the labour of one Man's hands, and confessing, that if the founder of so many and such magnificent edifices, really acquired great riches by the means of fervility and flattery, it was much to his honor, and we hope a full expiation of the frailties of a courtier, that he applied them, not to the vain purpofes of an *ufelefs* and *oftentatious* difplay of human power and greatnefs, but in the infinitely more commendable purfuit of erecting fuch magnificent monuments of piety, as promife to be the admiration of feveral fucceeding ages yet to come: and howfoever he might acquire the Surname of *Lofinga*, or be called *Vir Pecuniofus* (which is now no ftigma at all) we think that the private virtues and public charities of his riper years were fuch, as in more modern times would have been efteemed fufficient to atone for a multitude of the follies of youth.

WILLIAM BATEMAN, Bifhop of Norwich, in the fourteenth century, and founder of Trinity-hall, in Cambridge, was born at Norwich in the latter end of the reign of Edward I. He was from his tendereft years, of a docile and ingenious difpofition. Having therefore made a good proficiency in learning, wherein he furpaffed all his equals, he was fent to the Univerfity of Cambridge. After having gone through the ufual courfe of the fciences, he applied himfelf to the ftudy of the Civil Law, in which he took the degree of Doctor, before he was thirty years of age, a thing then uncommon. On the 8th of December, 1328, he was collated to the Archdeaconry of Norwich. Soon after this, he went and ftudied at Rome, for his further improvement; and fo diftinguifhed himfelf by his knowledge and examplary behaviour, that he was promoted by the Pope to the place of Auditor of his palace. He was likewife advanced by him to

the

the Deanery of Lincoln ; and so great an opinion had he of his prudence and capacity, that he sent him twice as his Nuncio, to endeavour to procure a peace between Edward III. King of England, and the King of France. Upon the death of Anthony de Beck, Bishop of Norwich, the Pope, by his usurped provisional power, conferred that Bishoprick upon him, on the 23d of January 1343, and consecrated him with his own hands. He was confirmed the 23d of June 1344. Being invested with that great dignity, he returned into his native country after many years absence; and lived in a regular, and withal in a generous and hospitable manner. Of Pope Clement VI. he obtained for himself and successors, the first fruits of all vacant livings within his diocese ; which occasioned frequent disputes between himself and his clergy. In the year 1347 he founded Trinity-hall, in Cambridge, for the study of the Civil and Canon Laws: and another Hall dedicated to the Annunciation of the Virgin Mary, for the study of Philosophy and Divinity. Being a person of great wisdom, eloquent, and of a fine address, he was often employed by the King and Parliament in affairs of the highest importance; and particularly was at the head of several embassies, sent on purpose to determine the great differences between the Crowns of England and France. In 1354, he was, by order of Parliament dispatched to the Court of Rome, with Henry, Duke of Lancaster, and others; to treat (in the Pope's presence) of a peace, then in agitation between the two Crowns abovementioned. This journey proved fatal to him; for he died at Avignon, where the Pope then resided, on the 6th of January 1364-5, and was buried with great solemnity in the cathedral church, near the Pope's palace in that city. With regard to his person, we are told that he was of an agreeable countenance, tall, handsome, and well made. He was likewise a man of spirit, justice, and piety, punctual in the discharge of his duty, a great lover and promoter of learning, and of a friendly and compassionate disposition. But he was a stout defender of his rights, and would not suffer himself to be injured, or imposed upon, or his dignity insulted by any one, may be inferred from the following anecdote, which our historians relate of him: Lord Morley having killed some of the Bishop's deer, infringed upon his manors, and abused the servants who opposed him, was obliged to do pennance by walking through the streets of the city, with a wax candle of six pounds weight in his hand, and kneel down before the Bishop in the cathedral to ask his pardon, although the King had sent an express order to the contrary.

He bestowed on the great altar of his Cathedral two images of the Holy Trinity, the one a large one, is a shrine made of solid silver gilt, of great value, the other a small one, with reliques of twenty pounds weight.

While he was Bishop there was such a dreadful plague in England, that it scarcely left a tenth part of the inhabitants living. And the Chronicle of Norwich says, that from the first of January to the first of July in the year 1348-9, fifty-seven thousand three hundred and seventy-four persons (besides ecclesiastics and

and beggars) died in the county of Norfolk only. This seems in some measure to be confirmed by the Bishop's having instituted and collated 850 persons to benifices vacant at that time.

MATTHEW PARKER, the second Protestant Archbishop of Canterbury, born August 6, 1504, was the son of a tradesman in Norwich: His father dying when he was but twelve years of age, his mother took particular care of his education, and in 1520, he was admitted a student in Corpus Christi college, Cambridge, of which society he was elected fellow, in the beginning of September 1520, in the seventeenth year of his age, and became chaplain to Anne Boleyn, whom he attended to the scaffold, and received particular instructions from her " to see that her daugh-" ter Elizabeth was brought up in the fear of God." He was a zealous promoter of the Reformation in the reign of Edward VI. who promoted him to the Deanery of Lincoln; he was obliged to abscond during the reign of Queen Mary; but on the accession of Elizabeth was advanced to the Archbishoprick of Canterbury, which he held till his death; which happened at his palace in Lambeth, May 17, 1575.

Parker being placed at the head of the church, and knowing that he should have all the art of the Papists to contend with, took care to have the Sees filled with the most learned and worthy men, and the Universities put under such regulations as should prevent Papists settling there. He was at great expence in rebuilding his palace at Canterbury, and founded a Free-school at Rochdale in Lancashire. It was by his interest chiefly that the great English Bible, commonly

monly called the Bishop's Bible, was first trranslated from the Hebrew and Greek in 1568, the former one having been mostly from the Latin of Erasmus. It is in one volume folio, on royal paper, and a most beautiful English Black Letter, embellished with several cuts of the most remarkable events in the old and new Testament, and Apocrypha; maps cut in wood, and other draughts engraven on copper, particularly under the names of the books to the second part of the Bible, beginning with Joshua, is a fine print of the Earl of Leicester, a half length in armour, holding a truncheon in his left hand. At the beginning of the first psalm, in the place of the initial letter is a copper-plate print of Secretary Cecil, in his gown and furs, holding in his left hand a Hebrew Psalter open, and having his right hand upon the letter B. standing before him.

A *complete* copy of this Bible is now extremely scarce; there is one in the Public Library at Cambridge, and the compiler of the Norfolk Tour, has another, *but a little imperfect*.

This Bible was in general use through England till the reign of James I. when the present translation was undertaken by his order, although the psalms of the former Bible are still used in the service of the church.

To Bishop Parker we are likewise indebted, for a treatise on the antiquity of the English Church, and the publication of four of our best ancient English Historians; Matthew of Westminster, Matthew Paris,

Asser's

Affer's Life of King Alfred, and Thomas Walfingham.

With all thefe fplendid qualifications, he has been blamed for his feverity to the Puritans, but whom would they not then have abufed? Upon the diffolution of Monarchy in 1649, Lambeth Houfe became the refidence of Colonel Scot, one of the Regicides, who turning the chapel into a hall or dancing-room, the venerable monument of the Archbifhop, ftanding in the way, was totally demolifhed, and out of hatred to the memory of the corpfe there interred, and to epifcopacy, the body was dug up; the lead that inclofed it was plucked off and fold, and the bones were privately buried under an adjoining dung-hill, near an out-houfe where poultry was kept, where they continued till after the Reftoration of Charles II. when Sir William Dugdale, the great Antiquary, acquainting Archbifhop Sandcroft where they were depofited, he procured an order from the Lords to fearch for them, and having been found, they were decently depofited again near the place where the monument formerly ftood, over which is engraven thefe words, CORPUS MATTHÆI ARCHIEPISCOPI TANDEM HIC QUIESCIT. Archbifhop Sandcroft, alfo caufed the fame monument to be again erected to his memory, with a long infcription, in Latin, written by himfelf.

JOSEPH HALL an eminent and learned divine, and fucceffively Bifhop of Exeter and Norwich, was born in Briftow Park, within the parifh of Afhby de la Zouch, in Leicefterfhire, July 1, 1574. He was educated in the Grammar School in his native place; and at the age of fifteen fent to Emanuel College in Cambridge,

Cambridge, of which in due time, he became fellow. He read the rhetoric lectures in the public schools, for two years with great applause; and distinguished himself as a wit and a poet, in this early period of his life, by the publication of his Satires in 1597.

After six or seven years residence in college, he was presented to the Rectory of Halstead in Suffolk, soon after which he married. In 1605 he accompanied Sir Edmund Bacon to the Spa, where he had an opportunity of examining into the state and practices of the Romish church. Having spent a year and a half in these travels, he returned to London, and was made chaplain to Prince Henry, and soon after presented to the Rectory of Waltham Abbey in Essex, which being convenient for his court attendance, he kept 22 years; during which time he was made Prebendary of Wolverhampton, and in 1616 Dean of Worcester, though he was then absent, attending the embassy of Lord Hay in France. The year after he attended the Earl of Carlisle into Scotland, and in 1618 was sent to the * Synod of Dort, but the air of the country not agreeing with him, he returned home in about three months; however, before his departure, he preached a Latin sermon to that famous assembly, which by their Precedent and assistants took a solemn leave of him; and the deputies of the States presented him with a gold medal, having on it the portraiture of the Synod.

This

---

* Cambridge sent two Divines to the Synod of Dort; the other was the Master of Sidney, both Puritan colleges: his medal is there in the public library.

This medal is now (1794) in the cuſtody of Dr. Farmer, maſter of Emanuel College.

Having refuſed in 1624 the Biſhoprick of Glouceſter, he accepted in 1627 that of Exeter, and in 1641 was tranſlated to the See of Norwich; but on December 30 following, having joined with other Biſhops in the proteſtation againſt the validity of the laws made during their forced abſence from the parliament, he amongſt the reſt was committed to the tower on the 30th of January 1642, but was releaſed in June following, upon giving 5000l. bail, and withdrew to Norwich; where he lived in tolerable quiet till April 1643. But then the order for ſequeſtering *notorious delinquents* being paſſed, in which he was included by name, all his eſtates real and perſonal were ſeized and ſold at public ſale, even (ſays Blomefield) to a dozen of Trenchers, nor did they forget to lay their hands upon his Eccleſiaſtical preferments, and turn him out of his palace.

About this time he wrote his Treatiſe, intitled " Hard Meaſare," in which he ſays, " They were " not aſhamed after they had taken away, and ſold " all my goods and perſonal eſtate, to come to me " for aſſeſſments and monthly payments for that " eſtate which they had taken."

In the ſame Treatiſe he informs us that Sheriff Tofts and Alderman Lindſey, attended by many zealous reforming followers came into his private chapel, known by the name of Jeſus chapel, and then ſituated on the North ſide of the great altar of the cathedral, to look for what they called *reliques of idolatry,* amongſt
which

which the painted glass in the windows, representing St. Ambrose, St. Austin, &c. were pointed out by them to Bishop Hall, to be particularly obnoxious, as representing so many Popes. The good Bishop to satisfy their scruples, promised to remove the cause, and that it might be done with the least injury to the windows, he caused the * heads of the pictures to be taken off, wittily observing, that he knew the bodies could not offend; but this partial compliance, not satisfying these zealous reformers, they soon after totally destroyed these beautiful windows.

To those Ecclesiastics whom the zealots of the day called delinquents, and whose church preferments they seized, they pretended to allow a fifth of their revenue, but this pittance was never regularly paid, and often wholly withdrawn.—Where power, fanaticism, and malignity are joined, no man's fortune can be secure for a moment. These refined oppressors had a nick-name for the unfortunate people who wished only quietly to enjoy their own property; they called them *heart malignants*, and fleeced them of their real and personal Estate, with as ittle ceremony as they plundered the clergy. These oppressions they called *the spoiling of the Egyptians*; and their rigid severity *the dominion of the Elect*; they interlarded their iniquities with long and fervent prayers; saved themselves from blushing by pious grimaces, and exercised in the name of the Lord all their cruelty on men.

Bishop

* This may in some measure account for our now seeing many figures in painted glass windows without faces, having only a piece of white glass to supply the place.

Bishop Hall published an humble Remonstrance in defence of Episcopacy; to which in 1641, five *Ministers, of whose names the first letters made the celebrated word Smectymnuus, gave their answer. Of this answer a confutation was attempted by the learned Usher, and to the Confutation, Milton published a reply.

In 1647 he retired to a little estate, which he rented, at Heigham, in the Western suburbs of Norwich, where he died September 8, 1656, in the 82d year of his age, and was buried in the church-yard there. In the chancel of Heigham church is his Monument, whereon is represented a golden picture of Death holding up an Escutcheon in his left hand, with these words, *Persolvit & quietus est.* and in another Escutcheon, in his right hand, *Debemus Morti nos nostraque*, and on the Monument this inscription;

> Induviæ JOSEPHI HALL
> Olim NORVICENSIS Ecclefiæ
> Servi repofite VIII. Die
> Menfis Septembris,
> Anno Domine 1656,
> Etatis fuæ, 82,
> Vale Lector,
> et Æternitati profpice.

And on the foot of the Monument,
JOSEPHUS HALLUS olim humilis Ecclefiæ Servus.

He was by learned foreigners called the English *Seneca*, and is universally allowed to have been a man of great wit

* Stephen Marshall -- Edmund Calamy --- Thomas Young --- Matthew Newcomen --- William Sparrow.

wit and learning, and of as great meekness, modesty and piety. His works are many and voluminous, having printed fifty single Treatises, since collected and published in three volumes, folio, in 1647, Bayle says they are filled with fine thoughts, excellent morality, and a great deal of piety.

In the beginning of his Satires he claims the honour of having led the way in this species of composition:

" I first adventure, follow me who list,
" And be the second English Satyrist."

This assertion of the Poet is not strictly true; for there were various satyrical writings previously to his appearance. But he was the first who distinguished himself as a legitimate Satyrist, upon the classic model of Juvenal and Persius, with an intermixture of some strokes in the manner of Horace. Succeeding authors have availed themselves of the pattern set them by Hall. The first three books were termed by the author *toothless* satires. He has an animated idea of the dignity of good poetry, and a just contempt of poet-asters in the different species of it. He says of himself, in the first Satire:

Nor can I crouch, and writhe my fawning tayle
To some great patron for my best avayle,
Such hunger-starven trencher-poetrie,
Or let it never live, or timely die.

His first book, consisting of nine Satires, is chiefly levelled at low and abject Poets. Several Satires of the second book reprehend the contempt of the rich, for men of science and genius. We shall transcribe
the

the sixth, being short, and void of all obscurity, and illustrative of some English manners two centuries ago.

> A gentle squire would gladly entertaine
> Into his house some trencher-chaplaine:
> Some willing man that might instruct his sons,
> And that would stand to good conditions.
> First, that he lye upon the truckle-bed,
> Whiles his young maister lieth o'er his head.
> Second, that he do, on no default,
> Ever presume to sit above the salt.
> Third, that he never change his trencher twise.
> Fourth, that he use all common courtisies;
> Sit bare at meales, and one half rise and wait.
> Last, that he never his young maister beat,
> But he must ask his mother to define
> How many jerks she would his breech should line.
> All these observed, he could contented bee,
> To give five marks, and winter liverie.

From this Satire it is evident how humiliating the terms were to which a private tutor was obliged to submit; without much probability of emancipation by the salary of 3l. 6s. 8d. and a great coat. — The author's characteristic of Satire is good.

> The satire should be like the Porcupine,
> That shoots sharp quils out in each angry line
> And wounds the blushing cheeke, and fiery eye
> Of him that hears and readeth guiltily.

The following stroke upon false descriptions of beauty is witty:

> Another thinks her teeth might liken'd be
> To two faire rankes of pales of ivory;
> To fence-in sure the wild-beast of her tongue,
> From either going far or going wrong.

Upon the whole, these Satires sufficiently evince both the learning and ingenuity of their author. The sense has generally such a sufficient pause, and will admit of such a punctuation at the close of the second line, and the verse is often as harmonious too, as if it were calculated for a modern ear: but the uncouth and antiquated terms and obsolete words which frequently occur in this writer, seem to require a short glossary to explain them.

In a catalogue of his works is a satirical piece, entitled *Mundus idem & alter*, &c. that is " The World " different yet the same." Bayle says, this is a learned and ingenious fiction, wherein he describes the vicious manners of several nations; the drunkenness of one, the lewdness of another, &c. and does not spare the court of Rome. Gabriel Naude says of this work, that " it is calculated less to divert the readers, than " to inflame their minds with the love of virtue."

Though the language of Bishop Hall begins to be obsolete, he may be ranked among the most eloquent of our English prose writers; he seems to have succeeded in the arduous attempt of assuming the different manners of Seneca and Cicero, and passages might be selected from his writings, which are in the best manner of both those Romans. We cannot avoid observing in this place, that an attention to the contemplations of

Bishop

Bishop Hall, is likely to be revived among critical readers, by a late detection of the plagiarisms of Sterne, by Dr. Ferriar of Manchester, in which many of the most striking passages in his writings are traced to this part of the works of our prelate, and to Burton's Anatomy of Melancholy.

JOHN COSIN a learned Bishop of Durham, in the seventeenth century, was the eldest son of Giles Cosin, a citizen of Norwich. He was born at Norwich, November 30, 1594. Having completed his studies at Caius College in Cambridge, he was appointed chaplain to Dr. Richard Neille, then Bishop of Durham, who pesented him to a Prebend in that cathedral, and procured him the Archdeaconry of the East Riding of the church of York. At the commencement of the civil wars, he was deprived of all his livings, being the first clergyman who underwent that punishment, and therefore went abroad, and fixed his residence at Paris; but returning in 1660, with King Charles II. was promoted to the Deanery of Peterborough, and afterwards to the Bishoprick of Durham, which he held till his death, January 15, 1672, in the 78th year of his age, and was buried under a little Monument, like one of those usually made in churchyards. His death deprived the wits and minor writers of much entertainment which they had promised themselves on his return to England. He was the author of several learned tracts, chiefly in controversial divinity.

Dr. SAMUEL CLARKE, a very learned and eminent Divine of the seventeenth and eighteenth centuries,

turies, was the son of Edward Clarke, Esq. Alderman of Norwich, one of its representatives in parliament for several years, and was born October 11, 1675. He made so rapid a progress in his studies at Cambridge, particularly in the mathematics, that before he had attained to the twenty-second year of his age, he had a considerable hand in introducing into the University the Newtonian philosophy. He afterwards applied himself to divinity, which he intended to make his profession, and was appointed chaplain to Dr. John Moore, Bishop of Norwich, who gave him the Rectory of Drayton, near the city. In 1706, he translated into Latin, Sir Isaac Newton's Optics; and being recommended to Queen Anne, by his patron the Bishop of Norwich, was presented to the Rectory of St. James's, Westminster. In 1710, he published a splendid edition of *Cæsar's Commentaries, in one volume royal folio; and in 1712 appeared his Scripture Doctrine of the Trinity, which made so much noise. He was afterwards engaged in a dispute with Liebnitz, concerning the principles of natural philosophy and religion; and the letters which passed between them on the subject, were published at London, in 1717. Upon the death of Sir Isaac Newton, he was offered the place of master of the mint; but this he refused, as inconsistent with his character. In the beginning of the year 1729, he published, in one vol. quarto, the first

* twelve

---

* This is one of the most magnificent books ever published in England, and a large paper copy of it is EXTREMELY SCARCE.

* twelve books of Homer's Iliad, with the Latin version accurately corrected, and learned notes, dedicated to the Duke of Cumberland; but before he had finished the rest, he was taken suddenly ill, and died on the 17th of May, in the same year. Since his death have been published from his original Manuscripts, by his brother, Dr. John Clarke, Dean of Sarum, an Exposition of the Church Catechism, and ten volumes of his Sermons. His works, which are numerous, and of which those we have mentioned form but a part, will remain a perpetual monument of his learning and abilities.

A picture of the Rev. Dr. Clarke is placed in the Royal palace at Kensington, under which is the following Inscription:

SAMUEL CLARKE, D. D.
Rector of St. James's, Westminster.
In every Part of useful Knowledge and critical Learning, perhaps without a Superior;
In all united, certainly without an Equal.
In his Works, the best Defender of Religion;
In his Practice, the greatest ornament of it:
In his Conversation communicative, and in an uncommon manner instructive:
In his Preaching and Writing, strong, clear and calm;
In his Life, high in the Esteem of the Great, the Good, and the Wise;
In his Death, lamented by every Friend to Truth, to Virtue and Liberty.
He died May 17, 1729, in the 54th year of his Age.

---

* The twelve last books of the Iliad were published 1732, in one volume quarto, by his son Mr. S. Clarke, who also published Homer's Odyssey, in the same manner, in two volumes quarto, 1740.

JOHN KAYE, or CAIUS, the prime glory among the phyficians of Queen Elizabeth's reign, was born October 6, 1510. Like Linacre, he united the firſt honours of literature with thoſe of medicine. His great attachment to his ſtudies was manifeſted by ſome very early productions, being chiefly tranſlations from Nicophorus, Calliſtus, Chryſoſtom and Eraſmus, and which were performed by him at the age of twenty-one. He ſtudied phyſic at Padua, under Johannis Baptiſta Montanus, the moſt eminent profeſſor of his time; and whilſt he reſided in that city, he lodged in the ſame houſe with the celebrated anatomiſt Andrew Veſalius, whoſe ardour he emulated in anatomical purſuits. On his return to his native country, he was incorporated Doctor of phyſic at Cambridge, and practiſed in his profeſſion at Shrewſbury and Norwich, where his reputation ſpread ſo faſt that he was ſoon called to London. Here he was ſucceſſively phyſician to Edward the Sixth, and the Queens Mary and Elizabeth. Being conſtituted a fellow of the College of Phyſicians, he was ever after the great ornament and ſupport of that body. He preſided, for ſeven years, at the head of the college, and diſplayed, on various occaſions, his zeal for the dignity and intereſt of the ſociety. To Cambridge, where he had received his firſt education, he was a ſignal benefactor. Gonville Hall, of which he had been a member, was erected by him into the * College, which now goes by his name. Dr. Kaye was diſtinguiſhed

as

* The ſquare added by Dr. Kaye to this College, was built in 1570, and coſt him 1,48cl. a ſum equal to 8,88ol. of the preſent time.

as a critic, a linguist, an antiquary, a physician and a naturalist; but it is only in the two latter capacities that he demands our present attention. For Galen he expressed the profoundest esteem and veneration; and he was a perfect master of that physician's voluminous writings. With this predilection, many new experiments or discoveries are not to be expected in Kaye's productions. His first work, "De Medendi Methodo," is of little consequence; but the next of his medical performances is indisputable original; and the subject of it forms a curious article in the annals of medicine. We mean his account of the "*Sweating sicknefs," or as he himself named it, the "Ephemera Britannica," published in 1556. Valuable, however, as this treatise is, not only as giving the fullest narrative of so singular a distemper, but as containing many judicious practical remarks, it is far from being a perfect piece of medical writing. What is most to be regreted is, that it affords but little light with respect to the first rise of the disease. It may be added concerning the work, that it is a good specimen of the *order*, though not entirely so of the *manner*, in which subjects of this kind should be treated. As a naturalist Dr. Kaye sustains a very respectable character. He was the correspondent and intimate friend of the celebrated Gesner, and drew up for his use "Short Histories of certain rare animals and plants," which were inserted in Gesner's works, and afterwards separately published, with corrections

* This disease broke out in 1551, at which time, Dr. Kaye lived in Norwich, and obtained the greatest reputation by the manner in which he treated it.

rections and enlargements. At the request, also of the same great naturalist, Kaye wrote a "Treatise on "British Dogs," in a method so judicious, that Mr. Pennant has inserted the whole piece in his "British "Zoology." In the opinion of the same gentleman, than whom none can be a better judge, all Dr. Kaye's other descriptions of animals are proofs of his great acquaintance with this branch of natural history.

As King James was passing through Caius College, the Master presented him Kaye's history of the University of Cambridge, upon which the King said, "give me rather Caius de Canibus." The first of these books, amongst other matters, tended to prove the superior antiquity of the place, as well as the pre-eminence of its learned members over the University of Oxford; and it remained uncontroverted for more than a century and a half, when in 1730, a person calling himself Thomas Caius, or Kaye, published a work in two octavo volumes, entitled, "*Vindiciæ An-*"*tiquæ Academiæ Oxoniensis,*" contra J. Caium.—The Cambridge historian certainly wrote elegant Latin, and though his arguments might be controverted, the elegance of his language could not be denied, and as such the book is always valuable to a scholar; but I never heard that the answer was worth any thing, till its scarcity stamped a value upon it.

Dr. Kaye died at Cambridge, after having foretold his death, on July 29, 1573. in the 63d year of his age, and was buried in the chapel of his own college. The following short inscription was put upon his tomb: FUI CAIUS.

There

There is a good profile head of him in Holland's Heroologia, fol. 183, and a catalogue of his works, amounting to 72 Treatises, in Aikin's Biographical Anecdotes of Medicine, and Pitt's English Worthies.

WILLIAM CUNNINGHAM, M. D. was born in 1531, and in 1559 published a book called the " Cosmographical Glasse," a folio of about 250 pages, containing as the title expresses, the pleasant principles of Cosmography, Geography, Hydrography, or Navigation ; with many cuts neatly executed upon wood, particularly a portait of the author in his Doctor's habit, and a plan, or rather a bird's-eye view of the city of Norwich, as it was in 1558, and on the back, an explanation of the plan. The book, though scarce, has long been useless, and the plan is no otherwise valuable than as a curiosity, and being the first that was taken of the city. He appears to have written seven other treatises, but dying at the age of 28, they were never printed.

Sir THOMAS BROWNE, an eminent English physician, and celebrated writer, was the son of Mr. Thomas Browne, a merchant of London, descended from an ancient and genteel family of that name seated at Upton, in Cheshire. He was born October the 19th, 1605, in the parish of St. Michael, Cheapside, in the city of London, and had the misfortune of losing his father in his minority, who left him however a considerable fortune, in which he was much injured by one of his Guardians. He was first sent for education to Winchester College, and thence removed to the University of Oxford, where he was entered a

Fellow-

Fellow-Commoner of Broadgate's-Hall, soon after stiled Pembroke College, in the beginning of the year 1623; took the degree of Batchelor of Arts, Jan. 31, 1626; proceeded in due time to his degree of Master of Arts, entered on the physic line, and practised that faculty for some time in Oxfordshire, which he quitted to accompany Sir Thomas Dutton, his father-in-law, to Ireland, hence he travelled into France and Italy, studied physic at Montpellier and Padua, at that time the celebrated schools of medicine; and in his return home through Holland, took his degree of Doctor in physic, in the University of Leyden. He returned to his native country in 1634, and the next year wrote his " Religio " Medici," or at least made the first sketch of it; an incorrect copy of which being handed about in manuscript, without his consent, he published an edition of it in 1643—In 1636 he settled himself at Norwich, and the year following was incorporated as Doctor of physic at Oxford. In 1641 he married Mrs. Deborah Mileham, of a good family in Norfolk, and five years after published his Treatise on " Vulgar " Errors." In 1655 he was chosen honorary fellow of the college of physicians, as a man " Virtute et " literis ornatissimus," eminently embellished with literature and virtue.

In 1658 he wrote a discourse on urn-burial, together with the garden of Cyrus; and in September, 1671, received at Norwich the honour of Knighthood from Charles II. and died in the city, on his birthday, Oct. 19, 1682, in the 77th year of his age, and was buried in the church of St. Peter of Mancroft; where,
upon

upon a mural monument, fixed to the South pillar of the altar, there are two inscriptions, one in Latin, the other in English, containing several particulars relating to his life. By his Lady he had ten children of whom only one son, and three daughters survived him.

In his person he was of a moderate stature, of a brown complexion, and his hair of the same colour. His picture in the college of Physicians, and the portrait prefixt to his works shew him to have been remarkably handsome, and to have possessed in a singular degree, the blessing of a grave and yet cheerful and inviting countenance. As to his temper, it was perfectly even and free from passions: he had no ambition beyond that of being wise and good, and no farther concern for money than as it was necessary; for otherwise he might certainly have raised a very large fortune in the way of his profession: but his charity, generosity, and tender affection for his children, to the expence of whose education he would set no bounds, contracted the wealth he left into a very moderate compass. His virtues were many, and remarkably conspicuous; his probity such as gained him universal respect, as his beneficence rendered him generally beloved: in respect to knowledge, he was extremely communicative in his conversation, and notwithstanding his rare abilities and established reputation, wonderfully modest. His religion was that of the Church of England, in which he shewed himself unaffectedly humble and sincere. As to sects in learning he followed none, but thought and wrote with the utmost freedom, illustrating every subject he touched

by

by such new and nervous remarks, as charmed every attentive reader, and has occasioned more care to be taken of the papers he left behind him, than has usually happened to the remains of learned men, a circumstance singular in itself, and which reflects on his memory the highest honour.

In 1684 Dr. Tenison, (afterwards Archbishop of Canterbury) published a small volume of Tracts written by Dr. Browne; and in 1686 his works were published in one volume folio. In 1712 his Posthumous works were published in one volume octavo, containing the antiquities of the cathedral church of Norwich. An account of the Urns found at Brampton in Norfolk, 1667, and some letters between Sir William Dugdale and Sir Thomas Browne, &c. This was adorned by several plates, and is become a scarce book.

His Religio Medici excited the attention of the public, by the novelty of its parodoxes, the dignity of sentiment, the quick succession of images, the multitude of abstruse allusions, the subtlety of disquisition, and the strength of language. What is much read will be much criticised, says his Biographer, and the remark was particularly applicable to the Religio Medici, which raised the author many admirers and many enemies.

It is not on the praises of others, but on his own writings, that he is to depend for the esteem of posterity; of which he will not easily be deprived, while learning shall have any reverence among men: For there is no science, in which he does not discover some skill; and scarce any kind of knowledge, profane

or

or sacred, abstruse or elegant, which he does not appear to have cultivated with success. Dr. Johnson.

BROWNE (EDWARD) an eminent physician the son of the preceding, was born about 1642. He was educated at the Grammar School in Norwich, and in 1665 took the degree of Batchelor of Physic at Cambridge. Removing afterwards to Merton College, Oxford, he was admitted there to the same degree in 1666, and the next year created Doctor. In 1668 he visited part of Germany, and the year after Austria, Hungary, and Thessaly, and passed through Italy. Upon his return he practised physic in London; was made physician to Charles II. and afterwards in 1682 to St. Bartholomew's Hospital. About which time he was concerned with many other eminent men, in a translation of Plutarch's Lives, in which he translated those of Themistocles and Sertorius. He was first censor, then elect, and treasurer of the college of physicians; of which in 1705 he was chosen president, and held that office till his death, which happened in August 1708, at his seat at Northfleet, near Greenhithe in Kent. He understood Hebrew, was a critic in Greek, and no man wrote better Latin, High-Dutch, Italian and French, which he spoke and wrote with as much ease as his mother-tongue; physic was his business and to the promotion of that, all his other acquisitions were referred. Botany, Pharmacy, and Chemistry he knew and practised. King Charles said of him, that he was as learned "As any of the College, and as well-bred as any at Court." He was married, and left a son and a daughter.

Upon his return into England in 1669, he published the first volume of his Travels, a thin quarto, with plates, in 1677 the second, and in 1685 a new edition of both in one volume, small folio, with many corrections and improvements. This work had a great character given it in the *Philosophical Transactions*, and was received with universal applause, which, without doubt, it very well deserved. His skill in natural history, made him particularly attentive to mines and metallurgy. The account of the countries through which he passed, is written with an uncommonly scrupulous and exact veracity.

JOHN SKELTON,- Rector of Disc, a celebrated wit and poet, was Poet Laureat to King Henry VIII. Erasmus called him the light and honour of British learning. Wood says his wit was biting, his laughter opprobrious aud scornful, and his jokes commonly sharp and reflecting. His propensity to satire created him abundance of enemies, amongst whom the Dominican Friars and Cardinal Wolsey were the most powerful and irreconcilable. The Dominicans were very obnoxious to his satirical pen, for their vices, and the Cardinal for his arbitrary proceedings; and, Skelton's foretelling Wolsey's downfall, was such a crime as a proud cardinal could not forgive in a poor priest, and accordingly Skelton was prosecuted for keeping a concubine; to which he replied. In his conscience he ever esteemed her for his wife, (which she really was) tho' he did not declare it, because Fornication in the clergy was thought a little sin, and Marriage a great one. He was forced to take sanctuary in Westminster Abbey. where he died June 29, 1529.

On Monday March the 24th, 1783, the Pageant of the GOLDEN FLEECE, or what is called BISHOP BLAIZE, was exhibited by the Woolcombers, in a ſtile ſurpaſſing all former proffeſſions of the kind in this city. The proceſſion began at ten o'clock in the morning, in St. Martin's at Oak, and thence paſſed through the principal ſtreets of the city.

The dreſſes were ornamented with all the embelliſhments that fancy and ingenuity could ſuggeſt, particularly the ſhepherds and ſhepherdeſſes:—The characters were extremely well ſupported, thoſe of Jaſon and the Biſhop met with diſtinguiſhed marks of approbation, and the whole was conducted with the greateſt order and regularity.

The GOLDEN FLEECE was borne in a grand palanquin, ſupported by four champions, and guarded by HERCULES and ORPHEUS. JASON rode on horſeback in a ſailor's habit, attended by CASTOR and POLLUX, HYLAS, THESEUS, BIRITHOUS, PELEUS, TELEMON, and forty-three other Theſſalian and Argive heroes, theſe Argonauts appeared in their proper dreſſes on horſeback. Biſhop BLAIZE, patron of the Woolcombers, was drawn in a phæton, or triumphal car; the cavalcade was accompanied by the ſocieties of Woolcombers in their different uniforms, and a Shepherd and Shepherdeſs to each ſociety; with proper bands of muſic, decorations of flags, and other emblemetical ornaments, to complete the proceſſion.

ORDER

ORDER OF THE PROCESSION.

FOUR TRUMPETERS.
MARSHAL-MAN.
P E A C E.
O R A T O R.
BANNER of BRITANNIA.
P L E N T Y.
D R U M S AND F I F E S.

TWENTY { ✻ ✻ ✻ ✻ ✻ ✻ ✻ / ✻ ✻ ✻ ✻ ✻ ✻ ✻ / ✻ ✻ ✻ ✻ ✻ ✻ } ARGONAUTS.

H E R C U L E S.
LYNCEUS.   THE GOLDEN FLEECE,   TIPHY.
ZETES. Borne on a GRAND PALANQUIN by 4 Men. CALAIS.
O R P H E U S.
CASTOR.   JASON DRAWN in a PHAETON   POLLUX.
BY FOUR HORSES.
STANDARD of THE ARGONAUTS.

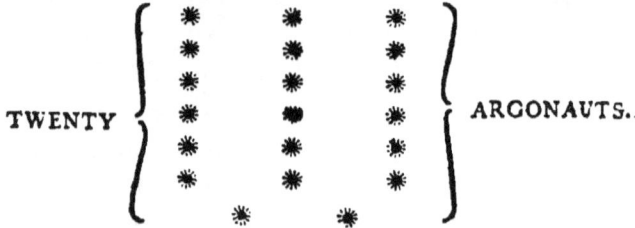

MILITIA BAND,
STANDARD of THE CITY.
TWO VERGERS.
O R A T O R.
BISHOP's CHAPLAIN
IN A PHAETON AND PAIR.
PAGE. •BISHOP BLAIZE PAGE.
IN A PHAETON DRAWN BY SIX HORSES.
STANDARD of THE CITY.
The BOOK-KEEPERS, SHEPHERDS and SHEPHERDESSES
belonging to the different Societies of Combers---12 Companies.
Seven Companies on Foot.---Five Ditto on Horseback.

CHRONOLOGY
OF
REMARKABLE EVENTS IN NORWICH.

446 THE foundation of Norwich.
575 The caftle firft built by Uffa King of the Eaft Angles.
872 King Alfred in Norwich, and improved the fortifications of the caftle.
912 King Athelftan in Norwich.
980 Norwich made a Borough, and governed by a Serjeant.
1004 Norwich burnt by Sweno, or Swain, the Dane, who then returned to his own country.
1010 The Danes returned into England, fubdued the Eaft Angles; and fettled in Norwich and Norfolk in 1011.
1014 The Danes driven out of England by Etheldred.
1016 The Danes again returned under Canute, who in 1017 became King of England, affigning Norfolk and Norwich to the cuftody of Turkill, a Danifh Earl.
1018 The prefent caftle is fuppofed to have been built about this time, by King Canute, and repaired, ornamented, and the outworks added, by Thomas de Brotherton in 1315.
1030 Norwich was a fifhing town, the ground on which St. Laurence church ftands being the ftaith.
1060 Norwich had 1,320 burgeffes and 25 churches.
1075 William the Conqueror, gave the Earldom, city and caftle, to Ralph de Waiet, who rebelling againft his benefactor, was fubdued, and t e city much injured in the conteft.

CHRONOLOGY OF EVENTS.

1086 Norwich contained 1,565 burgesses, and 480 bordars, i. e. labourers.

1087 William Rufus having suppressed the rebellion of Roger Bigot, granted the city many privileges.

1094 Herbert de Losinga removed the Bishopric from Thetford to Norwich, April 9, and in 1096, laid the first stone of the cathedral.

1122 Henry I. being at Norwich, granted the citizens a charter, containing the same franchises and liberties as London then enjoyed. From this time the city was governed by a Provost, chosen by the King, and the government of it first severed from the castle.

1135 King Stephen granted the custody of the castle to Hugh Bigot.

1140 The Jews *are said* to have crucified a child, named William, of 12 years old, and buried him in Thorpe wood; the body was dug up by the monks five years after, and became famous for the miracles performed at it's shrine, *by their pious frauds*.

1152 King Stephen made Norwich a corporation.

1174 The cathedral damaged accidentally by fire, and the city plundered by the Flemings, who came to assist Hugh Bigot, in his rebellion against King Henry II.

1193 King Richard I. granted a new charter, in which the people of Norwich were first called *Citizens*.

1216 Lewis, the Dauphin, having obtained a grant of the kingdom from the Pope, took the castle, and plundered the citizens, *a la Françoise*.

1252 The city inclosed with a ditch.

CHRONOLOGY OF EVENTS.

1266 The difplaced Barons feized the caftle, plundered the city, and killed many of the inhatants.

1271 The cathedral fteeple ftruck by lightning. A great flood.

1272 A quarrel between the citizens and monks, in which they alternately plundered and murdered each other. From this time to the reformation, animofities never ceafed between them; the ecclefiaftics were often pillaged and perfonally abufed by the populace, and the purfe of peaceable citizens compromifed the difference.

1278 The cathedral was finifhed and confecrated on Advent Sunday, by William de Middleton, the Bifhop.

1280 Confiderable damage done to the city and county by inundations and tempefts.

1285 The citizens obtained a new charter, but no extenfion of privileges.

1289 On Wednefday after the feaft of Epiphany happened a flood, which ran over White Friar's bridge, and deftroyed feveral houfes.

1294 The city walls firft begun. Finifhed in 1319, or 1320.

1296 Norwich firft fent reprefentatives to parliament 25th of Edward I.

1297 The cloifter began to be built. Finifhed in 1430

1315 A great dearth and mortality, fo that the living were fcarcely fufficient to bury the dead.

1328 A free trade for all Worfteds Manufactured in Norwich was granted: This may fhow how considerable the Manufactory of the city was, even in that early period.

1336 This year is memorable for the great increase of Worsted Stuffs, by a colony of Dutch, and Flemings, who were driven out of their country by an inundation. This trade was further encouraged by Edw. III. prohibiting the exportation of unwrought wool, and granting great privileges to foreign artificers; and by a sumptuary law, the first of its kind in England, ordering that none should wear any other than English cloth, except the Royal Family, and those who could afford to spend 10l. a year.

1340 From February to Easter following there was a public tournament in Norwich, at which King Edward III. and Queen Philippa were present. In the same year the gates and towers of the city were fortified and made habitable.

1341 The castle became the public gaol for the county of Norfolk.

1343 A very high wind, by which the passage-boat then coming from Yarmouth was sunk near Cantley, and 38 persons perished.

1348 The plague, destroyed, *it is said*, above 57,000 people in Norwich.

1350 A great tournament was held here, at which Edward the Black Prince, and many of the nobility were present. The city made a grand entertainment for the Prince and his retinue, at the expence of 37l. 4s. 6d,

CHRONOLOGY of EVENTS.

1361 A great dearth, attended by a plague; this was called the second pestilence. On the 15th of January the same year, the tower of the cathedral was blown down, and falling upon the choir, demolished great part of it.

1369 The plague broke out and carried off great numbers of people.

1377 The battlements on the walls and towers of the city amounted to 1630.—The inhabitants to 5,300.

1381 The rebels in Norfolk, amounting to 50,000 men, headed by Litester, a dyer of Norwich, totally dispersed at North-walsham, by the troops under Henry le Spencer, Bishop of Norwich.

1383 King Richard II. and his Queen visited Norwich, and were received with great pomp.

1390 A great mortality raged in Norfolk, and other counties, occasioned by the people eating unwholsome food.

1403 A Mayor and two Sheriffs appointed, instead of the four Bailiffs. William Appleyard the first Mayor.

1413 The city sustained great damage by fire.

1416 By the charter obtained this year, the mode of chusing the mayor, sheriffs, common-council, &c. in the city, was regulated.

1455 A statute was made, limiting the number of attornies to six for Norfolk, six for Suffolk, and two for the city of Norwich. In the preamble, an excellent reason is given for the regulation.

1463 The cathedral considerably damaged by fire.

1472 In this year, it is supposed, the day of electing

CHRONOLOGY OF EVENTS.

ing the Mayor, was changed from the firſt of March to the firſt of May, as it ſtill continues.

1477 A plague throughout England, which, Hollingſhead ſays, deſtroyed more people in four months, than had been killed in the laſt 15 years war.

1478 Another great peſtilence began in September and continued till November following, in which time, Nevyle ſays, there died an incredible number of people in the city.

1485 The kingdom was viſited by a new kind of diſeaſe, called the Sweating Sickneſs: ſcarce one in a hundred eſcaped the contagion, and great numbers died.

1501 John Rightwiſe, mayor, began building the croſs in the market, and finiſhed it in 1503. It was taken down in 1732 by, it is ſaid, a Mr. Otherwiſe.

1507 April 25 and June 4, two fires, by which 718 houſes in the city were deſtroyed.

1519 A great flood on St. Leonard's day, thence called St. Leonard's flood.

1530 King Henry VIII. was declared ſupreme head of the church; and acknowledged ſo by act of parliament, 1535, which gave to the King all abbies and monaſteries, not having grants of above 200l. a year value.

1534 The council chamber was built in the mayoralty of Auguſtine Steward, Eſq. About this time ſeveral people were burnt in Norwich and other places for Lollardy.

1539 The

1539 The prior and convent in the precinct, converted into a dean and chapter, and made a body corporate; and the precinct, which till then made part of the hundred of Blofield, declared to be part of the city and county of Norwich.

1544 The Mayor's feast for the first time kept in St. Andrew's Hall.

1549 Kett's rebellion broke out at Wymondham, July the 7th.

1551 The disease called the sweating sickness, broke out at Shrewsbury in April, spreading by degrees all over the kingdom, till October following. In London 960 persons died of it in one week, and prodigious numbers in other places. What was very extraordinary, no foreigner died of it.

1558 A great mortality raged through the kingdom; in Norwich 10 Aldermen died.

1561 The Earls of Northumberland and Huntingdon, with many other nobles and knights, dined with the mayor, on the guild-day, in St. Andrew's Hall.

1566 Three hundred and thirty Dutch and Walloons were invited to settle here, where they introduced the manufacturing of bayes, says, arras, mockades, &c. In 1571 their number had increased to 3,925, and in 1582, to 4,679.

1568 The west end of the guild-hall rebuilt.

1569 The Earls' rebellion in Norwich.

1570 Printing first practised in Norwich.

CHRONOLOGY of EVENTS.

1570 A great flood, from the feafon in which it happened, called Candlemas flood; it rofe confiderrably higher than that of St. Leonard's flood. The North fide of the city was totally overflown, and Fye-bridge broken down. The fame year John Throgmorton, Thomas Brooke, and G. Dedman, were hanged and quartered at Norwich, for high treafon.

1574 Norfolk had 6,120 able men on the mufter-roll, of which 3,630 were armed; and Norwich had 2,120 able men, of whom 400 were armed. This enrollment was made when an invafion was expected from Spain, by means of the boafted INVINCIBLE ARMADA.—There is reafon for believing that the county and city could now raife 24,000 men on a fimilar occafion.

1575 The Dutch fettled here invented the manufacturing of bombazines, for of which they obtained an exclufive privilege.

1578 Queen Elizabeth came to Norwich on Saturday the 16th of Auguft, and ftaid till the Friday following, during which fhe and her fuite lodged at the Bifhop's palace, and were entertained with pageantries, principally allufive to the trade and manufactures of the city. The Queen dined in public in the North alley of the cloifter. In the fame year, the Shirehoufe on the caftle-hill was built.

1579 A plague in Norwich, of which 4,817 perfons died, including 10 Aldermen, between Auguft 20, 1578, and February 19, 1579. This terrible

rible fcourge, was faid to have been bronght here by fome of the Queen's attendants in the preceding year,

1582 The water was conveyed from the New Mills to the Crofs in the market.

1583 The plague broke out again, and eight or nine hundred people died of it.

1588 Another plague, but it did not rage violently.

1591 White-friars bridge, and (fome accounts fay) Coflany bridge, were built with free-ftone. In the fame year 672 perfons died in the city in lefs than four months.

1597 It was agreed, that no one fhould ferve the office of Mayor a fecond time, unlefs at a diftance of nine years from the firft ferving.

1601 April 29, the cathedral fpire greatly damaged by lightning.

1602 Three thoufand and feventy-fix perfons died here of the plague.

1609 Sir John Pettus erected the building over the fpring without Bifhop's-gate.—In the fame year a plague, tho' but few people died of it.

1611 At a public rejoicing on Tomb-land with fire-works, 31 perfons were killed by the crouds of people-

1615 A great flood on St. Andrew's day, thence called St. Andrew's flood.

1620 The Boys Hofpital was begun, and 14 boys firft put into it.

1626 One thoufand four hundred and thirty-one perfons died here of the plague.

1629 A curious letter from Lord Pembroke, directed

to

to the mayor and sheriffs, complains of the quality of the herring pies sent to the exchequer.—The herrings were not of the first that were taken—the pies were not well baked—the herrings were deficient in number—they should be 120 herrings, and five in every pye—many of the pies were much broken, &c.—*Courtiers might surely be better employed.*

1648 John Utting, esq. the mayor, paying little regard to a petition presented to him by about 150 of the *godly* of the day, was sent for to London. He was a great favourite of the common people, who had like to have murdered the Messenger. After he was gone, the mob went to the Committee-house, standing on the site of the present Bethel, where the gunpowder was kept, and set fire to 80 barrels, which killed above 100 persons, and greatly damaged the adjacent buildings.

1654 An ordinance being published for raising 90,000l. a month for the maintenance of the army and navy. the city and county of Norwich raised 240l. and the county of Norfolk 4,660l.

1656 July 20 and 26. Two tremendous storms of hail, accompanied with thunder and lightning; many of the hailstones, measuring five inches in circumference, destroyed the windows in Norwich and its environs, and whole fields of corn were burnt by the lightning. The loss sustained amounted to above 3000l.

1665 Two thousand two hundred and fifty-one persons died of the plague.

1671 King

CHRONOLOGY OF EVENTS.

1671 King Charles II. and his Queen, with the Dukes of York and Monmouth, were sumptuously entertained at the Duke's Palace, by Lord Henry Howard.

1673 A great snow which laid upon the ground from February 24, till Easter, and suddenly thawing, occasioned a great flood, which damaged most of the bridges in Norwich.

1696 A new regulation of the coin, and a mint set up in Norwich.

1697 The water-works at the new-mills undertaken, and completed in about two years.

1701 A printing office opened in Norwich, by Francis Burges.

1706 Two great floods in Norwich in November.

1709 The New-mills re-built.

1711 The wherry in its passage from Yarmouth overset on Breydon, October 5, and 20 persons drowned.

1712 The act obtained for erecting a workhouse in Norwich.

1715 The artillery company of 100 men, first raised in Norwich.

1716 The gold chain, given by Mr. Thomas Hall of London, to be worn by the mayor, cost 100l. 11s.

1720 September 20. A mob in Pockthorp, under pretence of destroying callicoes, was dispersed by the artillery company.

1722 A great struggle of parties about the choice of a sheriff. The candidates were alderman Weld and Mr. Paul; the latter succeeded.

CHRONOLOGY OF EVENTS,

1725 St. Andrew's hall opened as an exchange, but continued so only one year.

1726 The Norwich tonnage act took place May 1.

1732 The stone pillar called charing-cross, and the market-cross, taken down.

1737 October 4, a great part of the city flooded.

1738 The ditches on the south side of the castle-hill levelled; ever since the cattle-market has been kept there, which within the last few years has greatly increased.

1739 A deep snow fell about Christmas, and remained upon the ground till March, when on the breaking up of the frost, a prodigious flood ensued. This has ever since been called the hard winter.—It's severity occasioned scarcity, and that produced riots, which were not quelled in Norwich without military assistance, and the loss of six or seven lives.

1741 It was ordered, that no foreigner, for the future be permitted to carry on any retail trade in the city, for longer than six months, without taking up his freedom.

1745 An artillery company raised in Norwich, under the command of the Right Honourable the Lord Hobart.

1746 September 30. The Shire-house on the castle-hill burnt down. Re-built in 1748.

1751 October 22. Bridewell and several adjoining houses burnt down.

1753 July 28. Bridewell greatly damaged by fire.

1754 Twelve dozen and six skeins of curious hard, even spun crape yarn, made by a woman at East

East Dereham, weighed only 16 ounces and nearly 2 drams.

1757 The militia act fixed the number of men to be raised for Norwich at 151. And the county 809—total 960.

1758 January 31. The new theatre opened with " The Way of the World."

1759 January 21. A violent hail storm, some of the hailstones, or more properly pieces of ice, were two inches long, and weighed ¾ of an ounce.--- The pageant of Bishop BLAIZE exhibited in Norwich.

1762 Oct. 22. A flood which continued to increase for three days, overflowed the lower part of the city, and laid near 300 houses, with eight parish churches under water. It rose 15 inches higher than that called St. Faith's flood in 1691; but not so high as the great flood in 1646 by eight inches, or St. Andrew's flood in 1614, by 13 inches.

1763 Hackney coaches first set up in Norwich, by William Huggins.

1766 The great scarcity of provisions occasioned a riot in Norwich; it broke out Saturday September 27, about noon, and was not suppressed till the following day at five o'clock, during which, part of the new-mills was damaged, and a large quantity of flour destroyed there; a malt-house without King's-street gates was burnt down; the furniture of several bakers demolished, and many other outrages committed; when, the magistrates and principal inhabitants determining to repel force by force, attacked the rioters whilst they were demolishing a baker's house on Tomb-land, and effectually dispersed them.

1768 August 2. A terrible thunder storm; the lightning fell on one of the towers between Brazen-doors and Ber-street-gates, and a boy of seven years old was killed on the spot.— Three hundred and eighteen freeholders for the county of Norfolk resided in Norwich.

1772 June 2. A violent tempest, in which the house now occupied by Counsellor Cooper, in Bethel-street, was much injured by lightning.

1773 A dreadful thunder-storm which lasted from seven in the evening, August 13, till ten the next morning, but did little damage.

1774 June 17. Another thunder-storm, by which the church of St. Peter Southgate was damaged. The same year St. Andrew's-hall underwent a a great alteration: several houses, the old gateway and the wall next bridge-street, were taken down, and a convenient opening left.

1779 The new-year was ushered in with one of the most terrible storms of wind attended by thunder and lightning; in which the lead upon St. Andrew's church was rolled up, and many other churches and houses greatly damaged.

1783 The pageant of Bishop Blaize exhibited by the Woolcombers, March 24.

1785 On Friday the 23d of July, at half past four, Major Money ascended in a Balloon, from the public garden without St. Stephen's-gates, and passing over Pakefield, a village between Yarmouth and Southwold, was carried near seven leagues from the land before the balloon touched the water, at about seven o'clock; and after beating about for four hours, was extricated from his perilous situation by the Argus revenue cutter.

1788 Part of the lower close was inclosed by Dean Lloyd, and a handsome garden made.

1791 The reservoir for water on Tomb-land taken down.

1792 Rochester-lane widened, and a good carriage road made cross the castle-ditches, through what till then had been called the Griffin-passage, into King's-street.

1792 The gentlemens walk paved with stone called Scotch granite.

1792 & 1793. Seven of the gates taken down, and two openings made through the walls, one between Ber-street-gate and Brazen doors, the other by chapel-field.

1793 Between Saturday morning and Sunday night December 22, one thousand seven hundred Turkies, weighing 9 tons 2 cwt. and 2 lb. value 680l. were sent from Norwich to London, in the various carriages; and two days after, half as many more.

1793 In September an American Aloe flowered in the hot-house of James Crowe, Esq. at Lakenham. In December the Hay-house in the market-place was taken down, and an underground engine, for weighing hay, constructed upon the castle ditches.

1793 The new county gaol built.

APPENDIX
TO THE CHRONOLOGY.

The following story is such as frequently occurs in our early histories, and may serve to amuse the reader, though not to inform the student of Natural History. It seems to be the offspring of fiction adopted by credulity.

1107 Ralph de Goggeshal affirms a man-fish to have been taken near Orford in Suffolk. As it had a human face and beard, it was presumed that it could speak, and many tortures were applied to the poor animal to overcome its silence, but in vain. With equal discernment, but less inhumanity, its captors took it to church, where, as might naturally be expected, 'it shewed no 'signs of devotion.' The diet which this tormented creature used was fish, out of which it had previously squeezed the moisture with its hands. One day, being neglected by its keepers, this 'lusus naturæ' found its way to the sea, and was heard of no more. Bartholomew de Glanville was Constable of Orford Castle when this event is said to have happened.

1243 The hospital in Bishopgate-street, built by Bishop Southfield.

1273 The King took away the liberties of Norwich, put down their bailiffs, and appointed governors of his own for three years together, on account of the late riot.

1286 The Jews synagogue, on the hay-hill, Norwich, destroyed.

1430 St. Peter's Mancroft church begun—finished in 1455.

APPENDIX to the CHRONOLOGY.

1448 King Henry VI. came to Norwich.
1472 The commons of Norwich yielded to the sheriffs 30l. per annum towards their fee-farm. Edmund Stalie, being sheriff, kept his shrievalty at Trowse.
1474 King Edward IV. came to Norwich.
14·6 King Henry VII. came to Norwich; also in 1498 with the Queen, and the King's mother.
1506 St. Andrew's church built.
1509 Great part of the cathedral burnt down.
1511 St. Michael's Coslany church built by sheriff Stalham.
1515 The Queen of France and Duke of Norfolk came to Norwich.
1517 Cardinal Wolsey came to Norwich; also again with Queen Catherine, 1523.
1522 Charles V. Emperor of Germany came to Norwich.
1523 Christian King of Denmark and his Queen, in Norwich.
1529 The Queen of France came to Norwich.
1550 The free-school purchased of K. Edward VI.
1553 St. Stephen's church built.
1558 Nine persons burnt in Norwich for heresy.
1592 A well built on the hay-hill.
1599 This year one Kempe came dancing all the way from London to Norwich.
1608 The city library began.
1621 Ber-street paved throughout.
1642 William Gosling, Esq. mayor of Norwich, carried prisoner to Cambridge, by Lord Grey, where he was confined three months, for refusing to confirm the orders for raising troops for the parliament.

APPENDIX TO THE CHRONOLOGY.

1643 The organs pulled down, and much other damage done to the cathedral.

1646 A plague in Norwich, and so great a flood Nov. 15, that boats were rowed in some of the lower streets.

1647 The lead taken off the Bishop's palace and chapel, by order of parliament.

1648 Sir Thomas Fairfax came to Norwich.—Six men hanged for attempting to rescue J. Utting, Esq. the mayor, and blowing up the magazine of gunpowder.

1650 Twenty-four persons hanged at Norwich, and other places in the county, for an intended insurrection in favour of K. Charles II.

1660 Sir Joseph Payne, the mayor, knighted by Charles II.

1663 The Lord Henry Howard gave the city a silver bason and ewer, worth 60l.

1677 Seven aldermen displaced.

1681 The Duke of York came to Norwich.

1682 A number of French workmen driven out of the city by the populace.

1684 Thomas Berney, Esq. executed in the town-close, for the murder of Mr. Bedingfield.

1687 Ten aldermen, and nineteen common-council, displaced.

1688 The Duke of Norfolk, attended by 300 knights and gentlemen, rode into the market-place, and declared for a Free Parliament—Dec. 7 and 8, the mob destroyed the catholic chapel at Black Friar's-yard, and pillaging many houses belonging to the catholics, were dispersed by the trained-bands.

1689 The polls for sheriff chanced to be twice equal, between Mr. John Drake and Mr. Roger Salter; on the third trial, the same day, Mr. Drake succeeded.

1693 Mr. Thomas Larwood, (a dissenter) fined five marks by the Judges, for refusing to serve the office of sheriff, to which he had been chosen in 1692, leaving the court to fine him, upon his refusal to serve if chosen again.

1697 A great flood in Norwich.

1698 Sir Henry Hobart killed by Mr. Le Neve.—A great snow

1704 A great struggle of parties about chusing an alderman. The candidates were Mr. Thomas Dunch, and Mr. Benjamin Austin: The former succeeded. — An election for members of parliament came on the same year, when William Blyth, Esq. the mayor, was committed to the custody of a sergeant at arms, for some irregular and undue proceedings during the contest.

1712 The steeple of St. Andrew's-hall fell down, Nov. 5.

1717 Two mayors of Norwich died within 10 months.

1730 Some labourers digging on moushold heath, in the manor of Thorpe, discovered the foundation walls of the church called St. William's in the wood, which were 33 inches thick.

1734 At the contested election for the county of Norfolk, 6,302 freeholders polled, which is the greatest number ever assembled here on a similar occasion.

APPENDIX TO THE CHRONOLOGY.

1759 July 4 and 5. The Norfolk Militia marched from Norwich, for Portsmouth, one batallion by way of Cambridge, the other by Colchester, to London, and passed in review before his Majesty, thro' the palace yard at Kensington.

1788 In a collection of Wild Beasts, exhibited at the sign of the Bear, in the market-place, a very large and beautiful Tiger broke loose in the night; and two small Monkies being left out of their boxes, he devoured one of them, with the collar and chain, which being unable to digest, he died within a few days: the other Monkey, creeping into a corner, sagaciously concealed himself by drawing a mat over his body, and deservedly escaped the imminent danger.

A LIST OF THE MEMBERS OF PARLIAMENT for the CITY OF NORWICH from the RESTORATION to 1700.

1660 William Barnham, Thomas Rant.
1661 Francis Carey, Christopher Jay; who dying, were succeeded by W. Paston, Augustin Briggs.
1678 William Paston, Augustin Briggs.
1679 Hon. William Lord Paston, Augustin Briggs.
1681 The same.
1685 Hon. Robert Paston, Sir Nevil Catline, Knt.
1688 Sir Nevil Catline, Knt. Thomas Blofeild.
1692 Thomas Blofeild, Hugh Bockenham, who dying in 1694, was succeeded by John Ward.
1695 Francis Gardiner, Thomas Blofeild.
1698 Robert Davy, Thomas Blofeild.
1700 The same.

THE NORFOLK TOUR.

*Seats and Principal Houses in the County.**

	Miles from Norwich.
Bayfield, Henry Jodrell, Efq.	23
Bixley, The Right Hon. Earl of Rofebery.	3
Brooke, Roger Kerrifon, Efq.	6
Bracon Afh, John Berney, Efq.	6
Beefton St. Laurence, Mrs. Prefton	10
Buckenham Houfe, The Right Hon. Lord Petre.	25
Burnham, The Right Hon. Lord Camelford.	32
Befthorpe, ... Vane, Efq.	12
Beefton, Andrew John Micklethwayt, Efq.	4
Cockley Cley, John R. Dafhwood, Efq.	28
Cromer, George Windham, Efq.	22
Creffingham, The Right Hon. Earl Clermont.	23
Ditchingham, The Rev. Bacon Bedingfield.	12
Earfham, Jofeph Windham, Efq.	13
Elmham, Richard Milles, Efq.	18
Eccles, William Woodley, Efq.	17
Eafton Lodge, Sir Lambert Blackwell, Bart.	6
Gillingham, Mr. Schutz.	16
Geldeftone, Thomas Kerrich, Efq.	14
Gunthorpe, Charles Collyer, Efq.	22
Honingham, The Honourable Charles Townfhend.	7
Hethel, Sir Thomas Beevor, Bart.	6
Hanworth, Robert Lee Doughty, Efq.	19
Hargham, Hugh Hare, Efq.	18
Heydon, William Earle Bulwer, Efq.	14
Hedenham, Charles Garneys, Efq.	12
Hillington, Sir M. Browne Folkes, Bart:	38
Heveringland, Wm. Fellowes, Efq.	9
Hilburgh, John Micklethwayt, Efq.	27
Honing, Thomas Cubit, Efq.	14
Kirby Bedo, Sir John Berney, Bart.	3
Letton, Brampton Gurdon Dillingham, Efq.	15
Lyndford, George Nelthorpe, Efq	27
Melton, Sir John Lombe, Bart.	6
Merton, The Right Hon. Lord Walfingham	20
Narborough, ... Tyfon, Efq.	32
Nacton, William Mafon, Efq.	24
Oxburgh, Sir Richard Bedingfield, Bart.	33
Quiddenham, The Right Hon. Earl of Albemarle.	17
Rackheath, Edward Stracey, Efq.	4
Rougham, Fountaine North, Efq.	29
Rifton, Edward Roger Pratt, Efq.	38
Shottefham, Robert Fellowes, Efq.	6
Scottow, Sir Thomas Durrant, Bart:	10
Saxlingham, The Rev. Archdeacon Gooch.	20
Shadwell Lodge, Robert John Buxton, Efq.	28
Spixworth, Francis Longe, Efq	4
Senham Lodge, Thomas Wodehoufe, Efq.	17
Stow Bardolph, ... Hare, Efq:	40
Snarehill, James Pell, Efq.	30

* The Seats particularly defcribed in the book are not inferted in this lift,

Taverham, Miles Branthwayt, Esq.	6
Toft W..., Stephen Payne Galway, Esq.	23
Thursford. Sir George Chadd, Bart.	26
Weston, John Cuftance, Esq.	8
Waxham and Worftead, Sir Berney Brograve, Bart.	18 and 14
Wretham, Wm. Colhoun, Esq.	26
Woodton, Mrs. Suckling.	10
Weafenham, Wm. Mafon, jun. Esq.	28
Witton, Mifs Norris	15
Weftacre High Houfe, Anthony Hammond, Esq.	30

COSSEY-HALL.

THE feat of Sir William Jerningham, Bart. who has made very fine improvements, raifed many beautiful plantations, and opened a view to the Hall upon the approach from Norwich, which has a pleafing effect: the winding of the river Wenfum at the bottom of a delightful lawn, through the meadows, and vifible from all the plantations to a great diftance, forms at once a ftriking and charming fcene. In every alteration made round Coffey, Sir William has fhewn an elegant and fuperior tafte in planting. The ruins and cottages in the plantations are well fancied and happily difpofed; there is a diftinguifhing neatnefs and pleafing combination of objects in various points of view, which pervades the whole, and renders the landfcape very delightful. From the BelleView, at a fmall diftance from the houfe, you have an extenfive profpect of the furrounding country. Norwich is very diftinctly feen.

The country about Coffey is finely broke into a romantic vale, the gentle afcent on each fide of which is beautifully dotted with wood. A flow, but clear brook meanders through one of the beft imagined parks in Norfolk. The houfe is an ancient building, of not very great extent, but it contains feveral good rooms, many paintings by eminent mafters, and an extenfive library of elegant and well-chofen books.

HOUGHTON.

THE firft appearance of this hall, the celebrated feat of the late Earl of Orford, built by Sir Robert Walpole, is that of feveral very magnificent plantations, which furround it every way. In the road from Syderftone, they appear, we think, to the greateft advantage; they are feen to a great extent, with openings left judicioufly in many places, to let in the view of more diftant woods; which changes the fhade, and gives them that folemn brownnefs, which has always a very great effect. The flatnefs of the country, however, is a circumftance, which inftead of fetting them off, and making them appear larger than they really are, gives them a diminutive air, in comparifon to the number of acres really planted. For were thefe vaft plantations difpofed upon ground with great inequalities of furface, fuch as hills rifing one above another, or vaft flopes ftretching away to the right and left, they would appear to be almoft boundlefs, and fhew twenty times the extent they do at prefent. The woods which are feen from the South front of the houfe, are planted with great judgment, to remedy the effect of the country's flatnefs; for they are fo difpofed as to appear one beyond another in different fhades, to a great extent.

The whole extent of the building, including the colonade and wings, which contain the offices, is 450 feet; the main body of the houfe extends 166. The whole building is of ftone, and crowned with an entablature of the Ionic order, on which is a baluftrade.

At each corner of the house is a cupola surmounted with a lanthorn.

This stately structure was begun in the year 1722, and finished in 1735, during which interval, the founder continued prime minister of state.

In the house, you enter first the great hall, a cube of 40 feet, which, bad as the proportion is, is certainly a very noble room; yet one would imagine the architect purposed to destroy the effect of so large a one, by sticking three quarters around it what is called a gallery: It is a balcony pushed out in defiance of all ideas of grace, elegance, or proportion. Opposite the chimney is an exceeding fine cast of the Laocoon. From the hall you enter the saloon; which but for height, would be one of the finest rooms in the world; it is 40 by 30, and 40 feet high, which is excessively out of proportion. To the left you turn into a drawing-room, 30 by 21, hung with a yellow damask. Out of that into the blue damask bed-chamber, $22\frac{1}{2}$ by $21\frac{1}{2}$; then into a very small dressing room, and next a small closet, out of which you enter the library, $22\frac{1}{2}$ by $21\frac{1}{2}$, which leads to the dining parlour, 30 by 21. and that opens into the hall; so one side of the house is taken up with the foregoing apartments. The other side of the saloon is another drawing-room, called the C. Maratt room, from having been covered with pictures by that master, 30 by 21; out of which you enter the green velvet bed-chamber, then a dressing-room, $21\frac{1}{2}$ by 18, then another bed-chamber the same size; next the cabinet, $22\frac{1}{2}$ by $21\frac{1}{2}$, which leads into the marble parlour,

parlour, 30 by 21, and is exceedingly elegant, one fide being entirely of white marble, and this concludes the right hand fide, opening into the hall.

Having thus ran through the rooms, the fitting up of which, for inftance in doors, door-cafes, windows, cornices, &c. is as magnificent as can be conceived, and in as great a ftile as any fingle room in England.

The *common* approach to the houfe is by the South end door, over which is engraved this infcription.

Robertus Walpole
Has Ædes
Anno S.—MD.CCXXII.
Inchoavit
Anno——MD.CCXXXV.
Perfecit.

On the right hand you enter a fmall BREAKFAST ROOM, in which there are: 1. A picture of hounds, by Wootton. 2. A concert of birds, by Fiori. 3. The Prodigal Son, Pordenone. 4. A horfe's head, a fketch, Vandyck. 5. A greyhound's head, Old Wyck. 6. Sir E. Walpole, grandfather to Sir Robert Walpole. 7. Robert Walpole, fon to Sir Edward, and father to Sir Robert Walpole. 8. Horatio Lord Townfhend, father to Charles Lord Vifcount Townfhend. 9. Mr. Harold, gardener to Sir Robert Walpole, a head, Ellis.

DINING PARLOUR. In which there are feveral good portraits belonging to Lord Orford's family.

HUNTING HALL. A hunting-piece. Sir Robert Walpole is in green, Col. C. Churchill in the middle, Mr. Thomas Turner on the one fide, by Wootton. Two Dogs.

Through the arcade you come at the COFFEE ROOM.

Returning through the arcade, you afcend the great ftair-cafe, painted in chiaro obfcuro, by Kent. In the middle four Doric pillars rife and fupport a fine caft in bronze of the Gladiator, by John of Boulogne, which was a prefent to Sir Robert, from Thomas Earl of Pembroke.

The DINING PARLOUR is 30 feet long by 21 broad. Over the chimney is fome fine pear-tree carving, by Gibbons, and in the middle of it hangs a portrait of him, by Sir G. Kneller; it is a mafter-piece, and equal to any of Vandyk.

King William, an exceeding fine fketch, by Sir G. Kneller. Mr. Locke, a head.—Carreras a Spanifh poet, writing, a half length, by Sir Godfrey Kneller. King George I.

The LIBRARY ROOM, is $21\frac{1}{2}$ feet by $22\frac{1}{2}$. Over the chimney is a whole length, by Sir Godfrey Kneller, of King George I. in his coronation robes, the only picture for which he ever fat in England.

The LITTLE BED-CHAMBERR, is all wainfcotted with mahogany, and the bed, which is of painted taffety, ftands in an alcove of the fame wood.

Over the chimney is a half length, by Dahl, of Catherine Shorter, firft wife of Sir Robert Walpole: This is an extreme good portrait.

A portrait of Maria Skerret, fecond wife of Sir Robert Walpole, three quarters, by Vanloo.

The LITTLE DRESSING ROOM. A landfcape, by Wooton, in the ftile of Claude Lorrain.

The BLUE DAMASK BED-CHAMBER, is of the fame dimenfions with the library, and is hung with tapeftry. Three landfcapes over the doors.

The DRAWING ROOM. Thirty feet by 21, is hung with yellow caffoy. The ceiling is exactly taken, except with the alteration of the paternal coat for the ftar and garter, from one that was in the dining room in the old houfe, built by Sir Edward Walpole, grandfather to Sir Robert.

Over the chimney is a genteel buft of a Madona in marble, by Camillo Rufconi.

Portraits of feveral of Sir Robert Walpole's children.

The SALOON is 40 feet long by 40 high, and 30 feet wide; the hanging is crimfon flowered velvet, the ceiling painted by Kent, who defigned all the ornaments throughout the houfe. The chimney-piece is of black and gold marble, of which alfo are the tables. In the broken pediment of the chimney ftands a fmall antique buft of a Venus, and over the garden door is a larger antique buft.

On the great table is an exceeding fine bronze of a man and woman.

The CARLO MARATT ROOM, is 30 feet by 21; the hangings are green velvet, the table Lapis Lazuli; at each end are two fconces of maffive filver.

The VELVET BED-CHAMBER, is $21\frac{1}{2}$ feet by $22\frac{1}{2}$. The bed is of green velvet, richly embroidered and laced with gold, the ornaments defigned by Kent; the hangings are tapeftry, reprefenting the loves of Venus and Adonis, after Albano.

Alexander adorning the tomb of Achilles, by Le Mer.

A sea-port, by old Griffier.

A landscape over the door, Ditto.

The DRESSING ROOM, is hung with very fine gold tapestry, after pictures of Vandyck. There are whole length portraits of James I. Queen Anne his wife, daughter to Frederick II. Kiug of Denmark, Charles I. and his Queen, and Christian IV. King of Denmark, brother to Queen Anne ; they have fine borders of boys and festoons, and oval pictures of the children of the Royal Family. At the upper end of this room is a glass-case filled with a large quantity of silver philegree, which belonged to Catherine Lady Walpole.

Over the chimney, the consulting the Sibilline Oracles, Le Mer.

Over the doors, dogs and still life, by Jervase.

The EMBROIDERED BED-CHAMBER. The bed is of the finest Indian needle-work. His Royal Highness Francis Duke of Lorrain, afterwards grand Duke of Tuscany, and since Emperor, lay in this bed, which stood then where the velvet one is now, when he came to visit Sir Robert Walpole, at Houghton. The hangings are tapestry.

Over the doors, two pieces of cattle, by Rosa di Tivoli.

The CABINET, is $21\frac{1}{2}$ feet by $22\frac{1}{2}$ hung with green velvet.

The MARBLE PARLOUR. One entire side of this room is marble, with alcoves for side-boards, supported with columns of Plymouth marble. Over the chimney

chimney is a fine piece of alto-relievo in ftatuary marble, after the antique, by Ryfbrack, and before one of the tables, a large granite ciftern.

Sir Thomas Wharton, whole length, Vandyck.
Two fruit pieces, Michael Angelo Campidoglio.
The Afcenfion, Paul Veronefe.

The HALL, is a cube of forty feet, with a ftone gallery round three fides; the ceiling and the frieze of boys are by Altari. The bafs reliefs over the chimneys and the doors are from the antique.

The figures over the great door, and the boys over the leffer doors, are by Ryfbrack. In the frieze are bafs reliefs of Sir Robert Walpole, and Catherine his firft Lady, and Robert Lord Walpole, their eldeft fon, and Margaret Rolle, his wife. From the ceiling hangs a French luftre.

Over the chimney is a buft of Sir Robert Walpole, Earl of Orford, by Ryfbrack.

Before a nich, over againft the chimney, is the Laocoon, a fine caft in bronze, by Girardon, bought by Lord Walpole at Paris, and for which the Emprefs of Ruffia offered the late Earl of Orford, 5000l.

On the tables, the Tiber and the Nile in bronze, from the antiques in the Capitol at Rome.

Two vafes in bronze, from the antiques in the villas of Medici and Borghefe at Rome.

The buft of a woman a moft beautiful antique.
The buft of a Roman Emprefs, antique.

On terms and confoles round the hall, are the following bufts and heads:

Marcus

Marcus Aurelius, antique. Trajan, ditto.

Septimus Severus, ditto. Commodus, ditto. These two were given to Gen. Churchill, by Cardinal Alex. Albani, and by him to Sir Robert Walpole.

A young Hercules, antique. Hesiod, modern. Baccio Bandanelli, by himself. Homer, modern. Faustina Senior, antique. Jupiter, ditto.
A young Commodus, ditto. A Philosopher, ditto. Hadrian, ditto. Pollux, ditto.

Going from the saloon, down the great steps, through the garden, you enter a porch adorned with busts of

Rome, by Camillo Rusconi. Minerva ditto. Antinous, ditto. A Philosopher's head, antique. Apollo Belvidere, ditto. Julia Pia-Severi, ditto.

Out of this you go into a vestibule, round which in the niches, are six vases of Volterra alabaster. This leads into the GALLERY, which is 73 feet long, by 21 feet high; the middle rises eight feet higher, with windows all round; the ceiling is a design of Serlio''s in the inner library of St. Mark's at Venice, and was brought from thence by Mr. Horace Walpole, jun. the frieze is taken from the Sybils Temple at Tivoli. There are two chimnies, and the whole room is hung with Norwich damask. It was intended originally for a green-house; but on Sir Robert Walpole's resigning his employments, on the 9th of February, 1742, it was fitted up for his pictures, which had hung in the house in Downing-street.

The late Emperor of Germany, when Duke of Lorrain, being in England, was entertained at Houghton,

ton, with the moſt magnificent repaſt that was perhaps ever given in England, though there was not a ſingle foreign diſh in the whole entertainment, relays of horſes being provided on the roads, to bring rarities from the moſt remote parts of the kingdom.

The capital paintings which formerly ornamented this magnificent houſe, and which unqueſtionably formed the firſt collection in the kingdom, next to the King's, we are ſorry to obſerve, were purchaſed by the Empreſs of Ruſſia, in 1779, for 45,500l.

The late Lord Orford gave Mr. Boydell permiſſion to take drawings of the principal pictures, which was executed by Mr. Farrington, jun. and engraved by the beſt maſters on 140 plates; and there being ſometimes two ſeparate prints upon one plate, the pictures copied are about 200. This magnificent work was publiſhed in 14 numbers, at two guineas each. The prints in metzotinto, by Mr. Earlom, are entitled to a high degree of praiſe. A print from the fineſt painting in this collection, the Doctors of the church, conſulting on the immaculateneſs of the Virgin, was engraved by Mr. William Sharp.

As it would be uſeleſs now to give ſo full a deſcription of theſe pictures as appeared in the former editions of the Norfolk Tour, we ſhall ſubjoin a catalogue only, affixing the price paid for each.

A CATALOGUE OF THE HOUGHTON COLLECTION OF PICTURES, SOLD TO THE EMPRESS OF RUSSIA.

A horſe's head, a fine ſketch, Vandyk, and a greyhound's, Old Wyck, 50l.

The battle of Conſtantine and Maxentius, a copy, by Julio Romano, of the famous picture, by Raphael, in the Vatican, 150l.

Suſannah and the two elders, Rubens, 150l.

A landſcape, with figures dancing, Swanivelt, 30l.

Jupiter and Europa, after Guido, Petro da Pietris, 40l.

Galatea, Zimeni, 40l.

A ſtud of horſes, Wovermans, 250l.

Venus bathing, and cupids with a car, in a landſcape, Andrea Sacchi, 180l.

A holy family, Raphael da Reggio, 70l.

A fine picture of architecture, in perſpective, Steenwyck, 8ol.

A cook's ſhop, Teniers, 800l.

Another cook's-ſhop, Martin de Vos, who was Snyders' maſter, 200l.

A bacchanalian, Rubens, 250l.

The Nativity, Carlo Cignani, 250l.

Sir Thomas Chaloner, Vandyk, 200l.

Sir Thomas Greſham, Antonio More, 40l.

Eraſmus, Holbein, 40l.

A friar's head, Rubens, 40l.

Francis Halls, Sir Godfrey Kneller's maſter, by himſelf, 40l.

The School of of Athens, a copy, Le Brun. 250l.

Rembrant's wife, half length, Rembrant, 300l.

Rubens' wife, a head, Rubens, 60l.

A man's head, Salvator Roſa, 40l.

Inigo Jones, a head, Vandyk, 40l.

Two pieces of ruins, Viviano, 40l.

Two daughters of Lord Wharton, Vandyk, 200l.

The Judgment of Paris, Luca Jordano, a sleeping Bacchus, with nymphs, boys and animals, it's companion, 50ol.

King Charles the First, whole length, Vandyk; Henrietta Maria of France, his queen, by Ditto. 40ol.

Philip Lord Wharton, Vandyk, 20ol.

Lord Chief Baron Wandsford, Ditto, 15ol.

Lady Wharton, Ditto, 10ol.

Jane, daughter of Lord Wenman, Ditto, 10ol.

Christ baptized by St. John, Albano, 70ol.

The stoning of St. Stephen, Le Sœur, 50ol.

The Holy Family, Vandyk, 160ol.

Mary Magdalen washing Christ's feet, Rubens, 160ol.

The Holy Family, in a round, Cantarini, 30ol.

The Holy Family, Titian, 10ol.

Simeon and the child, Guido, 15ol.

The Virgin with the child asleep in her arms, Augustin Carracci, 20ol.

An old woman giving a boy cherries, Titian, 10ol.

The Holy Family, Andrea del Sarto, 25ol.

The assumption of the Virgin, Morellio, 70ol.

The adoration of the Shepherds. It's companion, 60ol.

The Cyclops at their forge, L. Jordano, 20ol.

Dædalus and Icarus, Le Brun, 15ol.

Pope Clement the Ninth, Carlo Maratti, 25ol.

The Judgment of Paris, Carlo Maratti; Galatea sitting with Acis, tritons and cupids, it's companion, 50ol.

The Holy Family, an unfinished picture, Carlo Maratti, 8ol.

The Virgin teaching Jefus to read, Carlo Maratti, 200l.

St. Cæcilia, with four angels playing on mufical inftruments, companions to the former, 260l,

The affumption of the Virgin, C. Maratti, 100l.

The Virgin and Jofeph, with a young Jefus, by Carlo Maratti, in the manner of his mafter. Andrea Sacchi, 150l.

The marriage of St. Catherine, Carlo Maratti, 100l.

Two Saints worfhipping the Virgin in the clouds, Carlo Maratti, 60l.

St. John the Evangelift, it's companion, 60l.

A naked Venus and Cupid, C. Maratti, 150l.

The Holy Family, Nicholo Beritoni, Carlo's beft fcholar, 200l.

The affumption of the Virgin, ditto, 80l.

The pool of Bethefda, Giufeppe Chiari; Chrift's fermon on the Mount, Ditto ; Apollo and Daphne, Ditto ; Bacchus and Ariadne, Ditto, 450l.

Apollo, in crayons, Rofalba ; Diana, it's companion, 80l.

A profile head of a man, Raphael, 100l.

A profile head of St. Catherine, by Guido, 20l.

The birth of the Virgin, Luca Jordano ; and the prefervation of the Virgin, it's companion, 60l.

The flight into Egypt, Morellio, 300l.

The crucifixion, it's companion, 150l.

Hercules and Omphale, Romanelli, 100l.

The Holy Family, large as life, Nicholo Pouffin, 800l.

Rubens' wife, Vandyk, 600l.

Rubens'

Rubens' family, Jordano, of Antwerp, 40l.

A winter-piece, Giacomo Baſſan; and a ſummer-piece, by Leonardo Baſſan, 20ol.

Boors at cards, Teniers, 15ol.

Chriſt appearing to Mary in the garden, Pietro da Cortona, 20ol.

The Judgment of Paris, Audrea Schiavene; and Midas judging between Pan and Apollo, by Do. 60l.

Chriſt laid in the ſepulchre, Parmegiano, 15ol.

The adoration of the Magi, V. Brueghel, 100l.

The Vrgin and the child, Baroccio, 50l.

Naked Venus ſleeping, Annibal Caracci, 70l.

Head of Dobſon's father, Dobſon, 25l.

St. John, a head, Carlo Dolci, 90l.

Head of Innocent the Tenth, Velaſco, 60l.

A boy's head, with a lute, Cavalier Luti, 20l.

Friars giving meat to the poor, John Miel. Its companion, 15ol.

A dying officer at confeſſion, Bourgognone, 100l.

Its companion, 50l.

Boors at cards, Teniers, 5ol.

Boors drinking; its companion, Oſtade, 30l.

Chriſt laid in the Sepulchre, G. Baſſan, 40l.

Holy Family, with St. John on a lamb, Williberts, 40l.

Holy Family, Rottenhamer, 40l.

The Virgin and child, Alex. Veroneſe, 40l.

Three ſoldiers, Salvator Roſa, 50l.

The Virgin, with the child in her arms, Morellio, 80l.

The Virgin, with the child in her arms aſleep, Sebaſtian Concha, 20l.

T

Edward the Sixth, Holbein, 100l.

Laban, fearching for his images, Sebaftian Bourdon, 200l

The banqueting houfe ceiling, the original defign of Rubens, 100l.

Six fketches of Rubens for triumphal arches, &c. on the entry of the Infant Ferdinand of Auftria into Antwerp, 600l.

Bathfheba bringing Abifhag to David, Vanderwerfe, 700l.

Two flower pieces, Van Huyfum, 1200l.

Chrift and Mary in the Garden, P. Laura, 100l.

The Holy Family, John Bellino, 60l.

A landfcape, with figures, Lourgognone. Its companion, with foldiers, 100l.

Two fmall landfcapes, Gafper Pouffin, 40l.

The Holy Family, Matteo Ponzoni, 160l.

The murder of the innocents, S. Bourdon, 400l.

The death of Jofeph, Velafco, 200l.

Saint Chriftopher, Elfheimer, 50l.

Henry Danvers, Earl of Danby, Vandyk, 200l.

The apoftles, after the afcenfion, Paul Veronefe, 200l.

The Doctors of the church, confulting on the immaculatenefs of the Virgin, who is above in the clouds, Guido, 3.500l.

The Prodigal fon, Salvator Rofa, 1,800l.

Meleager and Atalanta, a cartoon, Rubens, 300l.

Four markets, Snyders. One of fowl, another of fifh, another of fruit, and a fourth of herbs, 1000l.

Marcus Curtius leaping into the gulph, Mola, 400l.

Horatius Cocles defending the bridge. Its companion, 400l.

A lioness and two lions, Rubens, 100l.

Architecture, said to be by Julio Romano, though rather supposed by Polydore, 30ol.

An old woman sitting in a chair, Rubens. An old woman reading, by Boll, 20ol.

Cupid burning armour, Elisabetta Sirani, Guido's favourite scholar, 60l.

The Holy Family, a group of heads, by Camillo Procaccino, 250l.

An usurer and his wife, by Quintin Matsis, the blacksmith of Antwerp, 20ol.

Job's friends bringing him presents, Guido, 20ol.

Europa, a fine landscape, Paul Brill, the figures by Deminichino. Africa, its companion, 30ol.

Dives and Lazarus, Paul Veronese, 100l.

The exposition of Cyrus, Castiglione. Its companion, 30ol.

The adoration of the Shepherds, Old Palma, 250l.

The Holy Family, Pinto, 200l.

A moon-light landscape, with a cart overturning; Rubens, 30ol.

A nymph and shepherd, Carlo Cignani, 20ol.

Two women, an emblematical picture, Paris Bourdon, 20ol.

Abraham, Sarah, and Hagar, P. Cortona, 1000l.

Abraham's sacrifice, Rembrant, 30ol.

The old man and his sons, with the bundle of sticks, Salvator Rosa, 250l.

The adoration of the shepherds, octagon, Guido, 400l.

The continence of Scipio, Nicholo Poussin, 600l.

Moses striking the rock, Nicholo Poussin, 900l.

The placing Chrift in the fepulchre, Ludovico Caracci, 300l.
Mofes in the bulrufhes, Le Sœur, 150l.
The adoration of the Magi, C. Maratti, 300l.
Cows and fheep, Teniers, 150l.
A landfcape, with a cafcade, and fheep, Gafpar Pouffin, 100l.
The laft Supper, Raphael, 500l.
Solomon's idolatry, Stella, 250l.
A fea port, Claude Lorrain. A calm fea by Ditto, 1200l.
Two landfcapes, Gafpar Pouffin, 250l.
The Joconda; a fmith's wife, reckoned the handfomeft woman of her time. She was miftrefs to Francis I. King of France, by Lionardo da Vinci, 100l.
Apollo, by Cantarini, 50l.
The Holy Family, with angels, Val. Caftelli, 200l.
The eagle and Ganymede, Michael Angelo Buonarotti, 10cl.
The Virgin and child, Dominichino, 100l.
The falutation, Albano, 200l.

HOLKHAM,

THE celebrated houfe of the Hon. Thomas William Coke, which may be feen any day of the week, except Sunday, by noblemen and foreigners, but on Tuefday only by other people. It was built by the late Earl of Leicefter, and cannot be viewed with too much attention. The center of this extenfive villa contains the principal or grand apartment, fituated in the middle

middle of four considerable wings, that are joined to it by rectilinear corridors. Under the basement story are the cellars. Each wing has its respective destination; one is allotted to the uses of the kitchen, and all its offices, a servants hall, and some lodging rooms: Another is the chapel wing; and therein are the dairy, wash-house, laundry, and some lodging rooms. At opposite angles on the western quarter, are situated the two other wings. One of these contains a complete family apartment. The other is wholly calculated to accommodate company, and called the strangers wing.

The house may be said to consist of five quadrangles, the center and the four wings; not that they are squares, but we use the term to give a general idea. Each of the two fronts thereof present a center and two wings. That to the South, and the grand approach, is as beautiful, light, airy, and elegant a building as can be viewed. The gilding of the window frames and sashes of this front, done in 1777, by the present Mr. Coke, gives it a magnificent appearance. The portico is in a fine taste, and the Corinthian pillars beautifully proportioned. This central front, in every respect that can be named, appears all lightness, elegance, and proportion: But when you advance near, you find no entrance to the house; there are no stairs up to the portico; and this circumstance, after so fine an approach, and so long seeing the portico, and expecting it to be the entrance, becomes a disappointment, and is a fault in the building.

We have spoken hitherto of the central front alone. The whole including the two wings, we cannot think so perfect; for there appears a great want of unity. The several parts are not so nicely connected as to form one whole. The center must be seen distinct, each wing the same; and likewise the small parts, which join the center to the wings. These are all distinct parts though joined together; nor is there any similitude of taste between the center and the wings; all the pieces of this front are light and elegant to a great degree: But when considered as the connected parts of one whole, the want of unity is striking. The center is uniform, and if we may be allowed the expression, elegantly magnificent. No building can deserve these epithets more than this; but they cannot be applied to the whole front, because the parts are not of an uniform taste, and the wings are at best but light and elegant; they have nothing magnificent in them: As to the *joining pieces* they are *pretty*. The North front consists of one row of Venetian windows, over another of common sashes in the rustics. This front is not so pleasing as the South one, but it is by far more of a piece with the wings, &c.

After venturing these criticisms upon the fronts of Holkham, common candour obliges us to acknowledge, that the inside of the house, in point of contrivance, is far preferable to any other we have ever seen; so admirably adapted to the English way of living, and so ready to be applied to the grand, or the comfortable stile of life, that convenience seems to have had the first place in Lord Leicester's mind, when he adopted the present plan; the general ideas of

which

which were firſt ſtruck out by himſelf and the Earl of Burlington, aſſiſted by Mr. Kent, and the deſigns of Palladio and Inigo Jones. Mr. Brettingham, of Norwich, ſuperintended the building.

You enter what they call the *great hall, but what is in reality a paſſage. It is called a cube of 48 feet; but 18 very large and magnificent Corinthian pillars having their pedeſtals reſted on a marble paſſage around it, and eight or ten feet high from the ground, the area at the bottom is but an oblong paſſage, walled, in with Derbyſhire marble, and upon that wall are the pillars, ſix in a line on each ſide, and ſix in front in a ſemi-circle around a flight of ſteps up to the ſaloon door. The paſſage or gallery as it may be called, runs around theſe pillars, and both together take up ſo much room, that all ſort of proportion is loſt; to look from it into the area, it appears exactly like a bath. The South front was one proof, and this hall is another, that the architect's genius was not of the magnificent or ſublime ſtamp; for in both he aimed at greatneſs: The impreſſion of the front is varied and conſequently weakened by the wings; and the want of proportion in the hall, ruins the vaſt effect which would otherwiſe attend the magnificence of ſuch pillars ſo nobly arranged: but in the elegant, the pleaſing, the agreeable, his taſte has never failed throughout

* The idea of this Hall was formed from the example of a Baſilica, or Court of Juſtice, by Palladio, and exhibited in his deſigns for Barbara's tranſlation of Vitruvius. The meaſures for the pillars are taken from Degodetz's deſigns in the Temple of Fortuna Virilis, at Rome.

throughout the whole building. The hall is entirely of Derbyshire marble.

The saloon is 42 feet by 27, a proportion much condemned, but it is by no means displeasing. Some call it a gallery; and perhaps a gallery is infinitely preferable to a cube, or to any proportion near a square enormously high. One of the finest rooms in England, is the double cube at Wilton, which is more of a gallery than the saloon at Holkham, and yet no one ever entered it without being struck with the justness of the proportions.— This saloon is hung with crimson caffoy, the pier-glasses small on account of the narrowness of the piers, each against a pillar of the portico, but in an elegant taste. The rooms to the left of the saloon are, first, a drawing-room 33 by 22, hung with crimson caffoy; the pier glasses very large, and exceedingly elegant; the agate tables beautiful beyond description. From thence we entered the landscape-room, which is a dressing-room to the state bed-chamber; 24 by 22, hung with crimson damask. A passage-room leads to the anti-room to the chapel, and then into the state-gallery. The walls are of Derbyshire marble; the altar and all the decorations in a very fine taste. Returning to the landscape-room, you pass into the state bed chamber, 30 by 24, which is fitted up in a most elegant taste. It is hung with French tapestry, except between the piers, which is by Mr. Saunders of Soho-square; the colours of the whole exceedingly brilliant. The bed is a cut velvet, upon a white sattin ground, and as it appears in common is a very handsome gilt settee, under a canopy of state: The design of the bed is equal to any

thing

thing in England. The chimney-piece remarkably beautiful; pelicans in white marble. The next apartment is Mrs. Coke's, confifting of a bed-chamber, dreffing-room, clofet with books, and a fmaller one; the bed-chamber 24 by 22, purple damafk, French chairs of Chiffel-ftreet velvet tapeftry; the chimney-piece a baffo relievo of white marble finely polifhed. The dreffing-room, 28 by 24, hung with blue damafk. So much for the fuite of rooms to the left of the hall and faloon.

On the other fide you enter from the latter, another drawing-room, 33 by 22 hung with a crimfon flowered velvet. The glaffes, tables, and chimney-pieces are well worth your attention. From this you enter the * ftatue gallery; which is without exception the moft beautiful room we ever beheld; the dimenfions are to the eye proportion itfelf; nothing offends the moft criticifing. It confifts of a middle part, 70 feet by 22, and at each end an octagon of 22, open to the center by an arch; in one are compartments with books, and in the other ftatues: thofe in the principal part of the gallery ftand in niches in the wall, along one fide of the room, on each fide the chimney-piece. Obferve in particular the Diana, the figure is extremely fine, and the arms inimitably turned; the Venus in wet drapery is likewife exquifite; nothing can exceed the manner in which

---

* This bears a near analogy to that in the Earl of Burlington's elegant Villa at Chifwick, which was evidently taken, tho' with fome variation, from the Marchefe Capri's, built by Andrea Palladio, near the town of Vicenza, in Italy.

which the form of the limbs is feen through the cloathing. The flabs are very fine; the ceiling the only plain one in the houfe, the reft being all gilt fretwork and mofaic.

The entrance we have already mentioned from the drawing-room is into one octagon, and out of the other opens the door into the dining-room, a cube of 28 feet, with a large recefs for the fide-board, and two chimney-pieces exceedingly elegant; one a fow and pigs and wolf, the other a bear and bee-hives, finely done in white marble; the nofe of the fow was broke off by a too common mifapplication of fenfe, *feeling* inftead of *feeing*. Returning into the ftatue gallery, one octagon leads into the ftranger's wing, and the other to the late Earl's apartment: confifting of, 1. The anti-room. 2. His Lordfhip's dreffing-room. 3. The library, 50 by 21, and exceedingly elegant. 4. Mrs. Coke's dreffing-room. 5. The bed-chamber. 6. A clofet with books. The rooms are about 22 by 20. The ftrangers wing confifts of an anti-chamber---dreffing-room---bed-chamber---clofet with books---bed-chamber---dreffing-room---bed-chamber---dreffing-room. The fitting up of the houfe in all particulars not mentioned, is in the moft elegant tafte; the Venetian windows beautiful, ornamented with magnificent pillars, and a profufion of gilding.

But now, let us come to what of all other circumftances is in Hoikham, infinitely the moft ftriking, and what renders it fo particularly fuperior to all the great houfes in the kingdom, *convenience*. In the firft place, with refpect to the ftate apartments. From the hall

hall to the saloon, on each side a drawing-room, through one of them to the state dressing-room and bed-chamber: This is perfectly complete. Through the other drawing-room to the statue gallery, which may be called the rendezvous room, and connects a number of apartments together, in an admirable manner; for one octagon opens into the private wing, and the other into the strangers on one side, and into the dining-room on the other. This dining-room is on one side of the hall, on the other is Mrs. Coke's dressing-room, and through that her bed-chamber and closets. From the recess in the dining-room opens a little door on the stair-case, which leads immediately to the offices; and it should be observed, that in the center of the wings, by the center of the house, by the saloon door, and behind Mrs. Coke's closet, are stair-cases quite unseen, which communicate with all the rooms, and lead down into the offices. We say *down*; for the hall is the only room seen on the ground floor; you step directly from a coach into it, without any quarry of winding steps to wet a lady to the skin, before she gets under cover. From the hall you rise to the saloon or first floor, and there is no attic. Thus there are four general apartments, which are all distinct from each other, with no reciprocal thoroughfares; the state---Mrs. Coke's---the late Earl's---and the strangers wing. These severally open into what may be called common rooms, the hall, statue-gallery, and saloon, and all immediately communicate with the dining-room. There may be houses larger and more magnificent,

but

but human genius can never contrive any thing more convenient.

To give a proper idea of the plantations, park, and other objects which environ this *museum* of taste and elegance; we shall enter Holkham parish by the road leading from Lynn to Wells, where twelve small clumps of trees surrounding the triumphal arch, first catch the attention, and give warning of an *approach*.—Turning into a gate on the left, the road leads under the TRIUMPHAL ARCH. This structure is in a beautiful taste, and finished in an elegant manner; it is extremely light, and the white flint rustics have a fine effect.—Crossing the Burnham and Walsingham road, a narrow plantation on each side a broad visto leads from hence to the obelisk, a mile and a half; this plantation ought to be much broader, for you see the light through many parts of it; but it is only a sketch of what the late Earl designed, and not meant as complete. At the bottom of the hill, on which the obelisk stands, are the two porters lodges, small, but very neat structures. Rising with the hill, you approach the obelisk, through a very fine plantation; and nothing can be attended with a better effect, than the vistos opening at once. There are eight. 1. To the South part of the house. 2. To Holkham church, on the top of a steep hill covered with wood; a most beautiful object. 3. To the town of Wells, a parcel of scattered houses appearing in the wood. 4. To the triumphal arch. 5. Stiffkey hills. The rest to distant plantations.

Vistos are by no means the taste of the present age;

age; but such a genius as Lord Leicester might be allowed to deviate from fashion, in favour of beauty and propriety. Nothing can be more regular than the front of a great house, the approach to it ought therefore to partake of this regularity; because straight cuts are out of fashion, it would be an absurdity to take a winding course to the house door, for the sake of catching objects aslant, and irregularly: such management is to the full in as false a taste, as regular cuts where the house is out of the question. For instance, those from the temple at Holkham, which, however, command exceedingly beautiful objects; 1. Wells church. 2. Holkham staith. 3. The lake in the park, which is seen from hence through some spreading trees, in a most picturesque manner; a planted hill, the sea. 4. Honcle-crondale.

The object most striking on the north side of the park, is the lake, which extends 1056 yards, in nearly a streight line, covering about 20 acres, including a small island; the shore is a very bold one, all covered with wood to a great height, and on the top stands the church. The stables, at the south west extremity of it, are plain, neat and commodious. The pinery and hot-house are equal to most in England. The plantations in general are sketched with more taste than any to be seen: in the number of acres many exceed them; but they appear to various points of view, infinitely more considerable than they really are. At the north entrance into the park they shew prodigiously grand; you look full upon the house, with a very noble back ground of wood, the obelisk just above the center, with an extent of plantation on each side that renders the view really magnificent. Nothing can be more beautiful than that from the church; the houſe appears in the midſt of an amphitheatre of wood, the plantations riſing one above another. Another point of view which we would recommend to a traveller's notice, is the vale on the eaſt ſide of the park. The north plantation ſtretches away to the right, with vaſt magnificence, the ſouth woods to the left, and joining in front, form an extent of plantation that has a noble effect.

The houſe was begun in 1734 by the Earl of Leiceſter, but, he dying in 1759, it was finiſhed by the Counteſs Dowager of Leiceſter, in 1764, who expended more than 10,000l. upon it and the additional furniture. It is built with curious white brick, the center and wings extending 345 feet in length and 180 in depth.

HOLKHAM CHURCH ſtands on a hill north of the town, one mile from the ſea, and is a noted ſea-mark, commanding an extenſive proſpect on the Britiſh ocean: It is dedicated to St. Withburga, and has a nave and two ailes with a chancel, all covered with lead. At the ſouth-weſt corner of the ſouth aile ſtands a ſtrong four-ſquare tower, embattled, having four bells, the lower part ſerves as a porch to the church: the north and ſouth ailes extend on each ſide of the chancel, and ſerve as butreſſes againſt ſtorms from the ſea. The eaſt end of both theſe ailes were chapels, and are incloſed. The church was thoroughly repaired by the Counteſs Dowager of Leiceſter in 1767, at the expence of 1000l. The pulpit, deſks, communion

nion table and rails thereto are mahogany, the font is marble, and every part of the building within and without, is in the neateſt taſte.

PAINTINGS, STATUES, and BUSTS, AT HOLKHAM.

GRAND APARTMENT.

HALL 46 by 70, and 43 feet high, finiſhed with fluted alabaſter columns, of the Ionic order.

STATUES in the Niches of the Colonade. Antonius —— Santa Suſannah —— Flora, or the Empreſs Sabina —— Bacchus —— Venus de Belle Feſſe —— Julia Mammea —— Faun with the Nacchare —— Antique Faun —— Septimus Severus —— Iſis, or Prieſteſs of Iſis —— Apollo.

SALOON. Twenty-eight feet by 40, and 32 feet high. The hangings of this room are of crimſon caffoy, the column chimney-pieces are Sicilian marble; and over the center door is a large marble buſt of Juno.

PICTURES in the SALOON. The continence of Scipio Africanus. The profile of the Spaniſh Lady, wonderfully graceful and fine. Scipio's, a very bad figure, his countenance without expreſſion; but the diſpoſition of the group very well imagined. *Gieuſeppe Chiari.*

Over the chimney-piece, Tarquin and Lucretia. *Procochiano.*

Over the other chimney-piece, Perſeus delivering Andromeda. Andromeda's figure a very good one, and the whole piece well coloured. *Gieujeppe Chiari.*

Coriolanus in the camp of the Volſci. The figure of
the

the old man kneeling before Coriolanus, and hiding his face is extremely fine; but the figure of Coriolanus himself, without dignity, haughtiness, or any great expression. The wife leading her two children, and smiling on them, forms a figure of no expression. The colouring however, and the back ground are good; the disposition indifferent. *Pietro Cortona.*

Two female portraits over the doors. *Carlo Maratt.*

Over the other side doors are two half length figures. *Agostino Sylla.*

DRAWING ROOM. Thirty by 22, and 22 feet in height. Statuary marble chimney-piece, two marble busts upon the cornice of the chimney-piece; one of the Emperor Caracalla, the other of Marcus Aurelius.

Over the chimney is the Madona in Gloria. *P. de Pietris.*

Two large bird pieces. *Hendieooter.*

A large landscape. *Claude Lorrain.*

A storm. *Nicholi Poussin.*

Portrait of the Duke of Aremberg on horseback, very fine. *Vandyk.*

Joseph and Potiphar's wife, a good piece. *Carlo Cignani.*

Four plaister casts of heads over the doors, Faustina, Pythagoras, Zeno, and Carneades.

Above them are four landscapes. *Horizonti.*

VESTIBULE to the STATUE GALLERY. An octagon of 21 feet diameter, and 32 feet high —— Antique marble busts, viz. Adrian —— Julia Mammea. Julia of Titus —— Marcus Aurelius —— Galienus. Geta.

STATUE GALLERY including its two large end niches, is in length 60 feet, 21 wide, and 23 in height.

STATUES and BUSTS in the GALLERY. Two young Fauns——A fine buſt of the elder Brutus——Seneca, its companion——A ſtatue of Neptune——Ditto of the God Faunus——Ditto of Meleager.

A ſtatue of the Pythian Apollo, ſtands in a nich over the chimney; a head of Sybele over that.

A ſtatue of Venus in thin drapery.

In a larger nich contiguous, ſtands the celebrated figure of Diana. The next is the figure of a Bacchus.

A buſt of Metrodorus.

In the ſmaller niches, the ſtatues of Minerva and Ceres.

A buſt of Cornelius Sylla.

Two tables of Alabaſtro Peccorella.

TRIBUNE of the GALLERY. A large ſtatue of Lucius Verus, in a Conſular habit.

A ſtatue of Juno.

Agrippina, the wife of Germanicus, in the character of Ceres.

Over the doors are two buſts; one of the elder Empreſs Fauſtina, the other of the Emperor Philip.

The whole length of the gallery, including the veſtibule and tribune, is 105 feet.

GREAT DINING ROOM. A ſquare of 27 feet, exclufive of its ſide-board nich, which is 9 feet by 10, in the clear of the opening.

Two chimney-pieces of a ſimilar deſign, compoſed of Sicilian jaſper truſſes, and ſtatuary marble.

The fide-board, table, frame and legs, are of porphyry; the table flab of Egyptian green marble; beneath a large bafon of mount Edgecombe red granite.

Two bufts, one of Geta, the other of Marcus Aurelius; two large heads above the chimney-pieces.

STATE BED-CHAMBER APARTMENT.

THE firft room from the faloon, is the ftate antichamber.

A large picture; the flight of the Virgin and Jofeph into Egypt. The figures difagreeable, efpecially Mary's, who is a female mountain; the drawing appears to be bad. *Rubens.*

A naked Venus; the colouring gone off, hard and difagreeable. *Titian.*

A landfcape. *Nicolo Pouffin.*

Over the chimney the reconciliation between Jacob and Efau; dark and difagreeable. *Pietro Cortona.*

Lot and his two daughters, dark and difagreeable. *Dominichino.*

A landfcape. *Nicola Pouffin.*

Jofeph and his miftrefs; not in Guido's bright and glowing manner; the colouring hard and difagreeable. *Guido.*

Over the four doors, portraits of Sir Lionel Talmarfh, and the Poet Waller. *Sir Peter Lely.*

A Pope. *Pomeranico.*

A Venetian lady; colours gone. *Titian.*

Two marble bufts; one is of the veftal Virgin, the other of the younger Emprefs Fauftina.

STATE DRESSING ROOM. A cube of 21 feet.
A landfcape over the chimney, *Claude Lorrain.*

Above

THE NORFOLK TOUR. 203

Above, St. John the Baptist preaching. *Luca Giordano.*

On each side of it a landscape. *Horizonte.*

Below them two. *Gasper Poussin.*

A landscape, Abraham preparing to sacrifice his son Isaac, rather in a dark stile. *Dominichino.*

A rock, very fine. *Salvator Rosa.*

The pendents that hang on each side. *Lucatelli.*

A landscape, St. John baptising our Saviour. *F. Bolognese.*

A landscape, it's companion; fine. *Gasper Poussin.*

A landscape, figures and cattle. *Claude Lorrain.*

Above it, one. *Claude.*

The pendents; one a sea piece, the other a landscape; both exceeding fine. *Vernet.*

The pair of landscapes below the above. *Claude Lorrain.*

The pendents below two pictures. *Ditto.*

In these landscapes, Claude's *elegant genius shines with uncommon lustre.*

STATE BED-CHAMBER. 20 by 30, and 17 feet high. Tapestry hangings; Europe, Asia, Africa, and America.

The four Seasons over the doors. *Zucarelli.*

A flowered Genoa velvet bed of three colours.

Over the chimney, Jupiter, caressing Juno; the colouring bad, her neck and face the best. *Gavin Hamilton.*

Medallion of Julius Cæsar.

STATE BED-CHAMBER CLOSET. Polyphemus and Galatea. *Annibal Caracci.*

Piece of macaws and parrots. *Rubens & Snyders.*

Two

Two flower pieces over doors. *Fil. Lauri & M. Angelo.*

A small Holy Family. *Albano.*

Two altar pieces. *Sebastian Conca.*

The portrait of a woman. *Leonardo da Vinci.*

A small portrait, in water colours, of Lord Chief Justice Coke. *Cornelius Jansen.*

Four landscapes in water colours, viz.

A copy of his Majesty's C Lorrain.

Ditto of a landscape, from N. Poussin. *Goupy.*

A copy of a landscape from Rubens. *Goupy.*

Ditto from N. Poussin. *Ditto.*

A view of Vignola's palace at Capraola. *G. Occhiali.*

A view of Rome from the banks of the Tiber. *Do.*

The marriage of Psyche. *Ignatius.*

Continence of Scipio.

Two landscapes. *Fillipo Lauri.*

A Saint bestowing the benediction. *Carlo Maratt.*

Bringing the Sick to a Saint preaching. *Andrea Mantegna.*

Sketch of the Salutation. *C. Maratt.*

Two landscapes in bister. *Claude Lorrain.*

A waterfall. *G Poussin.*

Nativity of the Virgin. *Di Rosso.*

A battle piece. *Bourgognone.*

Nativity of the Virgin. *Frederico Barocci.*

Landscape. *Salvator Rosa.*

Sketch of two figures. *P. Coravagio.*

Sketch for an altar piece. *Ciro Ferri.*

A naked woman. *Gieuseppe a' Arpino.*

CLOSET

CLOSET to State Bed-chamber. The Madona and young Chrift; drawing and colouring very fine. *Raphael.* But *quere* to the connriffeurs in originality.

A large landfcape. *Bartolomeo.*

Two perfpective views; the Doge's palace; the procuratia Nuova, the Mint, the Jefuit's college, and the church of the Salute. *Gafparo Occhiali.*

Over againft it, the bridge and caftle of St. Angelo. *Ditto.*

Cincinatus at the plough. *Luigi Garzi.*

Front view of St. Peter's church. *Occhiali.*

A view of the Colloffeum, and arch of Conftantine. *G. Occhiali.*

Judith with the head of Holofernes. *Carlo Maratt.*

A view of the Rialto at Venice. *Caneletti.*

Palace Cornaro. *Ditto.*

A portrait of Rubens' daughter. *Rubens.*

NORTH State Bed-chamber. A cube of 21 feet hung with tapeftry.

Mofaic table flab.

The chimney-piece. *Fior de Perfica.*

Over the chimney, a picture of a mufician. *Mola.*

Under it are two fmall paintings of fowls and fifh. *Dupret.*

A whole length portrait of the Earl of Leicefter, in the robes of the order of the Bath. *Richardfon.*

DRESSING - ROOM to the North State Bed-chamber. Twenty-feven by 17, and 20 feet high.

A whole length of Mrs. Newton, the Earl's grandmother.

Numa Pompilius giving laws to Rome. *Procaccini.*
A Cupid. *Guido Reni.*
Head of an Evangelift. *Ditto.*
The adoration of the Magi. *Cavalier Calabrese.*
The Virgin Mary reading. *Carlo Maratt.*
Youth and old age, two pieces; the old man very fine. *Lanfranco.*
Woman in a cave; more pleafing than any piece in this collection. The face very expreffive, extremely delicate, finely turned, and the drapery exquifite, difplaying the roundnefs of the limbs through it in the happieft tafte. *Parmegiano.*
Mary Magdalen anointing the feet of Chrift. *P. Veronese.*
Apollo and Daphne. *Carlo Maratt.*
Chrift fallen under the Crofs. *Giacomo Bassano.*
The Virgin, young Chrift, St. John and Jofeph. *An old copy after Raphael.*
Fruits and flowers, a fountain and a macaw. *Hondicooter.*
The deluge. *Carlendrucci.*
A landfcape. *Anibal Caracci.*
Small landfcape and figures, a repofe. *C. Lorrain.*
St. George, Santa Saba, and the dragon. *Studio.*
Full length of Lady Leicefter, and her fon Lord Coke. *Richardfon.*
A drapery figure of an Ifis.
CHAPEL. Sixty-three by 18, and 27 feet high. The affumption of the Virgin. *Guido Reni.*
Santa Cecilia, and St. Anne; the colouring very fine, the attitudes admirable, and the drapery graceful. *Cypriani.*

Abraham,

THE NORFOLK TOUR. 207

Abraham, Hagar, and Ifmael. *Andrea Sacchi.*
The Angel appearing to Jofeph in a dream, dark ftile. *Lanfranc.*
Rebecca at the well, and the fervant of Jacob. *Luti.*
Over the chimney-piece St. Mary Magdalen and an Angel. *Carlo Maratt.*

FAMILY WING.

ANTI-ROOM. Eighteen feet fquare by 16, the height of this floor.

On the chimney-piece, of purple and white Carrara marble, ftands the Egyptian God Canopus.

Two heads in marble; one of Alexander, the other of Homer.

A plaifter caft of Cupid and Pfyche.

Above the chimney is a portrait of John Coke, Efq.

Over the door, a head unknown.

A whole length of the Dutchefs of Richmond. *Kneller.*

A head of Lady Anne Tufton, Countefs of Salifbury.

A whole length of Lady Anne Walpole. *Kneller.*

A whole length of Lady Dover. *Ditto.*

Oval portrait of Mrs. Coke, Mother of the Earl of Leicefter.

A whole length of Mrs. Henningham. *Kneller.*

DRESSING-ROOM. Twenty-four feet by 18. A whole length of Edward Coke, Efq. Father to the Earl of Leicefter. *Kneller.*

Mrs. Cary Newton, Mother to the Earl of Leicefter, whole length. *Ditto.*

Oval portrait of Lord Clifford, over the door.

Above, is a head of Mr. Henningham.

Underneath, Lady Mary Henningham, his wife.

Below, Dorothy Walpole, Lady Townfhend. *Jarvis.*

Over the chimney is Catherine Tufton, Lady Sondes. *Dahl.*

Anne Tufton, Countefs of Salifbury. *Jarvis.*

Head of Richard Coke, Efq.

Lady Coke, wife of Sir Robert Coke.

The Dutchefs of Richmond.

The Duke of Leeds, and Lady Caernarvon. *Kneller.*

Over the library door, the Countefs of Leicefter.

Mrs. Price. *Sir Peter Lely.*

LIBRARY. Fifty-four feet by 18. Over the chimney, a fea piece. *Griffier.*

Mrs. COKE's DRESSING-ROOM. Eighteen by 24. Over the chimney, Lady Catherine and Anne Tufton.

Madona and St. Francis. *Cavedone.*

An altar-piece. *Solimene.*

Two landfcapes over the fide doors. *Lucatelli.*

Head of Chrift. *Frederico Borocci.*

Head of the Virgin Mary. *C. Maratt.*

The death of Lucretia; the lights and fhades very bad. *Luca Giordano.*

Over the door a moon-light piece. *Vandermere.*

Two pieces of poppies and thiftles. *Flemifh Mafter.*

Over the door towards the library, a ftorm at fea. This picture, and the four fmall ones in the lower tier. *Livio Meus.*

BED-CHAMBER. Eighteen feet fquare. Over the chimney, a view of the palace and place of St. Mark, at Venice. *Canaletti.*

The

The maid of the inn. *Rosalba.*
Two pieces of fowls over the doors. *Imperiali.*
This room is hung with tapestry, by Vanderbank.
Mrs. COKE's CLOSET. Over the chimney, a large coloured drawing of St. Ignatius's chapel. *Francesco Bartoli.*
Two papal crowns and a mitre. *F. Bartoli.*
Four circular drawings in red chalk. *Giacomo Frey.*
A portrait of Lord Coke, in Crayons. *Rosalba.*
Two girls heads. *Luti.*
Two views in water colours. *G. Occhiali.*
Assumption of the Madona, on agate. *Rotenhamer.*
Two drawings, framed and glazed. *Kent.*
Two drawings of views in circles. *Occhiali.*
An oblong sea view. *Ditto.*
Two young heads. *Kent.*
A drawing, the death of Cleopatre. *Ditto.*
A drawing, Augustus and Cleopatra. *Ignatius.*
Two views of Roman buildings, Trinita de Monti, and the palace Salviati.

Over the book-cases are two small portraits in oil colours, of Lord Leicester's father and mother.

Above the altar-piece is a small painting of Cupid, drawn in a car. *Guido Reni.*

A miniature head of St. John, upon copper.
Cardinal Gualtero, a ditto, upon copper.
A head of Christ, and a Diana's. *Ignatius.*
MINIATUERES, painted in Enamel. Earl of Leicester, Lord Coke, Henry Coke his son.
A Madona, a Leda.
Portrait of the Duke of Leeds.
Earl of Leicester. *Rosalba.*

Princess Borghese, in a vestal habit. *Ignatius.*

Lady Lansdowne, Mrs. Rouse, Mrs. Henningham, of a Lady, unknown, Sir Marmaduke Wyvill, two mens heads, unknown.

STRANGERS WING.

IN the corridor leading to it from the statue gallery, is a bust of the Emperor Saloninus.

A plaister cast of the little Apollo.

A ditto of Camillus.

A ditto of the Venus de Medici.

A ditto of the Muse Urania.

ANTI-ROOM. Over the chimney-piece, a whole length portrait of Lord Coke.

Over the doors, Lord Leicester's father.

Its companion, the same when a lad.

Facing the entrance, Richard Coke and his wife, Mary Rouse.

On the window side, is a whole length of Robert Coke.

Lady Anne Coke and her son, whole lengths. *Sir Godfrey Kneller.*

On the corridor side are two whole lengths, the Earl and Countess of Leicester. *Cavalier Casali.*

Two door pieces, the Earl of Leicester and his brother Edward, when young.

Busto of a Roma.

DRESSING-ROOM. Above the chimney is a whole length sitting figure of the Earl of Leicester. *Trevisani.*

Over

Over fide doors, Colonel Walpole, and Lady Mary Henningham.

Lord Chief Juftice Coke, and his firft wife, Mrs. Pafton. *Cavalier Cafali.*

Over a door, Archbifhop Laud.

Over the center door, Sir Thomas More.

Henry Coke, of Thorrington, fifth fon of Lord Chief Juftice Coke, and Margaret Lovelace, his wife. *C. Cafali.*

BED-CHAMBER, hung with tapeftry, from the defigns of Watteau.

Over the chimney-piece, a portrait of the firft Duke of Leeds. *Vandyk.*

DRESSING-ROOM. A landfcape and ruins, figure of Time. *Gifolfi.*

Deborah and Barack. *Solimene.*

A fmall view of Naples. *G. Occhiali.*

Two pieces of ruins. *Viviani.*

Over the center door, figures and ruins. *M. A. Caravagio.*

Two views; one of Naples, the other of Nettuno. *Occhiali.*

A woman's head, copied from Guido Reni. *Kent.*

Two heads of Madonas, after Raphael.

Over the fide door, nymphs bathing. *F. Lauri.*

The nativity of St. Anne. *Baccicia Gala.*

The genius of the Arts fupporting the figure of Time. *Sebaftian Conca.*

GREEN DAMASK BED-CHAMBER. Portrait of an Earl of Warwick. *Vandyk.*

GREEN DAMASK DRESSING-ROOM. Over

the chimney, a portrait of the Princess of Orange, mother to King William. *Sir Peter Lely.*

Diana and her nymphs. *Dominichino.*

St. Jerome in the desart. *Titian.*

Galatea, a large picture. *Albano.*

Landscape over the door. *Gasper Poussin.*

Figure of the magician mounted up in the air. *Tintoret.*

Elysian fields. *Sebastian Conca.*

BLUE and YELLOW BED-CHAMBER. A number of Cupids sleeping, and nymphs of Diana clipping their wings, *Albano.*

BLUE SATTIN DRESSING-ROOM. Above the center door is an original cartoon of Raphael, the Madona, young Christ, and St. John, in chiara oscuro.

Drawings in red chalk. *Juno Lanumvina.*

A man's head in black chalk. *C. Marrat.*

A landscape in red chalk. *Dominichino.*

A chiaro oscuro painting upon board; figures of men, some bathing, some dressing in a hurry, as if alarmed by the approach of an enemy. *M. Angelo Buonarotti.*

Hannibal passing the Alps with his army, in red chalk. *P. Cortona.*

Academy figure, in red chalk. *Andrea Sacchi.*

Ditto of Dominichino.

Ditto of Andrea Sacchi.

A pestilence, in bister, *N. Poussin.*

Head upon blue paper, in black chalk. *Dominichino.*

Over

Over the chimney-glafs, a fmall academy figure, drawn with a pen. *Raphael.*
A head of Madona, black chalk. *Francefco Chiari.*
Compofition, a tomb on the fore ground. *Van Lint.*
A head, red chalk, upon blue paper. *C. Maratt.*
Efculapius, from an antique ftatue, red chalk.
Middle row, the firft from the door, the Virgin embracing the Crofs, in black chalk.
Crucifixion of St. Andrea, red and white chalk. *C. Ferri.*
Chrift carrying the Crofs. *Luca d'Orlando.*
A ftudy from a Fox, with the pen. *Annibal Carracci.*
A battle piece. *Monfu Leander.*
Academy figure, in red chalk. *Bernini.*
A woman poffeffed, figures in red chalk. *School of Rapheal.*
Academy figure in black and white chalk. *Lanfranco.*
Over the doors, Venus and Adonis, in red chalk. *Guercino.*
Flora's head, in black chalk. *C. Maratt.*
A man's head, in black chalk. *Corregio.*
Wife men's offerings, in bifter. *Pietro. Perugino.*
A landfcape and figures, with the pen. *C. Lorrain.*
Soldiers breaking down a bridge, in bifter. *Parmegiano.*
The afcenfion, in black chalk. *C. Maratt.*
Madona and young Chrift, in red chalk. *Ditto.*
A drapery figure, a young man fitting. *Corregio.*
A Chrift with the Crofs. *Gieufeppe d' Arpino.*
A Salutation. *C. Maratt.*

An emblematic subject, in red chalk. *Lanfranco.*

Our Saviour and his apostles. *School of Raphael.*

An assumption of the Virgin, in bister. *Cirro Ferri.*

Battle piece, with the pen and India ink. *Monsu Leander.*

Drawing of Joseph and his brethren. *Polidor Caravagio.*

Taking down from the Cross. *Guercino.*

St. Francis healing a lame man. *Andrea Sacchi.*

An Apostle, drawn with the pen. *Titian.*

St. Paul preaching. *Carlo Maratt.*

An academy figure, pen and bister. *Guercino.*

Flight into Egypt, pen and wash. *Agostino Carracci.*

Cupid and Psyche, a red chalk drawing.

Two Roman Saints healing the blind. *Giovani Bonati.*

St. John baptising our Saviour, in bister. *C. Maratt.*

Academy figure, red chalk. *Andrea Camaseo.*

Cattle and countrymen. *Castiglione.*

Portrait of a woman, in red chalk. *Titian.*

Marriage of Joseph and the Virgin Mary, black chalk. *A. Masucci.*

Sketch of a female Saint, in red chalk. *C. Maratt.*

BUSTS and STATUES in the Vestibule under the Portico. A medallion, in marble, of Carneades.

Lysias, the Athenian orator.

Plato——Cicero——Seneca.

A large figure of Jupiter.

Two chinerary urns, in the form of altars.

Six

Six plaifter cafts in niches, viz.

Apollo of the Belvidere —— Meleager of Pichini. Ganymede of the Villa Medici—— Ptolemy—— Venus di Belle Feffe—— Dancing Faun.

Two large fide-board flabs of Mount Edgecombe, red granite.

PORTER's HALL, or GUARD-ROOM: Buft in plaifter, Earl of Leicefter. *Roubiliac*.

Buft of the Emprefs Salonina.

Buft of Lucius Lentulus.

Confular buft and pedeftal.

AUDIT - ROOM, 21 feet by 48. Above the chimney-piece, medallion of a Faun.

BUSTS in the Portico of the Steward's Lodge. Mecænas:

A caft of the Emperor Titus, in modern bronze.

Within; plaifter buft of the Earl of Leicefter. *Roubiliac*.

SEAT upon the Mount. A fmall antique figure of the river Nile, in white marble.

A coro marino antique; confifting of many figures, Sea Nymphs, Centaurs, and Cupids, in alto relievo.

GREEN - HOUSE. A plaifter caft, taken from an original mould of the Lion in the Villa Medici, afcribed to Flammius Vacca.

ORANGERY. A fine antique Corinthian capital, in white marble; alfo two antique marble bafes of columns.

COURT between the Kitchen and Chapel Wings. A large fluted antique Sarcophagus, without its cover; the body of it is very entire, and in good converfation.

TEMPLE.

TEMPLE. The little Apollo of Medici, Venus of Medici, dancing Faun of ditto, Ptolemy of ditto, all plaister casts from the antique.

WOLTERTON,

THE seat of the Right Honourable Lord Walpole, is an elegant and convenient house, built by the late Lord Walpole, about the year 1730, but the offices being concealed under ground, it does not make an appearance equal to its real size. The principal floor is, however, magnificent. The saloon, 30 feet square, is hung with elegant tapestry, and furnished with sophas and chairs, on which are richly wrought in needle-work, Æsop's Fables, the drawing and colouring being admirably executed. The hall, 40 by 27. A dining-room, 30 by 27. A good picture of King Charles. A dressing-room, 21 by 11, hung with tapestry of lively and spirited colours. A bed-chamber 25 by 22, the tapestry here is also very fine; the chimney-piece handsome. A drawing-room 25 by 21, the tapestry fine. A bed-chamber 22 by 21. A dressing-room 21 by 18. The pier glasses throughout the house are large and handsome. From the south east front of the house, is a beautiful view of a piece of water of about 14 acres, and the park, which appears more extensive than it is, from commanding a distant prospect of the woods and park of Blickling.

BLICKLING,

FORMERLY the seat of the Boleyns, of which family was Sir Thomas Boleyn, Knight of the Bath, and Earl of Wiltfhire: Anne Boleyn his daughter, wife of Henry VIII, and mother of Queen Elizabeth was born here. It now is the feat of the Honourable Afheton Harbord.

The houfe is unfortunately fituated clofe upon one end of the water, but it is a large and good one; the architecture is Gothic, a little blended with the Grecian. The weft front was built by the late Earl of Buckinghamfhire, in 1769. The principal rooms upon the ground floor are---the eating-room, 46 feet by 22, with two large bow windows---the common living-room, 57 feet by 21, with one large bow window---the hall, 42 by 33, and 33 feet in height; this contains a double-flight ftair-cafe, with a gallery of communication at the top: in two niches are the figures of Anne Boleyn, and her daughter, Queen Elizabeth. The principal apartments confift of a waiting-room, 22 feet fquare;---the old drawing-room, 46 by 22, with two bow windows; --the library 125 feet by 21, with three bow windows; the books are arranged on both fides. It is an excellent and very large collection, and an admirable rendezvous room: thefe rooms are 18 feet in height.---The new drawing-room is 42 feet by 25, and 22 in height. The ftate alcove bed-chamber, 33 feet by 21.

The Park and Gardens, containing about 1000 acres, furround the houfe on three fides. The park is nearly divided by a timber wood of about 180 acres; on one fide is a two-mile race courfe; the lower part is ornamented with large old timbers; the upper part is

diverfified

diversified by various plantations and buildings, one of which is a tower in the Gothic taste, resembling a church steeple; the ground is pleasingly irregular; the soil dry, and the views cheerful and extensive.

The Pleasure Garden, rather less than a mile in circumference, is surrounded on three sides by terraces, commanding pleasing though confined landscapes, of which the neat market town of Aylsham makes a principal feature.

The Green House is spacious and elegant, and the orange trees and other exotics particularly thriving.

The Lake is of a crescent shape, the bow of which extends a mile, and the string half a one, the extreme width being about 400 yards, is one of the finest in the kingdom: The colour is very bright; but what renders it uncommonly beautiful, is the noble accompanyment of wood. The hills rise from the edge in a various manner; in some places they are steep and bold, in others they hang in waving lawns, and are so crowned and spread with wood, that the whole scene is environed with a dark shade, finely contrasting the brightness of the water. Some woods of majestic oaks and beech, dip in the very water, while others gently retire from it, and only shade the distant hills: sometimes they open in large breaks and let in the view of others darker than themselves, or rise so boldly from the water's edge, as to exclude every other view. About the center of the water, on the right of it, is a projecting hill, thickly covered with beech; their stems are free from leaves, but their heads unite and form so deep a gloom, that not a ray of of the sun can find admittance, while it illuminates the water, on which you look both ways. This partial view of the lake, (for the branches of the beech hang over the water, and form an horizon for the scene) is strikingly beautiful.

NARFORD,

THE seat of Brigg Price Fountaine, Esq. built and furnished by the late Sir Andrew Fountaine. The house is a good one, but not the object of attention so much as the curiosities it contains, amongst which, nothing is more striking than the cabinet of earthen ware, done after the designs of Raphael; there is a great quantity of it, and all extremely fine. The collection of antique urns, vases, sphinxes, and other antiquities, is reckoned a good one; but what gives more pleasure than the venerable remains of this kind, is a small modern sleeping Venus in white marble, by Delveau; which in female softness and delicacy is exceedingly beautiful. The bronzes are very fine.

Sir Andrew Fountaine was celebrated for his elegant taste by Mr. Pope, and is said to have purchased for Sir Robert Walpole, some of the finest paintings in the Houghton collection. This seat is as deserving of the particular notice of a curious traveller as any in the county of Norfolk. From the appearance of the front of the house, which is not extensive, the observer finds himself most agreeably surprised by the number of rooms, which are unexpectedly presented to his observation.

The Library is very beautifully fitted up, and contains a moſt excellent collection of curious and valuable Books, not inferior to any one in the county.

PAINTINGS BUSTS, &c. at NARFORD.

HALL. At the eaſt end, a picture repreſenting the delivery of Achilles, by his mother Thetis, to the centaur, Chiron, for education.

On the north ſide, Europa carried by Jupiter, under the form of a bull, over the Helleſpont.

Next the chimney, Arachne turned into a ſpider by Minerva.

On the left of the chimney, Narciſſus.

On the ſouth ſide, the centaur Neſſus carrying away Dejanira, the wife of Hercules.

Over the door to the eaſt, Suſanna and the two elders.

Its companion, Angelica and Medor, from Taſſo.

Over the door to the north, the death of Lucretia.

Over the door to the weſt, Sophoniſba poiſoning herſelf. Theſe are by Pelegrino.

Over the chimney a portrait of Lord Burlington, who made Sir Andrew Fountaine a preſent of theſe pictures.

On the table next the chimney, a buſt of the Emperor Hadrianus.

On each ſide, two antique Sphinxes

On the other table, a ſleeping Venus, very fine, by Monſieur Delveau.

On the ſtair-caſe are the portraits of the reigning princes of England, beginning at the top with King James

James I. down to King George II. by different hands.

A Dutch market, the figures by Rubens, and the fruit by Snyders, very fine.

Some antique buftos and relievos.

BILLIARD - ROOM. To the north, the large picture reprefenting the marriage of the Sea at Venice, an annual ceremony, after Tintorett.

St. Thomas with a dead Chrift, in the manner of A. Durer.

On each fide the door, two landfcapes reprefenting the good Samaritan. Sebaftian Burdon.

Under the large picture, a landfcape. Rofa di Tivoli.

A Dutch fair, after Wouvermans.

A landfcape, the journey into the Wildernefs, from Egypt. Begham.

On the eaft fide, Danæ and the golden fhower, after Titian. Pouffin.

On each fide, two fea-pieces. Van Veld.

Dutch Boors. Hemfkirk.

The infide of the church at Antwerp. Teniff.

Three Cupids in a chariot drawn by doves. Albano.

A piece of Architecture.

A Dutch piece. Hemfkirk.

A landfcape.

Over the door on the left hand, a mufician, after Mola.

Over ditto on the right, Glaucus and Scylla. Salvator Rofa.

Titus's arch. N. Pouffin.

A fine landscape, with cattle. Tintoretto.

Over it a battle-piece. Michael Angelo della Battaglia.

A fine whole length of Mary de Medicis. C. Jansen.

In the bed-chamber next the Painter's room. Two landscapes in the style of Huisman, of Mechlin.

STAIR-CASE. A piece of sculpture of Prometheus chained to a rock. Cavalier David.

A fine head of a boy, antique.

Several antique statues.

DINING PARLOUR. Over the chimney, a bas relievo of the Roman charity. Camillo Rosconi.

Three antique busts.

On the right of the chimney, a portrait of a Dutch Burgo-master. Simon de Vos.

On the left of ditto, a portrait of Sir T. Chicely, master of the ordnance. Dobson.

On the south side, behind the door, a portrait of the Earl of Portland, when ambassador in France. Rigeau.

A portrait of the Duke of Richmond, of the Stuart family. Vandyk.

On the right of the door, a portrait of a Lady. Cornelius Jansen.

Its companion, a portrait of Sir Henry Spelman. Ditto.

LITTLE WITHDRAWING - ROOM. On the right hand of the door, a Holy Family. Titian.

Over it, a portrait of a youth. Sir Peter Lely.

Over the chimney, a portrait of Vandyk, by himself.

On the north side, Galatea, after Raphael. Andrea Sacchi.

Two landscapes. Old Brueghel.

On the left of the door, to the north, the death of Absalom. M. Angelo della Battaglia.

A picture of horses. Wouvermans.

St. Jerome, in the stile of Titian.

To the west, on the right of the window, a Madona. Andrea Schiavoni.

Below it, a view of Boxhill, near Epsom. Wyk.

On the right of the door, the Angel and Tobit. Lanfranc.

CLOSET. Is a very curious collection of earthen ware, painted from the designs of Raphael Urbino, John d'Udino, &c. It is the largest collection in England.

BLUE DRAWING-ROOM. Over the chimney, a fine picture of the children of Israel gathering manna, A Bloemart.

The marriage in Cana. Old Franks.

Behind the door, a Bravo. Spagriolet.

An old woman. M. A. Caravagio.

A portrait of Ramboet, a disciple of Rubens, by himself. Scarce.

Julius Cæsar, and its companion, an emblem of victory, by Julio Romano, out of the collection of King Charles I.

Two landscapes, hand unknown.

A very fine picture of spaniels. Fyt.

A bull hunting, its companion Rosa di Tivoli.

A fine picture of the Holy Family. Andrea del Sarto.

A Bacchus. Pouffin.
A portrait. Vandyk.
Underneath, on the right, an ufurer and lady. Rembrant.
The interview of King Henry VIII. and Anne of Cleves, by H. Holbein, or John of Mabufe.
Over the door, St. John in the Wildernefs. Annibal Caracci.
A young Roman. M. Ang. Caravaggio.
A flower piece. Old Baptift.
STUCCO DINING-ROOM, is hung with family pictures.
PICTURE CLOSET. Apollo and Daphne, by Simone Memmi, a difciple of Giotto.
On the right, at the top, a Madona and child. Albert Durer.
Ditto, its companion, by a fcholar of Raphael Urbino.
Part of the Holy Family. Vanderwerffe.
Its companion, ditto. Carlo Maratti.
At the bottom on the right, a Holy Family. Le Loire.
In the middle, Corregio's family, by Corregio. Its companion, a Holy Family. Hand unknown.
On the left, Mofes found by Pharaoh's daughter. Tintoretto.
The crucifix'on. Magnafci.
A head of Rubens' wife. Rubens.
The adoration of the Shepherds, in the ftile of Corregio.
In the middle, the afcenfion. Solimeni.
On the left, the converfion of St. Paul, on marble, Pietro Cantarini.

Two old men. Quintin Matfis, of Antwerp.
Two battle pieces. Burgognone.
On the left, our Saviour curing the blind. Old Franks.
A Colombine and Pierot. Vatteau.
A landfcape. Wouvermans.
A Madona. Carlo Dolci.
A Flemifh merry-making. P. Angelles.
The death of St. Sebaftian. Tintoretto.
On the weft fide, at the top, two fine landfcapes. Salvator Rofa.
In the middle, our Saviour in the garden. P. le Genoefe.
On the left, a Holy Family. Schidoni.
On the right, two Cupids. N. Pouffin.
A head of old Dobson, on paper. Dobfon.
On the right hand, Euridice wounded by a ferpent. Poelenburch.
On the left, the feaft of St. Cæcilia, on marble. Van Balen.
Two boys heads, Francis Hals.
Three children of the Earl of Dorfet's. H. Holbein.
A Bacchanalian. Pelegrino.
A facrifice. J. Ricci.
DRESSING - ROOM. To the eaft, Galatea. Ricci.
Two views of Venice. Cagnaletti.
A Cupid. Gieufeppi Chiari.
The labourers in the vineyard. Dominico Fetti, *very fine.*

Over

Over the cabinet, a facrifice. N. Pouffin.
Its companion. Ditto.
Mofes found by Pharaoh's daughter. Pelegrino.

The LIBRARY, is 40 feet by 21; in it are feveral antique Roman and Egyptian vafes, and portraits of eminent men.

LIBRARY CLOSET. To the eaft, the middle picture is St. Cæcilia, a copy from a picture, by Carlo Maratti, in the collection of the Earl of Orford, by J. Davis, Efq. of Watlington.

On each fide, two pictures. Pietro da Pietris.
A veftal Virgin. J. Raoux.
A Holy Family. N. Beretoni.
On each fide, two Holy Families. C. Maratt.
Over the chimney are feveral antique bronzes.
The Apollo with the golden drapery, is antique.
A veftal Virgin. Carlo Maratti.

RAINHAM-HALL,

THE feat of the Marquis Townfhend, was built about the year 1630 by Sir Roger Townfhend, Bart. under the directions of that excellent architect Inigo Jones. It is perhaps the moft delightful fituation in the county of Norfolk, and has been greatly improved by the prefent noble poffeffor. The building itfelf is rather in the ftile of an exceeding good habitable houfe, than a magnificent one. The country around is rich and charmingly cultivated. The park and woods, containing about 800 acres, are beautiful, and the lake below, peculiarly ftriking. Extenfive lawns, and opening views into the country enrich the enliven-
ing

ing scene, and display the bounties of nature in its most enchanting and luxuriant pride.

There are several very valuab.e pictures in this house; amongst the rest, the famous picture of Belisarius, by Salvator Rosa: This picture was given to Charles Lord Viscount Townshend, secretary of state, by the late King of Prussia: And Mr. Strange engraved a much admired print from it. Mr. Arthur. Young says, the picture has, he thinks, more expression in it, than any he had ever seen. Some connoisseurs are of opinion that it is not the picture of Belisarius, but of Caius Marius.

There are three flower-pieces and two landscapes with beasts, *very fine,* and many other paintings by Sir Peter Lely, Jervase and Richardson, but being chiefly portraits of Lord Townshend's family, it is not necessary to insert a catalogue of them here.

Lady Townshend's dressing-room is ornamented with prints, stuck with much taste on the green paper.

MELTON-CONSTABLE,

THE seat of Sir Edward Astley, Bart. was built by Sir Jacob Astley, grandfather to the late Sir Jacob, about the year 1680, and within a few years has been much ornamented and improved; particularly the west front, but not being a very modern building, is still rather in the stile of a neat habitable house, than an elegant one; the chapel, the grand stair-case, the ceilings, and many of the rooms are highly finished. Sir Edward has a fine collection of prints, many curious

ous and valuable books, with some original paintings by the best masters. The park contains between six and seven hundred acres, is four miles in circumference, has lately been judiciously ornamented, and the great canal made with uncommon difficulty and much judgment; which when properly united with wood will have a fine effect; still something more may be done to improve this charming villa. The temple, managery, church, porters lodges, stables, and belle-view, are seen to advantage in various directions as you approach the house from the south. In the managery Lady Astley has a curious collection of birds. Half a mile from the house, in the road to Holt, Sir Edward has built a tower about forty feet high, called Belle-view: It is commodiously fitted up, the apartments and furniture are elegant, and from the look out at the top, there is an extensive prospect of twenty-five miles, of a rich wood-land country, finely intermixed with villages and corn-fields.— Norwich, Northwalsham church, Lord Buckingham's tower, Holt, Cley, and the sea breaking through the hills at about five miles distance, and much superior in point of view to any artificial piece of water, all combine to render this prospect one of the most perfect and pleasing in the county.

The country round Melton gradually rises for some miles to the house, from the top of which there is an extensive prospect to the east, south and west; there is a stair-case and door to the roof, which is of lead, and flat.

FELBRIGG,

FELBRIGG,

THE seat of The Right Hon. William Windham, is by nature one of the most beautiful situations in Norfolk, as in this park, which is very extensive, there is more uneven ground than in any other in this county; nor has art been less bountiful: the woods are large and ancient. In the center of the great wood is an irregular oval of about four acres, surrounded by a broad belt of lofty silver firs: on entering this oval, the eye is wonderfully pleased, without at first perceiving why it is so; we suppose it must be from the contrast which this sameness of green makes to the varied tints of the other forest trees, every where mixed in the rest of the grove, and which these lofty evergreens entirely exclude.

From another part of the wood an extensive prospect demands attention through a break in the grove, whence the uneven ground of the park is seen to the greatest advantage: Norwich spire at full 18 miles distance, terminates the view.

From the upper part of the wood the sea presents itself, but not in so striking a manner as it will from the new plantation, which in a few years will conceal that pleasing object from the eye, and then at once display all its awful majesty.

Mr. Windham's plantations are designed to answer two purposes, to ornament and belt round his park, and to extend his great woodland scene nearer the sea, towards which, at two miles distance it forms a grand

bulwark,

bulwark, and from which he looks down an easy declivity, over a bold shore, to an unlimited prospect on the German ocean.

The general utility of inclosing commons and waste lands has long been a subject of much debate. Mr. Kent is a strong advocate for it, and the facts stated in his account of the improvement made upon Mr. Windham's estate, at Felbrigg, seem to justify his conclusions. He says, "the parish of Felbrigg consists "of about 1300 acres of land, and till the year 1771, "remained time out of mind in the following state: "400 acres of inclosed, 100 of wood-land, 400 of "common-field, and 400 of common or heath. By "authentic registers at different periods, it appeared, "that the number of souls had never been known to "exceed 124; which was the number in 1745; in "1777 they were only 121; at this time (1794) they "amount to 174." This rapid increase Mr. Kent attributes chiefly to the recent improvements made in the parish, by inclosing all the common-field land, and converting most of the common into arable land and plantations. Farther to strengthen his opinion of the benefits of inclosure, Mr. Kent remarks, that the parish of Weyburn, consisting of about the same quantity of unenclosed common and common-fields, as Felbrigg did, has not increased of late in population.

The house, which has been considerably enlarged by the Windham family, is elegant and convenient, and the old stile of architecture observable in the South front, has been happily kept up in the hall, and in the library, which is well furnished with the most
valuable

valuable authors, and contains a capital collection of prints, from the beſt maſters.

WESTWICK,

THE ſeat of John Berney Petre, Eſq. is ſituated within eleven miles of Norwich and three miles of North Walſham. It is deſervedly eſteemed one of the moſt delightful ſpots in the county; the moſt judicious and happy efforts of art having laid open and diſplayed in the moſt agreeable manner, the natural beauties of the place. The kitchen garden and hot-houſes are inferior to few in this part of the kingdom. The lawn and plantations are extenſive and beautiful. It was long thought impracticable to obtain an ornamental piece of water for the farther improvement of the ſcene, on account of the elevated ſituation of the place, and the nature of the ſoil: but that difficulty is at laſt fully ſurmounted; Mr. Petre having been able by an ingenious application of two Archemedean ſcrews, to raiſe a ſufficient ſupply from a large reſervoir below the ſummit of the hill. Theſe ſcrews are worked by a windmill, and will diſcharge about 500 barrels an hour when the wind is briſk. The lower ſcrew raiſes the water eleven feet, into a ciſtern, from which the other takes it eleven feet higher, into a channel made for the conveyance of it to its place of deſtination. This channel winds along near three miles; ſometimes through hills, where it is 14 or 15 feet deep; and ſometimes over low grounds, where it is elevated to a conſiderable height above the ſurface of the earth—and at laſt forms a fine ſheet of water upwards of a mile in length, completing the beauty of the lawn and plantations.

At a little diſtance from the houſe is an ornamental building, called a Gazebo or Belle-view, ninety feet high; a ſquare pedeſtal of 20 feet tapering round upwards, with a ſtair-caſe in the inſide up to a lanthorn at the top, faſhed, and neatly fitted-up, whence there is a remarkable fine proſpect of a large extent of ſea-coaſt of near 30 miles on one ſide; and on the other a rich inland country, as far as the eye can reach; the whole in the higheſt ſtate of cultivation, and moſt beautifully cloathed with wood.

KIMBERLEY,

THE firſt ſeat here belonged to the ancient family of the Faſtolffs. It ſtood in the weſt part of the town, but Sir John Wodehouſe in the reign of Henry IV. demoliſhed it, and built a noble ſeat on the eaſt part, where the family continued till 1639, and then Sir Philip Wodehouſe demoliſhed it, and removed to the preſent ſeat at Downham-Lodge, which is juſt acroſs the river, dividing the pariſhes of Kimberley and Wymondham, to which Downham is a hamlet; the piece of water which lies in this pariſh, and is there ſaid to contain about twelve or fourteen acres, is now extended into a noble lake of about twenty-eight acres, which ſeems to environ a large wood, or carr, on its weſt ſide, rendering its appearance to the houſe much more grand and delightful; the rivulet that ran on its eaſt ſide is now made a ſerpentine river, laid out in a neat manner, and is the boundary to the park, on the weſt and north ſides, being above a mile in length: the declivity of the hill on the northern part is a fine lawn, with the ſerpentine river at the bottom of it, which is ſeen at one view from the grand entrance of

the

the houfe, which was built by the late Sir John Wodehoufe, Bart.

Great improvements have been made fince the deceafe of Sir John, by the late Sir Armine Wodehoufe, both in the waters and the park; Sir Armine likewife greatly improved the family feat, adding four rooms, one to each angle of the houfe, and made other confiderable alterations.

Kimberley houfe is a handfome building, with convenient offices detached, but not particularly an object of attention to a traveller, tho' it contains feveral good rooms, and a confiderable library. One piece of painting, an original head of Vandyk, by himfelf when young, is *very fine*. But if a park profufely garnifhed with a multitude of the moft venerable oaks in the county, and a beautiful piece of water, can give pleafure to the traveller, he will be highly gratified in viewing them at Kimberley.

Sir Roger Wodehoufe was knighted by Queen Elizabeth, at Sir Edward Clere's houfe at Blickling, Auguft, 1578. And the Queen on her return from Norwich, in her progrefs to Cambridge, on the 22d of the fame month, lodged at Sir Roger Wodehoufe's.

There is ftill in the family a noble throne, which was erected for the queen, in the grand hall at Kimberley; it is of crimfon velvet, richly embroidered with gold, having on it the arms of Wodehoufe and his quarterings, with the fupporters, all in curious work, and on the top are the fame arms impaling Corbet.

GUNTON-HALL, the feat of the Right Honourable Lord Suffield, is not particularly calculated for the infpection of a traveller, but the offices added to it it about ten years ago, under the direction of Mr. Wyatt, are said to be superior to any in the kingdom.

Not far from the house stands the parish church, which was re-built by the late Sir William Harbord, Bart. and has a handsome portico of the Doric order.

LANGLEY - HOUSE, the seat of Sir Thomas Beauchamp Proctor, Bart. is a very handsome building, with a park and extensive plantations.

RAVENINGHAM - HOUSE, the seat of Sir Edmund Bacon, premier Baronet of England, is a modern built handsome house.

In the north side of the nave of Raveningham church, between the two upper pillars, is the following curious inscription:

Here lyerh buried under this stone of marbyll:
Margret Sumtyme the wife of Humfry Castyll.
Late wife to Rauf Willoughby:
Squire for King Richard the thyrds body.
The zere of God M : cccc. lxxx & 111 :
on the 1x day of March departed Sche.
For whose Soule I beseech you hartely to pray :
And devoutly a pater-Noster & eve-mary to say.

At DENTON, three miles and a half from Bungay, Mr. Stackhouse Tompson, of Norwich, has a country house, with about 40 acres of land, laid out in a most pleasing taste. There is a neat cottage, a garden, a rural Chinese temple, a grotto, and many natural curiosities; so happily disposed, and the whole is so different from every other place in the county, that it well deserves a traveller's notice. You have a pleasing view of Flixton Hall, the residence of Alexander Adair, Esq. at about a mile's distance, situated in the centre of extensive woods.

WARHAM, the feat of Sir M. Browne Folkes, Bart. is one of the moſt beautiful ſituations in Norfolk. The houſe ſtands on the brow of a gently riſing hill, backed to the north with very fine plantations of fifty years growth. They have ſomewhat the appearance of a creſcent form, ſheltering from the north, eaſt, and weſt, and opening to the ſouth, down over a beautiful winding vale, and then commanding a rich varied proſpect of diſtant incloſures. Some villages and churches, ſcattered about the view, and a large though regular, water in the valley, all tend to make it cheerful, while the thick woods which crown the tops of ſeveral hills, and the groves that ſink into the vale, throw a picturesque beauty over the ſcene that cannot fail to ſtrike the ſpectator.

The view that breaks at once upon you on coming through the dark fir wood in the approach from London, is very beautiful. You look at once upon a range of lofty plantations around the houſe, whoſe dark ſhade forms a contraſt to the brilliancy of the landſcape, that ſets it off in the fineſt colours. In front you look upon various clumps, riſing boldly from the water, united in ſome places with thick hedges, and in others broken by incloſures, which ſpreading over the hill to the left, the water is loſt under a dark grove: the fields riſe ſo thick about it, as to unite with a diſtant plantation which crowns the hill; a church is happily ſituated on the point of it; and beyond is ſeen a more diſtant rich woodland. Full to the left, is a large Daniſh camp* of three

---

* An encampment of Sweno the Dane. One of the Meadows is called Sweno's Meadow.

three entrenchments, which are quite perfect. Turning to the right, you look upon an inclosure which breaks into the plantations; it is fringed with open wood that half obscures the village, scattered thickly with trees, and Warham steeples, one peeping over the thick plantations near the house, and the other more open, compleat the view.

As you advance through the vale in the way to the house, the scenes change, but all are beautiful. The varied lawns, and hanging slopes, crowned in some places with woods, and in others broken by rich inclosures, and all truly picturesque and beautiful.

The ride from Warham to Stifkey, is through a much more picturesque country than is commonly met with in Norfolk; the road runs on the brow of the hill looking down on Stifkey vale. The vale, which is composed of meadows of the finest verdure, winds in a very beautiful manner from out of a thicket of woody inclosures, and retires behind a projecting hill, an humble stream glides through it, and adds a cheerfulness, which water can alone confer. The hills rise in a bold manner; they are bare of wood, but that is compensated by the thick inclosures, in which the village is scattered, forming with its church in a dip of the hill, and that of Blakeney above it, in a prouder situation, a most complete and pleasing picture.

COCKTHORPE, a village of only three houses, has furnished three famous Admirals. Sir Christopher Mimms, Sir John Narborough, and Sir Cloudesley Shovel.

Near

Near Blakeney is another uncommon view, quite different from that at Stifkey : the road winds into a fequeftered valley fhut out from the fea, by a bold uncultivated hill. To the right the grounds fhelve from the road into a narrow vale. In this little wooddy hollow is a village half feen among ftraggling trees : the fteeple is uncommonly picturefque ; half of it is hid by a rifing flope, and the church three fourths obfcured by a thicket of trees. The oppofite hill rifes very boldly ; it prefents a large inclofure, under the thick fhade of a noble fpread wood, which hangs to the right into another valley, but is loft behind a regular bare hill of a conic form, which rifes from the junctiou of the vales, in a very remarkable manner ; and almoft fcreens a diftant range of rifing inclofure. Immediately to the right, is a floping tract of fields, and above them wild ground, with a white tower rifing from behind it. The whole forms one of thofe half gloomy, and yet not unpleafing fcenes, in which Pouffin delighted ; it is a fpot worthy of fuch a pencil.

Sherringham Cliff is a very high fteep fhore : it looks on one fide full upon the fea, and on the other over a various country abounding with inequalities of ground ; many hills fcattered widely about, numerous cultivated inclofures, and fix or feven villages are feen. Sherringham is prettily overlooked, backed by a rifing hill.

LYNN REGIS,

LYNN REGIS, or KING's LYNN,

CAMDEN was of opinion that Lynn derived its name from the British word Lhyn, which means a lake, pool, or spreading waters; but Spelman affirms that the right name is Len, in Saxon, a farm or tenure in fee, and Len Episcopi, as it was formerly called, meant the Bishop's Farm. It retained the name of Bishop's Lynn till the time of King Henry VIII, who exchanging the monastery of St. Bennet in the Holme, and other lands, for the revenues of the Bishopric, this town amongst the rest, came into his hands, and with the possessor, changed its name to Lynn Regis.

Camden says that the town is not of any antiquity, but sprung up out of the ruins of what is called Old Lynn, or West Lynn, which lies on the opposite side of the river.

Camden's opinion of this town's not being of great antiquity is probably right, but in saying it sprung out of the *ruins of Old Lynn*, or West Lynn, he is certainly mistaken, it no where appearing that Old Lynn ever was any thing but what it now is, an inconsiderable village, which may have been the case with Lynn Regis, before the advantages of commerce were understood, by which it has gradually been raised from its primitive obscurity, to that of being the most considerable sea-port town in the county, and inferior only to London, Bristol, Liverpool, Hull, and Newcastle, in England.

It is a large rich, handsome and very thriving town, standing upon the eastern bank of the Great Ouse, at about ten miles distance from the British ocean. It is one mile and a quarter long from the South-gate to the the Block-house, at Fisher's-end, and about half a mile from the river to the east-gate, which is the broadest part; it contains about 2,500 houses and 12,000 inhabitants, is encompassed on the land side by a deep wet ditch and an ancient wall; was formerly defended by nine bastions, and might now easily be made a place of considerable strength. It is divided by four small rivers, over which there are fifteen bridges. At the north-end there is a platform of twelve cannon, eighteen pounders, called St. Anne's-Fort, but having no cover for the men, it could be of very little use, if the town was attacked from the river side.

This town has been honoured with no less than fifteen royal characters; but we shall mention only those which more immediately apply to our purpose, King John, after chastising the revolted Barons of Norfolk, assembled his forces here in the sixth year of his reign, 1204, and during his stay, and on the petition of John Grey, Bishop of Norwich, granted the town a charter to be a free borough for ever, and the Burgesses to choose themselves a *Prætor*, or *Provost*, on condition that he should be subject to the *Bishop*, and take an oath yearly to that end, at the Bishop's palace at Gaywood, whence he was called the *Bishop's Man*. At the same time King John presented the corporation with an elegant double gilt embossed and enamamelled cup and cover, weighing 73 ounces,

73 ounces, and holding a full pint, which is well preserved, and upon all public occasions and entertainments used with some uncommon ceremonies, at drinking the health of the King or Queen, and whoever goes to visit the mayor, drinks sack out of this cup. He also then gave them from his own side, *'tis said*, a sword with a silver mounting, to be carried before the mayor; but as the charter dated Sept. 14. in the 6th year of this King's reign calls him *Præpositus* or *Provost*, a title not clearly defined, it has been denied that King John granted the town a Mayor, but that it had one in the last year of his reign, is evident from his letters patent, dated June 7, 1216, directed

To the Mayor and good men of Lynn.

Bishop Gibson in his additions to Camden observes, that this sword, which by the inscription, is said to have been given by King John, was really the gift of King Henry VIII. after the town came into his possession, and he changed their Burgesses into Aldermen, and granted them several privileges. The charter granted by King John, does not mention the sword, but that granted by Henry expressly says, " He " granted them a sword to be carried before their may- " or." A loose paper of Sir Henry Spelman's dated September 15, 1630, says, one Thomas Kenet, townclerk of Lynn, assured him, that John Cooke, swordbearer, in 1580, went to Mr. Ivory the school-master of the town, and desired him to compose an inscription, to be engraved upon the plain hilt of the town-sword, to this effect, " King John gave this sword to the " town," hereupon he caused the person who gave

this

this information, and was then his scholar, to write these words.

*Ensis hic Donum fuit Regis Johannis,
à suo ipsius Latere datum.*

In ENGLISH.

King John *took this sword from his own side, and gave it to this town.*

which the sword-bearer carried to Mr. Cooke, a Goldsmith, who engraved it upon one side of the hilt. If this story be true, the inscription of which the town so much boasts, is of no authority. On the other side of the hilt is *Vivat Rex* Henericus *Octavus. Anno Regeni sui* xx.

The Gentlemen of the Corporation insist, that the sword now borne before the Mayor, was given by King John, and has been used for that purpose from the time of Henry III. and that when some Kings have honoured the town with their presence, the mayors themselves have carried this sword before them; and it is remarkable, says Mr. Mackerell, that in a window on the north side of the choir, near the altar of St. Nicholas chapel, the town arms and the sword are depicted in glass, and most probably were fixed there soon after erecting the chapel and glazing the windows, which is supposed to have been in the reign of Edward III. between the years 1326 and 1376, or about 150 years after K. John is said to have given the sword to the town. Upon the whole it is pretty clear, that the sword was given by King John, but whether from his own side, and to be carried before a Provost or a Mayor, must still remain doubtful.

doubtful. If there be any error in the infcription upon the fword, it is in faying that King John *took it from his own fide*, thereby intimating, that it was the fword he commonly wore, which it is not eafy to believe, it not only being much too large for an offenfive weapon, but alfo, like all other fwords ufed for purpofes of ftate by corporate bodies.

The Mayor is annually elected Aug. 29, and fworn into office September 29, when he gives an elegant entertainment at the Hall, to the corporation and the country gentlemen and ladies, in the neighbourhood. At this feaft, King John's cup, after dinner, is handed to the mayor, he prefents it to his predeceffor, who takes off the lid, and the mayor drinks the King's health, the lid is then replaced and after certain ceremonies of turning the cup round, the mayor delivers it to the late mayor, and in like manner it paffes down the mayor's table; thence it is carried to the mayorefs and the ladies.

On the 29th of Auguft the mayor calls a hall for the election of a fucceffor, who is chofen by the common council, as they are by the court of Aldermen; but if any difpute fhould arife, and the mayor break up the affembly, the common council may fit down upon the fteps of the hall and choofe a mayor, if ten out of the eighteen are unanimous, and this election the court of Aldermen cannot controvert.

The corporation confifts of a mayor, recorder, twelve aldermen, and eighteen common council men, a town-clerk, chamberlain, &c. The town has fent two Burgeffes to parliament ever fince the 26th of Edward I. (1298) and the election is in the whole body of the freemen and free-burgeſſes, in number about 330, and the mayor is the returning officer.

In 1768 there was a ſharp conteſt for members to repreſent this Borough in parliament, when the number of voters upon the poll amounted to 312.

The Honourable Thomas Walpole - 200
Sir John Turner, Bart. - - 174
Criſp Molineaux, Eſq. - - 159

The harbour is about the breadth of the Thames above bridge, and is capable of containing 200 ſail of ſhips: The ſpring tides flow more than twenty feet perpendicular if a north-eaſt wind accompanies, and ſometimes force the ſhips in the harbour from their moorings, tho' ten miles diſtant from the ſea. This rapid influx of the the tide is very properly called the *Eager*.

There are no freſh-water ſprings in this town, but the inhabitants are plentifully ſupplied from the Gaywood river, with that great neceſſary of life, by the water-works near the eaſt-gate, called Kettle Mill.

St MARGARET the VIRGIN, being the tutelary Saint and patroneſs of this town, in honour of her; its arms are three dragons heads, each wounded with a croſs (for ſhe is ſaid with a croſs to have conquered a dragon) and its public and common ſeal is the effigies of St. Margaret ſtanding in a triumphal manner, wounding the dragon with a croſs, and treading him under-foot, with this inſcription round it, *Stat Margareta draco fugit in cruce læta*.

The principal church is dedicated to St. MARGARET. It was firſt built by Herbert de Loſinga, Biſhop of Norwich, about the year 1100, and had a lofty lanthorn in the middle of the cross aile, and at the west-end two towers, in one * of which are eight bells: On the other there was a very elegant spire, which from the foundation was 258 feet high, and equal to the length of the church and chancel; but this being blown down in the year 1741, and greatly damaging the body of the church, the ruins were entirely taken down, and it was re-built with a nave and 2 large ailes, and is now one of the largest parochial churches in England. The breadth to the outside of the foundation of of the walls, is 130 feet.

St. NICHOLAS CHAPEL, supposed to have been built between the years 1327 and 1377, in the reign of Edward III. is 200 feet long and 78 broad, and it is 170 feet from the foundation to the top of the spire. The body consists of a nave and two ailes divided by two rows of ten neat pillars each, forming acute angles at the top.

Sir Benjamin Keene, many years ambassador at the court of Madrid, where he died, being a native of this town, was brought from thence, and buried in this chapel in 1759, and a very handsome monument of white marble, in the form of an antient urn, with an inscription, specifying his places and employments, which he filled with dignity and honour to his country and himself till the time of his decease, is placed over him.

The THEATRE is very convenient and neat, neither profusely ornamented, nor disgustingly plain, and

---

* A turret was erected on the top of this tower, about the year 1774.

and although not free from faults, yet has none but what refulted from the architect being confined to fill up the fhell of an old building which was raifed for another purpofe.

The ASSEMBLY - ROOMS are capacious, and handfomely fitted up; they confift of three on a line. The firft, an old town hall, 58 by 27, and of a well proportioned loftinefs, would be a very good ball-room, had it a boarded floor; but at prefent forms a very noble anti-room. It opens into the ball-room, 60 feet by 27, and 22 feet high, which would have been a proper one, if the architect had given his mufic-gallery a hitch backwards; for at prefent it is a mere fhelf ftuck between the chimnies, an eye-fore to the room. If he did it through confinement for want of fpace, he fhould undoubtedly have formed his mufic-feats upon the plan of thofe at Almack's, at the end of the room; they might have waved in a fcroll round the door of the card-room, mingled with branches of candles, which would have been a great ornament.

The card-room is 27 by 27, and 22 feet high.

As the three are upon a line, it would have given them an uncommon elegance, had the openings from one into another been in three arches in the centre, fupported by pillars, inftead of the prefent glafs doors, which are mean.

The eye would then at once have commanded a fuite of 145 feet, which with handfome luftres properly difpofed, would have rendered thefe rooms inferior to few in England.

The CHAPEL of St. JAMES, since the diffolution of the priories, being in part demolished, and the reft become ruinous, was rebuilt in the year 1682, by the liberal benefactions of the mayor, burgeffes, and principal inhabitants, and converted into a workhoufe for fifty decayed old men, women, and poor children, where a good endowment and provifion is made for their work, inftruction and maintenance, and for putting the children out to trades. Great additions have lately been made to this place, and it is now the general workhoufe for the whole town.

In the year 1683, Sir John Turner, Knt. three times mayor here, and many years one of their reprefentatives in parliament, erected, at his own expence, a handfome building of free ftone, with two orders of columns, intending it for an exchange. Upon the fecond floor, in a nich in the front, is a ftatue of King Charles II. and within is the cuftom-houfe, fitted up with feveral commodious apartments for that purpofe; on the platform above is raifed an open turret, upon pillars of the Corinthian order, with an exchange bell therein, being finifhed with an obelifk and ball, whereon ftands fame, inftead of a weathercock, the whole being 90 feet high.

The Tuefday market-place, is a fpacious fquare area of three acres, having on an afcent of four fteps, a very handfome market *crofs of free ftone, of modern architecture, built in 1710, adorned with ftatues and

---

* The foundation feems to have given way on the north fide, and confequently the building inclines that way.

and other embellishments, with a peryſtile round below, ſupported by ſixteen pillars of the Ionic order; as alſo another walk above, encompaſſed with an iron paliſade, enriched with tracery work and foilage, incloſing a neat octangular room; the upper part is finiſhed with a cupola and turret, wherein hangs the market-bell, the whole being about 70 feet in height. On each ſide ſtand in a ſemicircular form, the butchers ſhambles; and behind is another building, for a fiſh-market.

By the ſecond charter of King Henry VIII. to this town, in the 29th year of his reign, two Fairs or Marts were granted, one to be held on the 27th of Auguſt, this is called the cheeſe fair, and is kept in Chequer-ſtreet; the other on the 14th of February, which is called the Mart, and is proclaimed for ſix days: it is kept in the Tueſday market-place, and is much reſorted to by genteel company from moſt parts of the county, but the trades-people who attend it are not half ſo numerous as they were thirty years ſince. The markets, on Tueſdays and Saturdays, are plentifully ſupplied with all kinds of proviſions, at reaſonable rates. Before the year 1782 the Saturday-market was kept in high-ſtreet, near St. Margaret's church; which being found inconvenient, the wall on the north-ſide of the church-yard, and the buildings between that ſide of the church and the gaol, which contained the butchery, and two large ſchool-rooms, were taken down; a handſome new butchery was built cloſe to the north-weſt corner of the church, and a convenient area left for holding the market, yet ſo difficult is it to remove the moſt obviour abfurdities, when founded on long eftablifhed cuftoms; that the market people reluctantly leave the many inconveniencies of a market kept in a narrow and dirty ftreet, to enjoy fafety and every neceffary accommodation, in a fituation well adapted to the purpofe.

The new walk or mall, from the bars by the workhoufe to Gannock Gates, is about 340 yards long, and eleven yards wide between the quick hedges. At convenient diftances on each fide of the walk, a recefs is left in the hedge in a femicircular form, where benches are fixed, and twenty people may fit down at a time. Upon a gentle afcent on the right, is a plantation and fhrubbery, laid out in a pleafing tafte by the late Charles Turner, Efq. on the bottom of this winds a pretty lively ftream of water, which after paffing through Lady Bridge, empties itfelf into the Oufe. At the end of Mr. Turner's fhrubbery, is a fmall plantation of lime trees and Scotch firs intermixed, whence there is a good view of Lynn, and the adjacent villages, where wood, water, modern buildings, and ancient ruins, are fo happily blended as to form a moft charming profpect.

About half way between the South and Eaft gates, ftand the remains of an ancient oratory, an odd fort of building, with feveral vaults and cavities under ground, over which are fome dark cells for the priefts to take confeffions in, and above them a fmall chapel in the figure of a crofs, arched above, and enriched with carvings; it is dedicated to the bleffed Virgin, and commonly called *The Lady's*, or *The Red Mount*, whither the Romifh penitents, in their pilgrimrge grimage to the holy wells and monaftery of our Lady at Walfingham, ufed to refort, and perform their devotions.

In this town there have been feveral priories, oratories, and religious houfes, which are now demolifhed, except a hexagon fteeple of the Grey Friars, near the Workhoufe.

The fituation of this town, near the fall of the Oufe into the fea, gives it an opportunity of extending its trade into eight different counties; fo that it fupplies many confiderable cities and towns with heavy goods, not only of our own produce, but imported from abroad. It deals more largely in coals and wine, than any other town in England, except London Briftol, and Newcaftle. In return for thefe articles of merchandife imported, it receives back for exportation the corn produced in the feveral counties which it fupplies. Its foreign trade is very confiderable, efpecially to Holland, Norway, the Baltic, Spain, and Portugal. It has been faid, that the four Norfolk ports export as much corn as all the reft of Enggland. The following extract, taken from the cuftomhoufe books, at Lynn, is to be confidered as the *yearly average* which has been exported to foreign markets and coaftways, for the years 1791, 1792, and 1793, which were far from being greatly productive.

	Quarters.	per Qr.			Amount.		
		L.	S.	D.	L.	S.	D.
Wheat,	30116	2	4	0	66035	4	0
Wheat Flour,	3158	2	16	0	8786	8	0
Barley,	17294	1	4	0	135532	16	0
Malt,	10703	2	0	0	21406	0	0
Rye,	12298	1	5	0	15372	10	0
Peafe,	3855	1	8	0	5397	0	0
Beans,	4708	1	4	0	5639	12	0
Vetches,	73	1	10	0	109	10	0
Rape Seed	2423	1	16	0	4001	8	0
					262050	8	0

In the year 1190, a Jew of this town having embraced the Christian Faith, the Levitical Tribe determined to assassinate him, and meeting him in the street, set upon him, on which he fled for sanctuary to the nearest church, whither they pursued him, and breaking open the doors, attempted to force him away. On this the Town's-men, joined by many foreign mariners, not only rescued him, but pursued the offenders to their houses, which the foreigners burnt and plundered, and killing some of the Jews, retreated to their ships, and immediately setting sail, carried away the spoil to their own country.

Mary Smith was burnt at Lynn, Jan. 12, 1616, for Witchcraft, which she was accused of having practised upon various persons, by means of a vocal contract with the Devil. This poor creature, who no doubt was insane, acknowledged the truth of these foolish accusations. And Alexander Roberts, calling himself a preacher of God's word, at King's Linne, in the same year published a treatise on Witchcraft, in which the story of Mary Smith is included.

An infallible cure for WITCHCRAFT.

It is not many years since an inhabitant of Boston in New England, took a fancy to accuse his neighbour of Witchcraft, and the crime being *clearly proved,* the poor culprit suffered *according to law.* The contagion spread, and their Session's-house was crowded with Witches, as much as our Old Bailey with Pickpockets. To the Tribe it brought fees,—and so far was well.—But a man having been cheated by his Lawyer, made oath that *said Lawyer* was a *Wizzard.* This

This was too much, the clan was in danger,—The Court had a special meeting, and unanimously determined, that they would not receive any more informations against Wizzards. The Bye Law had the effect of a charm, and Sorcery was no more.

In the year 1643 the burgesses and inhabitants of Lynn, reinforced by the country gentlemen, amounting in all to about 5000 men in arms, defended this town against 18,000 of the parliamentary forces, under the Earl of Manchester, from the 28th of August till the 16th of September, when it was surrendered; and to preserve it from plunder, was obliged to pay to every foot soldier of his army ten shillings, and to every foot officer, under the rank of a Captain, a fortnight's pay, amounting in all to 3,200l. after which it was made a garrison town for the parliament.

Preparatory to the restoration of Charles, II. it was fortified afresh, by Sir Horatio Townshend, ancestor to the present Marquis Townshend, of Rainham, who was created a Baron by King Charles II. for his loyal services, by the stile and title of Lord Townshend, of King's Lynn.

Voltaire, in his Essay on Universal History, vol. iii. pages 182 and 183, observes, that the first who certainly made use of the Compass, were the English, in the reign of Edward III. What little science still remained was confined to Monasteries;—and in a note by the translators, at the bottom of page 182, extracted from Hackluyt's voyages, we are informed, that Nicholas de Lenna, or of Lynn, in Norfolk, a

franciscan

franciscan friar, and an excellent musician, mathematician and astrologer, bred at Oxford, after having applied his studies chiefly to astronomy; by the help of his *astrolabe, made five voyages to the North Seas. In the first he sailed from Lynn to Iceland, with company, whom he left on the sea coast, while he travelled up into the island, in search of discoveries. He presented his charts of the northern seas, at his return, to Edward III. in the year 1360, and they were afterwards made use of in the reign of Henry VI. Chaucer had a great esteem for him, stiling him *Frere* Nicholas Linn, a Rev. Clerke. He is said to have wrote a book of Discoveries, called *Inventio Fortunatæ*. He died in the year 1369, and was buried at Lynn.

Alan of Lynn, a Carmelite Friar, had the industry to make Indexes to 33 writers, among which was Augustin, Anselm, and Aquinas. He died about 1428.

WILLIAM WATTS, M. A. of Caius-college, Cambridge, an admirable critic and divine, was born in this town. Vossius calls him, *Doctissimus, & Clarissimns* Watsius, *qui optime de Historia meruit,* &c. He, by his travels became master of divers languages; and at his return was made chaplain to King Charles the First, minister of St. Alban's, Wood-street, in London, and prebendary of Wells; but being sequestered, plundered, and his wife and children turned out of doors, he fled to the King, served under Prince

---

* The Astrolabe was an instrument well known to the Ancients, by the help of which they could steer from one point of the Old Continent to another.

Prince Rupert, and was in moſt of the battles fought with the parliament forces. Upon the declining of the King's cauſe, he ſtuck ſtill to the Prince, and ſerved at ſea; till being blocked up with him in the harbour of Kinſale in Ireland, he was overtaken with an incurable diſtemper, of which he died in 1649. He was a conſiderable writer, and had a principal hand in Sir Henry Spelman's Gloſſary; and corrected and added notes to and publiſhed Matthew Paris's Hiſtoria Major in 1640, as alſo divers Treatiſes in Engliſh, as, the hiſtory of Guſtavus Adolphus; Mortification Apoſtolical; a Treatiſe of the Paſſions, &c.

THETFORD,

IS on the great poſt road from Norwich to London, twenty-nine miles from the former, and ſevnty-nine from the latter. It ſtands in an open country, upon the Little Ouſe, which is the boundary between the counties of Norfolk and Suffolk, and navigable for ſmall craft from hence to Lynn Regis.

It is the opinion of our moſt reſpectable topographical Hiſtorians, that the Romans, and after them the Saxons, continued the names of the principal towns of the Ancient Britons, where they found them ſuitable to their ſituation. The Romans called Thetford *Sitomagus*, which in the *Celtic* language means the City or Habitation of the Sinones or Sitones, upon the Ford. The Sinones were an ancient people of Gaul; the Sitones an ancient people of Germany. *Tedford*, *Tetford* and *Tefford*, the Saxon names, are evidently but ſmall variations in ſpelling, meaning alike

The

The Ford, or moſt frequented paſſage over the waters, before the uſe of bridges was generally known. The modern name, Thetford, ſaid to be derived from its ſituation upon the river Thet, is undoubtedly a miſnomer, there being no river in the county of that name.

Thetford very probably was the ancient *Sitomagus* mentioned by Antoninus in his Itinerary, and even before the Roman invaſion, had been famous for the reſidence of the chiefs of the Britons, but under what name is not known, nor is it very material: The beſt towns belonging to the Britons were very obſcure, (as are thoſe of all uncivilized people) and hiſtory does not furniſh us with any particular account of them. Under the Romans it was the royal city of the *Iceni*, and during the Saxon domination, the ſeat of the Eaſt Anglian Kings.

Martin in his hiſtory of this place ſays, it was a fenced and royal city, from the unfortunate overthrow of Boadicea, to the eſtabliſhment of the Saxon Heptarchy in 575, when Norwich, Lynn, and Yarmouth were yet in their infancy: But as there have been many doubts on this ſubject among hiſtorians, his exultation ſeems to be premature; however, if his honeſt zeal and partiality for his native place, of which he was writing a hiſtory, led him into haſty or erroneous concluſions, it is but fair to let that paſs for granted, which, though we may not implicitly believe, we cannot ſatisfactorily refute.

Though this town had flouriſhed amidſt all the misfortunes, occaſioned by the furious contentions of the
.Britons

Britons with the Saxon and Danish invaders: and had twice been destroyed; in Edward the Confessor's time it still contained 947 burgesses, when Norwich had not more than 1320 persons of that description; but owing to causes with which we are not acquainted, it declined so rapidly, that at the time of making the Conqueror's Domesday-book, there were only 720 burgesses, and 224 houses were empty; and in 1088, when Bishop Herbert removed the See to Norwich, it continued to decay, from which it has never recovered.

The town at first lay wholly on the Suffolk side of the river, had twenty churches and several monasteries, and is supposed to have been fortified by the Romans; this part now contains but few houses, and on approaching it, a traveller must be sensibly struck with the vestiges of antiquity which invite his attention on every side, and point out its once flourishing condition: It has now the appearance of a decayed village. On the Norfolk side of the river are several streets constituting a town of considerable extent; in which there are many well-built houses, but the streets are ill paved, and it has not by any means a prosperous appearance.

It was a burgh by prescription only, till the charter granted to it by Queen Elizabeth, March 12, 1573. The corporation consists of a mayor, ten aldermen, and twenty common council, who elect the members, the mayor being the returning officer. The Lent Assizes for the county, are held in its Guild-hall. It has a weekly maket on Saturday, and annual fairs, May 14, August 2, and September 25. The first re-

B b   presentatives

presentatives to parliament for this borough, was in the first year of Edward VI. (1547). The arms are a castle triple towered, on each of the two outermost towers, a centinal armed with an halbert proper.

St. Peter's Church stands on the Norfolk side of the river, and is now the principal church. It is built of free-stone and flint, whence it has the vulgar name of the *Black* church. It consists of a chancel, nave and two ailes, the chancel tiled and the rest leaded. Its square west tower is built on arches, open on the north and south sides, which is much cracked, and contains six bells; on the largest is engraved:

Nos Thome meritis mereamur gaudia lucis.

There are two other churches in the town, but they have nothing in them deserving particular notice. The names and situations of twenty churches formerly standing here, are given in Martin's history.

On the east side of the town stands the Castle-hill, which Camden confessed himself unable to determine, whether it was the work of the Romans or Saxons; Martin thought the latter.

The exterior figure of this work seems to have been a right angled parallelogram with the angles rounded off, its greatest length lying from east to west. It consisted of two ramparts, each defended by a ditch. Within these, near and parallel to their west sides, is a high and steep mount keep, entirely encompassed by a ditch. East of this mount is a large area or place of arms 300 feet square. This mount is about 100 feet in height, and the circumference of the base 984; the diameter measures 338 feet at its base, and 81 on its summit, which is dishing or concave upwards

THE NORFOLK TOUR.

wards of twelve feet below the outer furface, owing probably to its having been once furrounded by a parapet. The flope or ramp of this hill is extremely fteep, forming an angle with the plane of the horizon of more than 40 degrees, and yet no traces remain of any path or fteps for the purpofe of carrying up machines or any weighty ammunition. The chief entrance feems to have been on the north fide, where in the fecond or inner rampart, a paffage is fo formed, that troops attempting to enter muft have prefented their flanks to a double line of the garrifon looking down upon them. Such was, it is prefumed, its form, when entire. At prefent the whole of the fouth fide is covered with buildings, and towards the eaft it has been nearly levelled, and is cut through by the road, only part of the eaft fide, near the north eaftern angle remaining. The enclofing ramparts are ftill near 20 feet high, and their ditches at the bottom from 60 to 70 feet wide, which confidering the double flope of 40 degrees, gives a confiderable width at the creft of the ramparts. The ditch round the mount meafures 42 feet wide at bottom.

The chief magiftrate found here at the Conqueft, was ftiled a Conful, whence it is fuppofed to have been a Roman town. In the eleventh century it was the See of a Bifhop, and a place of great note, but declined on the tranflation of the See to Norwich; yet in the reign of Henry VIII. it was a place of fuch confequence as to be made a fuffragan See to Norwich.

In the reign of James I. an hofpital and a grammarfchool were founded here, by Sir Richard Fulmerfton.

Sir Joseph Williamson, Secretary of State to King Charles II. built the council-house, and gave the corporation a sword and a mace. Here is a common gaol, a bridewell and a workhouse.

This place has been honoured with the presence of many of our Sovereigns. particularly Henry I. and II. Queen Elizabeth had a house here which she frequently visited, and King James I. making it one of his hunting seats, had a palace here, which is still called the King's house.

In the church of St. Mary, there was a society of religious persons as early as the reign of King Edward the Confessor, if not before: and hither Arfastus, Bishop of the East Angles, removed his episcopal seat from North Elmham, in 1075; but it continued here only nineteen or twenty years, and then was translated to Norwich; after which, a monastery for Cluniac monks was built here by Roger Bigod, and made subordinate to the abbey of Cluney in France; but this house and place being found inconvenient, the same Roger began a most stately monastery without the town, and on the other side of the river, dedicated to the Virgin Mary. This monastery was finished in 1114, and was made denison the 50th of Edward III. and upon the dissolution, was found to be endowed with yearly revenues to the amount of 312l. 14s. 4d.

EAST DEREHAM,

EAST DEREHAM,

IS one of the neateft and moft populous market towns in the county, delightfully fituated on the eaft fide of a rivulet, and nearly in the centre of Norfolk. It has a weekly market on Friday, and fairs February 3, and September 28. Here is a genteel affembly-houfe. A new butchery was built a few years fince, and though it may not be handfome, 'tis convenient. At the north end of the market-place ftands a pillar, marking the diftances to moft of the principal towns and feats in the county.

It has been twice almoft deftroyed by fire, the firft was on July 1, 1581, the fecond July 3, 1681, when 170 houfes were burnt, and the whole lofs was eftimated at 19,443l.

The Church is dedicated to St. Nicholas, and has a chapel belonging to it at Hoe. It is a large pile, built in the form of a cathedral; has a nave, north and fouth ailes, two tranfepts, and chancel, all leaded. There is a tower between the body of the church and the chancel. The fouth porch was built by Roger and Margaret Boton, whofe names are now to be feen in the ftone-work. The font is octangular and very handfome; on it are carved the reprefentation of our Saviour's crucifxion, and the feven facraments of the Romifh church, below which are eight of the Apoftles at full length, and at the eight corners beneath them, the four evangelifts, and the fymbol of each, namely, an angel, a lion, bull, and eagle. The afcent up to it, is by a double octagon; the upper octagon is curiously worked in the Gothic taste; it was erected in 1468, and cost 12l. 13s. 9d. To this stone font a Gothic top was added in 1678, ornamented in the taste of the time, and supported by four fluted pillars. Before the font, stands a large brass eagle, on a pedestal of the same, supported by three small lions; it is gilt, and was formerly used as a litany desk. In the middle of the centre aile hangs a brass branch, with a double circle of candlesticks, twelve in each circle; it was purchased in 1738, and cost twenty-five pounds. The church is very handsomely seated, the fronts of the seats towards the middle aile being all panneled wainscot. Edmund Bonner, L. L. D. and afterwards Bishop, of flaming memory, was collated to this Rectory, by the Bishop of Ely, in 1534.

The tower in the middle of the church being thought too weak for the bells, part of it, and the bells were taken down, about 1501, and the large tower (then called the new clocker) in the church-yard, on the south side, and about twenty yards from the chancel, was begun; it was several years in building; in it is a clock and eight bells.

At the west end of the church yard, are the ruins of a very ancient baptistry, over which was formerly a small chapel dedicated to St. Withburga, At the east end of this, there is the remains of a curious old Gothic arch, from which runs a spring of clear water, formerly said to have had many healing and medicinal qualities. The fabulous account is, that this spring took its rise in the church-yard, from the place where St. Withburga was first buried. It was arched ed over and converted into a cold bath in the year 1752.

Here was a famous guild, or fociety of St. Withburga, which had a ftrong brick houfe, called the Guild-hall, where their feafts were kept, and other ceremonies performed. This was pulled down, and a handfome houfe built on its fite by James Smyth, Efq. now of Bradenham.

SWAFFHAM,

ONE of the neateft market towns in the county, ftands upon a rifing ground, in an open champaign country, on a gravelly foil, contains about 3000 inhabitants, and is efteemed a very healthy fituation. There are many handfome modern-built gentlemens houfes in it, and a genteel neighbourbood around, which render it a pleafant and defirable retreat. The market-hill is fpacious, and a handfome crofs was a few years fince erected on it by the late Earl of Orford. The butter market formerly kept at Downham is removed to this place. The market is on Saturday, and plentifully fupplied with good provifions. The town ftands fo high, that fome of the wells are fifty yards deep.

The races annually commence about the 25th or 26th of September, and continue for three days, at which time there is a great meeting of the nobility from Newmarket, and the gentlemen and ladies in the county. There are affemblies the firft an! third nights, and frequently a concert of mufic the intermediate night. An affembly-room has been built on the

weft

west side of the market-hill, in which subscription assemblies are held every month.

In the months of November and March, great coursing matches for greyhounds are held here for a a week. The matches are regularly entered, and the greyhounds names, play or pay, half forfeit, &c. put down in the book, iu the same order as the running horses at Newmarket.

The church was begun about the end of the reign of Edward IV. when the chancel was finished, but the church was not completed till the reign of Henry VII. It is built in the form of a cathedral, having a nave, north and south ailes, chancel, and two transept chapels, making it in the form of a cross. It is a very handsome building ; the tower steeple is particularly light, well proportioned and elegant, surmounted with a * turret, erected in 1777 ; the whole is covered with lead, and built with free-stone, flint, and brick : The upper part of the nave is coped and embattled ; the steeple is entirely free-stone, and embattled, in which there is a clock and eight bells; above the water table, and under the battlements, are two shields, in one of which are the cross-keys, and in the other, two swords a-cross, the emblems of St. Peter and Paul, to whom the church is dedicated. The tower was begun in 1507 and finished in 1510. Over the door of which are several niches for images. From the west door to the entrance into the chancel is about 41 yards, and the breadth of the nave, together with the

---

* The turret is too small in proportion to the steeple, tho' it is said to have cost the town near 500l.

THE NORFOLK TOUR.

the ailes within the walls, is about 17 yards. The vault of the church, and the fide ailes, are fupported by fine flender pillars, confifting each of four fmall pilafters joined together, forming fourteen handfome arches, feven on a fide : Over which are twenty-eight neat light windows. The roof is wonderfully beautiful, of oak, neatly wrought and carved.

The north aile and fteeple of this church, are faid to have been built by John Chapman, erroneoufly ftated to have been a travelling tinker, *who was enriched by a dream*. There formerly was the picture of him, with his wife and three children, in ftained glafs, in every window of this aile, with the following infcription running through the bottom of each window :

Orata pro bono Statu Johannis Chapman ——— Uxoris ejus, et Liberorum fuorum, qui quidem Johannes hanc Alam cum feneftris, tecto et—fieri fecit.

In this aile a large and lofty gallery is erected for the fingers ; the afcent is by a ftone ftair-cafe in the adjoining wall, the way no doubt to the ancient roodloft.

The arch of the chancel, and that at the weft end, are very grand and fpacious, rifing almoft to the fummit of the roof of the church. The chancel is about fifteen yards in length, and feven in breadth, the roof is of oak, fupported by Angels.

From the moft ancient times there was a vicar under the rector, prefented by him, fo that the rectory was a *finecure*. The patronage of the vicarage is in the Bifhop of Norwich.

CASTLE

CASTLE RISING.

SIR HENRY SPELMAN obferves it is a Burgh of fuch antiquity, that the royal Archives and Records give no account of it; and he thought that the Romans had a place of defence here, where fome of their coins had been found, and a Conftantine had been brought to him. That it is the moft ancient Burgh in the county feems evident from its mayor being always called over firft, at the reading of the King's commiffion of the peace before Judges of affize. It was formerly governed by a mayor, recorder, high fteward, twelve aldermen, a fpeaker of the commons, and fifty (fome fay feventy) burgeffes. At prefent the corporation confifts of two aldermen only, who alternately ferve the office of mayor, and return two members to parliament, the mayor being the returning officer. The burgage tenures are the property of the Earls of Suffolk and Orford, and though five or fix names generally appear upon the poll at an election for members of parliament, it is very doubtful whether there is a fingle *legal voter* belonging to the burgh, except the Rector.

This town, from its vicinity to the Great Oufe, the flatnefs of the adjoining marfhes, the name of a ftreet in it called Haven-gate-lane; in which a piece of an anchor was dug up fome years ago, and feveral other corroborating evidences, is fuppofed, in ancient times, to have been a fea-port. Tradition the faithful preferver of many a fact which hiftory may have overlooked, defpifed, spifed, or forgotten, has handed down to us the two following lines:

Rifing was a fea-port-town, when Lynn was but a marfh,

Now Lynn it is a fea-port town, and Rifing fares the worfe.

The caftle was built after the grant of the town and lordfhip by King William II. to William de Albani, that King's pincerna, or butler, and probably by his fon William, the firft Earl of Suffex, who died in 1176. It ftands upon a hill, on the fouth fide of the town, whence is a fine profpect over land, and an arm of the fea: great part of the walls of the keep, or inward tower, are ftill ftanding, being a Gothic pile, much refembling that of Norwich, and little inferior, the walls being about three yards thick, confifting chiefly of free-ftone with iron or car-ftone, encompaffed with a great circular ditch and bank of earth, on which ftood alfo a ftrong ftone wall. The ditch, now dry, was probably formerly filled with water; there is but one entrance to it, on the eaft fide, over a ftrong ftone bridge, about thirty paces long, (with a gate-houfe thercon) about eight or nine paces broad, and is fupported by one arch. The inward part of the caftle, or keep, is all in ruins, except one room, where the court-lete of this lordfhip is held. No doubt the apartments were grand and fumptuous, when queen Ifabel refided here, and when the great King Edward III. with his queen and court were often entertained, and lodged here. On the walls which are decaying, having no cover, were towers, or turrets, which the lords of the manors of Hunftanton, Roydon, and the Wootons,

Woottons, were by their tenures obliged to guard and defend. The compass of the ditch that incloses the whole is above one thousand and eighty paces.

In this castle Isabel, Queen of Edward II, and mother of Edward III. after the death of her favourite, Earl Mortimer, was confined from 1330 till her death in 1358, where she was visited by Edward III. and his Queen in 1340, and again by the King, 1344.

LITTLE WALSINGHAM,

A CONSIDERABLE market town delightfully situated on the banks of a nameless river, which runs into the sea below Stifkey, at six or seven miles distance. The grounds on each side rising in a bold manner gives the country here an appearance not often to be met with in this county. Mr. Warner's plantations, the abbey and church with a small spire, are fine objects, presenting themselves in different points of view on approaching the town.

The curioes traveller should not omit seeing the gardens of the late Henry Lee Warner, Esq. in which are the ruins of an ancient monastery, and shrine dedicated to the Virgin Mary,* and formerly as much frequented as that of Thomas a Becket at Canterbury. The chapel was built in the year 1061, by Richolde, a noble widow and Lady of that manor, in imitation of the chapel of Nazareth.

In those days of darkness and superstition, when Priests and Monks ruled not only the consciences but the

* Here are two wells called by her name.

the purses of the Laity, then they who had not made a pilgrimage and an offering at the shrine of the blessed Virgin of this place, were looked upon as impious and irreligious. — *Erasmus*, who had been here, gives the following description of it. "The Church is splendid and beautiful, but the Virgin dwells not in it; that, out of veneration and respect, is granted to her Son. She has her church so contrived as to be on the right hand of her Son; but neither in that doth she live, the building being not yet finished. In this church there is a small chapel of wood, into which the pilgrims are admitted on each side at a narrow door; there is but little or no light in it, but what proceeds from wax tapers, yielding a most pleasant and odoriferous smell; but if you look in, you will say it is a seat of the Gods, so bright and shining it is all over, with jewels gold and silver."

Sir Henry Spelman tells us, when he was a child, there was a common tradition, that King Henry VIII. in the second year of his reign, went barefoot from Barsham to Walsingham, and offered a necklace of great value to the Virgin Mary; but in the thirtieth year of the same reign, Thomas Cromwell, then Lord High Chamberlain of England, carried her image from hence to Chelsea, where he took care to have it burnt.

FAKENHAM,

IS a neat market town: The market is held on Thursday, where the merchants from Wells constantly ly attend to buy corn of the farmers for exportation. There is a court-house, which is now used as a school, where occasionally concerts of music are held: It was intended for a sessions-house, the quarter sessions of the peace being formerly held alternately at Fakenham and Walsingham, but of late years at Walsingham and Holt.

The church is a large regular pile, having a nave, a north and south aile covered with lead, and a chancel covered with tiles; at the west-end a tower steeple with eight bells, and is dedicated to St. Peter. Round the cover of the font is, *Orate pro aia Ade Powryte, et Alicie uxoris ejus, et omnium benefactor, fuor. qui istud opus fieri fecerunt in honore Dei omnipotentis. Amen.* On the eight sides of the stone bason, or font, are several religious emblems, viz. an angel, ox, lion, and eagle, to represent the four Evangelists; also that of the Trinity, a cross crown of thorns, the King's-arms; also on the pillars of it, the Letter H, or L, in an old character, and a crown over it, to represent it as being in the Duchy of Lancaster, or built in the reign of Henry VI.

HOLT,

IS a market town, and the principal town in the hundred, pleasantly situated on rising ground, and in a fine country, that may justly be called the garden of Norfolk. The scenes around, and the prospects it commands, are more variegated than in any part of the county. The air is sharp but healthy. There are some good houses in it, but the want of water is
severely

severely felt, the inhabitants being obliged to fetch it at some distance. The Quarter Sessions of the Peace are held here and at Walsingham alternately, and the Sessions-house is used as an assembly-room for the monthly assemblies. It is 124 miles from London. The market is on Saturday. Great part of this town was destroyed by fire, on Saturday May the 1st. 1708.

The church is dedicated to St. Andrew. Before the fire it had a nave, two ailes, a square tower, and a spire so high as to be a good sea-mark: the chancel after this was fitted up for the reception of the parishioners.

Sir John Gresham was born in this town in 1507: He entered into partnership with his brother Sir R. Gresham, an eminent merchant, in London, and served the office of sheriff during the year his brother was Lord Mayor, and founded a free-school in Holt, which is under the direction of the company of fishmongers.—He and his brother projected the scheme of building the Royal Exchange, which was afterwards completed by Sir John, Son of Sir Richard. He died 1556.

CROMER,

THERE was formerly a town called Shipden, betwixt this town and the ocean, but the sea has entirely swallowed up that town, and makes hasty strides towards devouring Cromer also, which now stands so near the edge of the cliff, that in the memory of many people now living there, upwards of twenty houses have at different times been precipitated into the sea.

At very low tides there is an appearance of something, which the fishermen call Shipden steeple. It is hardly probable, but that a large tower, whose foundations were an hundred feet perpendicular from the surface of the sea, after being tumbled into it, with the immense body of earth that supported it, and after being washed for many centuries by the waves, must have been so shattered and dashed to pieces, that no remains can be visible.

There is now no harbour at Cromer, yet a trade is carried on from this place, whence corn is exported, and coals, deals, &c. are imported. As the method of trading from the place is curious, we shall mention it.

The vessels used are from 60 to 100 tons burden, few larger: at high water they are laid upon the beach, and, as soon as the water is sufficiently ebbed, carts are drawn to the side of the ship, and the coals are shot into them, as they are into lighters in other places. The carts carry only half a chaldron at a time, as the road up the cliff is very steep. In this manner the carts continue working, till the water flows so high as to wash the horses bellies, and float the carts: they can unload sometimes 60 chaldrons in a tide. When the vessel is empty, it floats on a high tide, and continues at a little distance from the shore, and is loaded with corn by boats, as they seldom run the hazard of loading them when laid on the beach, lest contrary winds should prevent their getting off with the cargo.

Robert

Robert Bacon a mariner of this town difcovered Iceland, and is faid to have taken the prince of Scotland, James Stuart, failing to France for education, in the reign of Henry IV.

THE CHURCH has been a magnificent ftructure of flint and free-ftone. It was built about the year 1396: its fteeple, which is 159 feet high, is fquare, and richly ornamented with free-ftone fculpture: the chancel is in ruins.—About a mile to the eaft of the town is the light-houfe. — Here is a great fifhery for lobfters and crabs, and within the laft few years, a confiderable number of herrings have been taken on the coaft.

There is a fair on Whitfun Monday, which draws together all the neighbourhood within ten miles. To a mind that can receive pleafure from feeing others pleafed, without defpifing the reafons of their being fo, this is a moft ftriking fcene; feveral hundreds of both fexes, and all ages, in their holiday cloaths, are feen from the cliff in boats, which beautifully enliven the fea, whilft fwarms of people who cannot get boats enough to gratify their defire of floating, impatiently wait on the beach, which is covered with them.

This town is likely to receive confiderable improvements, from its having lately become a fafhionable bathing place.

AYLSHAM,

AYLSHAM,

THIS town in the time of Edward II. and III. was the chief town in the county for the linen manufacture. But about the time of Henry VIII. that had much decreased, and the woollen manufacture flourished. In the reign of James I. it was famous for knitters. At present no manufacture is carried on.

It is a neat market town situated on the river Bure, in the most agreeable part of the county, eleven miles from Norwich, seven from North Walsham, eleven from Cromer, eleven from Holt, and contains about one hundred and twenty families. The river Bure was made navigable from Coltishall to this town, for boats of 13 tons burden, and drawing two feet four or five inches water. The work was completed in October 1779, and cost 6000l.

The Church, dedicated to St. Michael the Arch-Angel, is a noble regular building, and was erected by John of Gaunt, Duke of Lancaster; it has a nave, two ailes, two transcepts and a chancel adjoining; a square tower with a small broach or spire on the top, an organ, clock, and ten bells; the porch and the whole building being covered with lead. On the south window there is a neat painting of the salutation, finished in 1516. On the font is neatly carved the emblems of the four Evangelists, the instruments of the passion, a crucifix, and the arms of John of Gaunt, Duke of Lancaster, Lord Morley, Bouchier, St. George, and a crofs flore.

The

The county Bridewell ſtands near the market-place, and has this curious inſcription, cut in wood. *God preſerve. our. ſupreⅿ. bed. Kyng. Henry. Theight. Pray. for. the. good. proſperyte. and. aſſiate. of. Roberd. Marſham. and. Ione. his. wyfe. the. wiche. this. bowſe. they. cawſed. to. be. made. to. the. honor. of. the. towne. be. thir. qwick. lives. fines.* 1543.

The free-ſchool ſtands near the church, it was founded by Robert Jannys, Mayor of Norwich, in 1517, and endowed with 10l. a year.

The Market is on Tueſday, and the Fairs are March 23, and September 26,

GAYWOOD,

IS a village adjoining and within a mile of the Borough of Lynn Regis, to the Eaſt. This town and Lordſhip belonged to the Biſhops of the Eaſt Angles, in the time of the Saxons, and was given by ſome of their Kings. It continued in the See of Norwich till it was granted by an act of parliament, February the 4th, in the 27th year of Henry VIII. to the Crown, with other of the Biſhop's manors and barony, by way of exchange for the abbey manors and lands belonging to the monaſtery of St. Bennet in the Holme.

The church is dedicated to St. Faith the Virgin and Martyr; it conſiſts of a ſquare ſteeple of brick, in which there are three bells; a nave with north and ſouth croſs ailes, covered with thatch. It is a Rectory, and the Tythes amount to 256l. per annum. The Rev. Samuel Beatniffe was Curate and Rector of this pariſh, 55 years, and lies buried in the chancel, with the following inſcription upon his tomb-ſtone.

In

In Memory of
The Rev. Samuel Beatniffe, M. A.
Who died at Lynn, August 10, 1781,
In the 79th year of his age.
Having been Curate, and Rector of this Parish,
And Bawſey, 55 years.

He was benevolent and charitable,
His mind was cheerful, eaſy, and unſuſpicious ;
To all mankind he was juſt and friendly,
And to his relations generous.
He lived reſpected, and died lamented. *

John de Gray Biſhop of Norwich, built a noble palace in this village in 1210, for himſelf and ſucceſſors : At this time Lynn belonged to the Biſhop of Norwich, which very probably occaſioned the Biſhop's building a palace here ; and it is worthy of remark, that when King John was at Lynn, and granted the corporation many extenſive privileges, it was upon the expreſs condition, that the provoſt, or chief magiſtrate, ſhould at the Biſhop's palace at Gaywood, annually acknowledge himſelf ſubject to the Biſhop of Norwich.

There is no edifice now in this village, bearing marks of ſuch high antiquity, and it is difficult to gueſs in what part of the town it ſtood, unleſs it was on the ſite of what is now called Gaywood-hall, which is

---

* If faſtidious criticiſm ſhould diſcover, that too much is here ſaid of an obſcure village; and an obſcure man, let gratitude be permitted to make the following reply.----The Compiler of this humble performance, here ſpent a great part of his early years, and being the adopted ſon of this worthy man, pays this ſmall tribute to his memory.

is surrounded by a very large and deep moat or wet ditch, and ramparts, certainly of no modern date, and which could never be made for any other purpose than that of defence; a very common and necessary precaution, when the great Barons of the kingdom frequently took up arms against their Sovereign, or against each other. For petty tyrants then acknowledged no law beyond the point of a sword, or the flight of an arrow.

About forty years ago there was an oak tree of extraordinary size standing at the entrance thro' the rampart on the north side of this hall; it was quite hollow, and had a table in the middle, round which eight or ten people might conveniently sit.

In 1684 the militia of the county were reviewed in compliment to Charles II's. presence, 'tis said "On "Gaywood Green," but there being no place in the village now known by that name, leads us to conjecture, that the review was upon Sayer's marsh, a fine common belonging to this town, and between it and Lynn to the south, where the Western Battalion was reviewed by the late Lord Orford in 1759, previous to being called out into actual service.

There are about 300 inhabitants in this village; the land is not inferior to any in the county, and lets at from 25s. to 3l. per acre, but the village has not by any means that cheerful appearance which it bore 40 years ago; this perhaps has been occasioned by the great advance of rents, which in general are so high as to keep the little farmers wretchedly poor.

In Reffley wood in this parish, there is a fine spring of

of Chalybeat water, which upon being taken into a bason has a black and dirty colour, but on mixing it with spirits, becomes quite clear, and is of a pleasant flavor. This is a kind of Vauxhall to the inhabitants of Lynn, who resort here in great numbers during the summer season.

A considerable Fair is held at Gaywood, on the 22d and 23d of June.

St. BENNET in the HOLME,

THAT is " in the River Island." Canute, the Danish King of England, returning from Rome, founded a monastery in a fenny place, called Cowholm, and sometimes Calvescroft ; where before the Danes came into England, one Sweman an Hermit, with others his brethren, lived about fifty years ; whose successors, the Hermits of this place, being slain in the Danish persecution, occasioned King Canute, to expiate his countrymens' murthering them, to begin the foundation of this monastery, which was then dedicated to St. Benedict, and endowed by him, and his successor Edward the Confessor, with great privileges and revenues. It was afterwards so strongly fortified by the monks, that it looked more like a castle than a cloister. It was besieged by William the Conqueror in vain, till a monk betrayed it on condition that he should be made abbot ; which he accordingly was ; but shortly after the King ordered this new * abbot to be

* Barber's MS. says that this Abbot, whose name was Ethelwold or Elewold, fled into Denmark to escape the fury of William the Conqueror.

be hanged for a traitor, and thus he received the juft reward for his treachery. The lands were valued on the diffolution of the monafteries, the 26th of Henry VIII. at fix hundred and fixty-feven pounds, nine fhillings and eight-pence, per ann. which lands, being a little before the diffolution exchanged for thofe belonging to the See of Norwich, the Bifhops of Norwich for this reafon, are at this day privileged to challenge the title of abbot of Holme, and, may accordingly fo ftile themfelves. What remains at prefent of the buildings of this monaftery is very little, the church, &c. being all entirely deftroyed, except fome part of the old gate-houfe : However fince the publifhers of the Monafticon have met with a Draught or Reprefentation of the church in a manufcript in the Cottonian Library, and printed it there, I fhall refer the reader to that work; whereby he will be able to guefs at the nature of the fabric. See Monafticon Anglicanum. Vol. 1. p. 282.

The greater part of the preceding, and the following account of St. Bennet's Monaftery is extracted from a MS. of Mr. T. Barber, late of the Cuftom-houfe, Yarmouth, to which he had fubjoined a complete lift of the Abbots to the diffolution, but it being too long to be inferted here, we fhall felect fome remarkable paffages only.

William Rugge, alias Repfe, or Reppes, (the fortieth Abbot of this place) D. D. and Fellow of Gonvill Hall, in Cambridge, and fon of Wm. Rugge, of North Repps in this county, was made Abbot April 26, 1530. Six years after which being promoted by King Henry VIII. to the See of Norwich, he by

virtue

virtue of a private act of parliament, parted with all the lands of his Bishopric (except the site of his Episcopal palace in Norwich) to the King, by way of exchange for the revenues belonging to the Abbey of Holme, and priory of Hickling; which last being soon after alienated by him, the whole income since his time appertaining to the See of Norwich, has been only the Estate of Holme monastery, which his successors still enjoy, according to the purport of the said act; which continuing unrepealed gave occasion to Bishop Richard Montague, *temp. Caroli primi*, to subscribe himself in his leases executed before the great rebellion, Richard by divine permission Lord Bishop of Norwich, and head Abbot of St. Benedict's de Hulm. But to return to Bishop Rugge, alias Repps; he died anno 1550, September 21, and was buried in the middle of the cathedral church of Norwich, having been deprived by order of King Edward VI. on January 31, preceding, notwithstanding he had been a zealous stickler for the King's Supremacy, and influenced his Convent, 21 in number, to subscribe to the same anno 1534. Two years before this monastery was annexed to the See of Norwich, by act of parliament as aforesaid, which limited the Bishops of Norwich before the reformation took place, to maintain only a prior and twelve monks; all which were so well provided for before the year 1553; that not the least sum remained payable out of the abbey, either in pensions or otherwise at that time.—Willis's mitered abbys, v. 1. p. 118.

The exchange of the lands of the Bishopric, with those of St. Bennet's Holme and Hickling, was made

in

February 4,27th, Henry VIII. at which time Abbot Repps was nominated to the See of Norwich, though not elected till May following.

Bishop Repps, alienated from the Bishopric, not only the priory of Hickling, but many good manors belonging to the abbey, some by absolute gift, others upon trifling exchanges, and made long leases, so that at last he was unable to maintain the State of the Bishopric, and forced to resign, with a pension of 200 marks, (as I have somewhere met with.) 'Tis certain he was not deprived, because in the patent of commission of John Hopton, the Bishopric is said to be void by the resignation of William the last Bishop.—The porter or some servant of the Bishop, is said to have made a copy of verses, beginning thus,

Poor Will, thou rugged art, and ragged all,
  Thy abbey cannot bless thee in such Fame;
To keep a palace, state, and lordly hall,
  When gone is thence what shou'd maintain.
the same, &c.

When the Bishops of Norwich were freed from maintaining the prior and twelve monks, is not known; 'Tis no wonder any of them are not in the pension Bishopric, anno 1553, because if any then remained unprovided for, they were supported out of the Bishopric, and not from the Crown.

Bishop Repps lived at St. Bennet's, for I have seen processes or citations, to call persons before him or his Auditor, *Causar in capellâ sancti Salvatori infra manerium nostrum de Hulmo*; and sometimes, *in Capellâ sancti mariæ infra manerium nostrum de Hulmo*,

D d   1542.

1542. However, in his or the succeeding Bishop's time, the abbey was suffered entirely to fall to ruin. Bishop Jagon sued the administratrix of Bishop Redman for 3,161l. dilapidations about the monastery; but it had been done so long that he recovered nothing.

Bishop Freake repaired a handsome hall or grange called Ludham-hall, built by the Abbot Martin, anno 1450, about a mile from the abbey, in a better situation, which was the country seat, and indeed chief place of residence of all the succeeding Bishops, who had here round them about 300 or 400l. per ann. domains, with all sorts of meats, venison, wild fowls, rabbits and fish in great plenty, of their own; and thereby were enabled to live honourably and hospitably, till Bishop Montague came, who leased it out upon lives to provide for his family; since which the Bishops have resided at Norwich.

The ground in the Island of St. Bennet in the Holme is so fenny, that if the little strings and roots of the shrubs in it are cut they will swim upon the water; and it has been conjectured from the cockles now and then dug up there, that the sea has formerly broken in so far. The river Thyne or Thyrn joins the Yare near Clipsby, forming a kind of peninsula called Flegg, where the soil is very rich and fruitful. It is in this part of the county that the Danes are supposed to have first settled, both because it is nearest their landing, and being nearly surrounded with water, is pretty well fortified by nature; and also, because in that little compass of ground we find 13 villages ending in *by*, a Danish word, at the end of a name,

name, signifying a village or dwelling-place, hence our by-laws in England come to signify such laws as are peculiar to each town, village, corporate body, or society.

CONCISE REMARKS ON THE COUNTY.

According to the Roman division of England, Norfolk was part of the *Iceni*. In the Saxon division it made a part of the kingdom of the East Angles. It is called *Simeni* by Ptolemy only, who most certainly means the same country by it, as other authors by the *Iceni*. This appears from the situation he has ascribed to it after *Cattieuchlani*, and having the *Trinobantes* on the East, toward the estuary of the Thames. The modern name Norfolk, or *Northern-folk*, is, without question, by way of distinction from Suffolk, or the *Southern-folk*.

Norfolk is a maritime county, nearly of an oval form, and so surrounded by water, that except at a small causeway, near Lopham, it is an island. The British ocean forms its boundary on the north and east, for near 100 miles: on the south it is divided from Suffolk by the river Waveney and Little Ouse. From Yarmouth haven to near Littleport, is about 70 miles, whence the isle of Ely is its boundary to Gunthorpe sluice, an irregular course of 37 miles: Cross-keys wash divides it from the county of Lincoln.

According to Sir Henry Spelman, it lies between 52 deg. 28 min. and 53 deg. 3 min. of north latitude, and between 13 deg. and 1 deg. 42 minutes of East longitude: being 63 miles long from Yarmouth to Wisbeach, and about 40 in breadth from the parallel of Billingford to Wells; by the roads it measures 71 miles by 43. Its circumference is nearly 210 miles, containing an area of (a) 1,148,000 acres, or 1,793¾ square miles, each being 640 acres. It is divided into 33 hundreds, in which are, one city, four burghs, twenty-four market towns, and about 700 (b) villages. In these are reckoned 47,780 houses, and 240,000 inhabitants. It sends 12 members to parliament, has about (c) 6000 county freeholders, and provides 960 men to the militia. It lies in the diocese of Norwich, and province of Canterbury; pays 22 parts of the Land-tax raised in Great Britain; to the poor rate 83,739l. 4s. 10d. and with respect to the general situation of the kingdom, is accounted to be " in the " East of England," and East Dereham, near the centre of the county, is 94 miles, north-nor-east from London.

The county, says Camden, is large and almost all champaign, except in some places where there arise gentle hills. 'Tis very rich, well stored with flocks of sheep, and abounds with rabbits. The soil is different according to the several quarters; in some places fat, luscious and full of moisture, as in Marshland and Flegg; in others, especially to the West,

it

(a) Hence it appears to be in magnitude, nearly one thirty-fifth part of England.

(b) The Index to the poll-book, published in 1768, makes them 716, exclusive of the city and county of Norwich. By the list at the end of this book, they amount to 728.

(c) In the great contested election for Knights of the Shire in 1734, the Freeholders upon the poll amounted to 6,302, in 1786, they were 5,568.

it is poor, lean, and sandy; and in others clayey, and chalky. The soil is more various than perhaps that of any other county, and comprehends all the sorts that are to be found in the island; arable, pasture, meadow, wood-lands, light sandy ground, deep clays, heaths and fens.

What Camden advances in general terms, on the soil and produce of the county, was written more than two centuries ago; since which the improved state of agriculture has made such changes, that we hope it will be acceptable to our readers to be informed what Mr. Kent has more particularly said upon the same subjects in 1794. His words are — The greatest part of the arable land is sandy. The prime parts of the county lie north, and north-east of Norwich; which may be denominated a true sandy loam, equal in value to the best parts of the Austrian Netherlands, which it resembles. The district south and south-east of Norwich, though chiefly sand, has an occasional mixture of clay, and is, in many parts, wet, and full of springs; but yet this part is fruitful, though in a less degree than the former.

The largest proportion of the county lies west and north-west of Norwich. There is some very good land in different parts of this district; but upon the whole, it is very inferior to the two preceding. This is called West Norfolk; and on account of the three great houses, Houghton, Holkham, and Rainham, is the part which strangers are most acquainted with.

The part of the county lying south-west of Norwich, runs upon a still lighter sand; so light, that in the hundred

dred of Greenhoe, the sand very often, in a high wind, drifts from one parish to another. Here are the great rabbit warrens.

Marshland may be considered as a hundred by itself. The soil is a rich ooze, evidently gained from the sea; the north part is highly productive; but the south part very much injured for want of a better drainage.

The air on the sea coast is in general sharp and healthy, in the hundreds of East and West Flegg damp and unwholesome, at Lynn and in Marshland cold, damp, gloomy, and aguish, so that when a stranger comes to live in Marshland, and gets the ague, which he seldom escapes, he is said *to be arrested by the bailiff of Marshland.* The inland part of the county is extremely pleasant and salubrious. On the whole, the people of Norfolk have long been celebrated for their activity, healthy constitution, subtlety, and sharpness of wit, which Camden reproached them with turning to one of the worst of purposes,—that of harassing each other with petty law suits. If this reproach were well founded in Camden's time, we believe it to be no longer applicable, and that no county in England, of equal extent and opulence, presents fewer instances of this kind. Perhaps the inhabitants have discovered, that he who goes to law on frivolous and vexatious occasions, gratifies his resentment at the expence of his purse, and the injury of his reputation.

The Diocese of Norwich comprehends the counties of Norfolk and Suffolk, and a few parishes in Cambridgeshire, excepting Emneth in Freebridge-Marshland,

THE NORFOLK TOUR. 285

land, which belongs to the Bifhopric of Ely; Hadleigh, Monks-Illeigh, and Moulton, in Suffolk, as peculiars to the Archbifhop of Canterbury, and Frekenham, to the See of Rochefter.

It is divided into four Archdeaconries, and thofe fub-divided into deanries, parifhes, parochial benefices, and medieties.

Archdeaconries	Deanries	Parifhes, &c.
Norwich	13	365
Norfolk	12	468
Sudbury	8	}523
Suffolk	14	

The number of eftablifhed Clergy refident within the Diocefe of Norwich, as calculated in 1772, was:

Of the beneficed Clergy, about 550.
Curates not beneficed, about 150.

The county has the greateft number of parifh churches of any in the three kingdoms, and if, as before has been ftated, it contains 1793¾ fquare miles, or 1,148,000 acres, and 240,000 inhabitants, it is 134 perfons to every fquare mile, and one to every three acres and 1-third, a population furpaffing any other county in England, at the fame diftance from the metropolis: And, it being fuppofed that one perfon out of every eight or nine, but we will fay, in every ten, is able to bear arms, the county and city have 24,000 men fo qualified.---The mufter-roll in 1574 contained 8,240 names; whence it appears, that within 225 years, the defenfive power of the county

county is increased in nearly a threefold proportion.

The civil government of the county is in the High-Sheriff for the time being. He is annually appointed by the King, and presides at the assizes, and other county meetings. The Lent Assizes are held at Thetford in March, and the Summer Assizes at Norwich, in August.

The military and marine government of this county is committed to the care of a Lord-Lieutenant and Vice-Admiral, who is also Custos Rotulorum. The Lord-Lieutenant is the *locum tenens* of the King, and, as his Vice-roy, governs in the county. It is an office of great distinction, appointed by the King for managing the standing militia in the county, and all military affairs therein. He has the power of commissioning all officers in the militia, (his Majesty's approbation as a mere matter of form, being obtained); he appoints the Deputy-Lieutenants, whose names must also be presented by the King. As Custos Rotulorum, he puts such gentlemen as are properly qualified, into the commission of the peace, and is supposed to have custody of the rolls, or records of the Sessions of peace. In both these capacities he appears rather a Minister than a Judge, though he is, in his own person, a Justice of Peace and Quorum. Lord-Lieutenants of counties were first instituted July 24, 1549.

The county hath the honour of having raised the the first battalion of militia, which marched out of the county, and did duty at Hilſea-barracks, near Portſmouth in 1759.

There were ſeventy-ſeven monaſteries and religious houſes in Norwich and the county of Norfolk, at the time of the general diſſolution by Henry VIII. in the year 1535. — It is obſerved that eccleſiaſtical colleges are always in the moſt pleaſant and fruitful places: While the world allowed the Monks their choice, it is ſurely no diſhonour that they choſe well.

There are in Norfolk more *reſident proprietors* of 400l. a year, landed eſtate, than in any other county in England.

The Quarter-ſeſſions for the county are held in the Shire-houſe, on the Caſtle-hill of Norwich, in January, April, July and October. The ſummer Aſſizes, monthly county courts, and the various county meetings are alſo held in the Shire-houſe, and the county elections, upon the Caſtle-hill.

The roads are naturally ſo good, that when King Charles was here in 1671,* he ſaid, the county ſhould be cut into ſtrips to make roads for the reſt of the kingdom.

* At that time there was not a ſingle Turnpike Road in the county.

TURNPIKE

TURNPIKE ROADS in NORFOLK.

	MILES.
From Norwich to Thetford	29
Norwich to Swaffham	28
And to Mattifhall	4
Weft Bilney to Lynn	9
Norwich to Yarmouth	22
St. Olave's Bridge to Beccles	8
Lynn to Gayton	7
Lynn to Caftle Rifing	5
And to Hillington	4
To Grimfton	3
Ditto to Methwold	19
And to Little Oufe Bridge	14
Ditto to Wifbeach	17
Fincham to near Wifbeach	17
Norwich to Scole Inn	20
And to New Buckenham	12
Ditto to Watton	21
Ditto to Aylfham	11

Mr. Kent has ftated the value of the fuperabundant produce of the county to be as follows :

Corn annually exported	£. 901,521 9 0
Bullocks, fheep, wool, fwine, rabbits, dairy articles, poultry, game, herrings,	275,500 0 0
	1,170021 9 0

If ten pounds be apportioned for the annual fubfiftance of every human being, one with another, which is acknowledged to be a liberal allowance, it follows, that the county fends out a foreign fupply for upwards

wards of 117,000 persons; and as the soil of Norfolk is far from being naturally good, it muſt, undoubtedly, be to art and induſtry, that this great ſource of treaſure is to be aſcribed.

The inhabitants of Norfolk are rather below the middle ſtature, of a clear complexion, an active, induſtrious, enterpriſing diſpoſition, and particularly ſkilful in agriculture. Its extenſive ſea coaſt and inland navigation, furniſh 6000 experienced and hardy ſailors: the worſt parts of the county, a prodigious number of rabbits, and every part of it excellent mutton, and the beſt turkies in England.

The extenſive culture of turnips as now practiſed in Norfolk, for the purpoſe of fattening bullocks, was introduced into the county by Charles, Viſcount Townſhend, who brought it from Hanover in the year 1715, and firſt tried it upon the light lands in the vicinity of Rainham. In 1727 it was very general in that part of the country, and has ſince become the baſis of the Norfolk Huſbandry. For the various ſpecies, culture, and application of this moſt uſeful plant, we refer our readers to Marſhall's Rural Œconomy of Norfolk, vol. 1. p. 256 to 298.

LIST OF RARE NORFOLK PLANTS.

VERONICA TRIPHYLLOS, *Trifia Speedwell.* Near Cockley Cley; it grows in Suffolk, and is a very rare plant in other counties of England.

UTRICULARIA MINOR, *Leſſer-hooded Milfoil.* St. Faith's Newton Bogs, near Norwich.

SCHOENUS

SCHOENUS COMPRESSUS, *Compreſſed Bog-ruſh.* St. Faith's Bogs, and near Ditchingham Bath.

SCIRPUS PAUCIFLORUS, Fl. Scot, *Little chocolate headed Club-ruſh.* Poringland heath and Ellingham fen.

SCIRPUS SYLVATICUS, *Wood Club-ruſh.* Ditchingham.

ERIOPHORUM VAGINATUM, *Hare's-tail ruſh.* Bawſey Bottom, near Lynn.

PHALARIS ARENARIA, Fl. Ang. or PHLEUM ARENARIUM, Lin. *Sea Canary-graſs.* On Yarmouth Downs, and likewiſe near Swaffham, far from the Sea.

PHALRIS PHLEOIDES, Lin. *Cat's-tail Canary-graſs.* Firſt diſcovered in Great Britain in 1780, near Swaffham.

ALOPECURUS VENTRICOSUS, Fl. Ang. MILIUM LENDIGERUM, Lin. *Panic fox-tail graſs.* Gillingham cornfields.

AIRA SETACCA, Fl. Ang. *Mountain hair-graſs.* Stratton Strawleſs Heath.

POA ANGUSTIFOLIA, *Norrow leaved Meadow-graſs.* On the walls of Caſtle Riſing Caſtle.

ÆGILOPS INCURVA, *Sea hard-graſs.* Yarmouth Downs.

ELYMUS ARENARIUS, *Sea lime-graſs.* On the Norfolk coaſt.

TILLÆA MUSCOSA, *Procumbent Tillea.* Dry Heaths in Norfolk and Suffolk, and as yet not noticed in any other county of England.

HOLESTEUM UMBELLATUM, Lin. CERASTIUM UMBELLATUM, Fl. Ang. *Umbelliferous Chick-weed.*

Originally

THE NORFOLK TOUR.

Originally found at Norwich, since at Bury, but no where else in England, as yet known.

GALIUM ANGLICUM, *Small Ladies bed-straw, or Goose-grass.* On the walls of Binham Church.

ASPERULA CYNANCHICA, *Squinancy-wort.* Swaffham Heath.

ANCHUSA SEMPERVIRENS, *Evergreen Alkanet.* About Norwich plentifully, but rare in the county.

VERBASUM LYCHNITIS, VAR. β. Fl. Ang. *Hoary yellow Mullim.* It has been noted for growing about Norwich in great abundance for many years back; it is not uncommon likewise in the county. It grows also at Bury, and Wollerton in Northamptonshire, is mentioned by Ray, otherwise this beautiful plant seems to be claimed by Norfolk and Suffolk alone, and by the first in particular.

GENTIANA PNEUMONANTHE, *Marsh Gentian, or Calathian Violet.* Stratton Heath near Norwich; the intelligence of its growing there was first communicated to the world, by the late Mr. Stillingfleet.

BUPLEURUM TENUISSIMUM, *Least Hare's-Ear.* Near Cley and Lynn.

SELINUM PALUSTRE, *Marsh Selinum.* Very near Norwich, and in many places in Norfolk. This plant was not known to be English by Mr. Ray.

OENANTHE PIMPINELLOIDES, *Parsley water Drop-wort.* Marshes near Yarmouth, and but of late known to be a native of Norfolk at all.

CICUTA VIROSA, *Long leaved water Hemlock.* This very poisonous plant grows very near Norwich, and in many places in the county.

STATICE RETICULATA, *Matted Sea-Lavender.*

Norfolk alone has the honour of producing this plant on its sea shore, viz. at Wells Blakeney and Cley; it was not known to Mr. Ray.

MYOSURUS MINIMUS, *Mouse-tail.* St. Faith's and Lakenham, near Norwich.

NARTHECIUM OSSIFRAGUM, *Lancashire Asphodel.* Dersingham Moor.

ACORUS CALAMUS, *Sweet smelling Flag or Calamus.* It has been noticed by Ray many years back, as growing on the river Yare.

FRANKENIA LÆVIS, *Sea-heath.* Near Yarmouth.

RUMEX PULCHER, *Fiddle-dock.* In Norfolk, very common.

VACCINIUM OXYCOCCOS, *Cranberries.* Dersingham Moor.

CHRYSOSPLENIUM ALTERNIFOLIUM, *Alternate leaved golden Saxifrage.* Poringland Heath, near Norwich.

PARIS QUADRIFOLIA, *Herb Paris, True-love or one-berry.* Rackheath wood, and near Bawburgh.

MONOTROPA HYPOPITHYS, *Yellow Bird's nest.* Shottisham and Stoke.

DIANTHUS PROLIFER, *Proliferous Pink.* Near Norwich.

CUCUBALUS OTITES, *Spanish Campion.* Near Swaffham.

ARENARIA TENUIFOLIA, *Fine leaved Sandwort.* Near Cley. On Sir Richard Bedingfield's garden walls, at Oxborough.

SEDUM ANGLICUM, *English Stone crop.* Norfolk coast.

CHELIDONIUM GLAUCIUM, *Yellow horned Poppy.* On the Norfolk coast.

CHELIDONIUM CORNICULATUM & HYBRIDUM, *red and purple horned Poppy.* Both discovered in Norfolk by Mr. Stillingfleet, and sent to Mr. Hudson, author of the Flora Anglica.

PAPAVER HYBRIDUM, *Bastard Poppy.* Near Norwich.

STRATIOTES ALOIDES, *Fresh-water Soldier.* In Norfolk, very frequent.

ANEMONE PULSATILLA, *Pasque flower.* Lexham, at a place called Tulip-hills.

TEUCRIUM CHAMÆDRYS, *Common Germander.* Norwich city walls.

MELAMPYRUM ARVENSE, *Purple Cow-wheat.* Near Coffey and Litcham, and some other places in Norfolk. This beautiful species appears to be rare in other counties.

COCHLEARIA DANICA, *Danish Scurvy-grass.* At Wells.

IBERIS NUDICAULIS, *Naked rock-cress.* About Norwich, frequent; rare in other counties.

TURRITIS GLABRA, *Smooth tower-mustard.* Near Norwich, and has been noticed by Ray, as a scarce Norfolk plant.

CRAMBE MARITIMA, *Sea Colewort.* Norfolk coast.

GERANIUM SYLVATICUM, *Wood Crane's-bill.* Holt wood in Leziate, near Lynn.

LATHYRUS PALUSTRIS, *Marsh Lathyrus.* At Ranworth Norfolk.

HIPPOCREPIS COMOSA, *Tufted horse shoe vetch.* Swaffham Heath.

TRIFOLIUM ORNITHOPODIOIDES, *Bird's foot trefoil.* Moushold Heath, Norwich.

MEDICAGO FALCATA, *Yellow Medick, or wild Lucern.* Been noted for growing in Norfolk, and particularly about Norwich.

CREPIS FOETIDA, *Stinking Crepis, or hawk-weed.* In the road from Swaffham to Downham, very sparingly.

HYOSERIS MINIMA, *Least Swine's Succory.* Corn-fields near Norwich and New Buckenham.

HYPOCHÆRIS GLABRA, *Smooth Hypochæris, or hawk-weed.* In a field betwixt Norwich and Coffey.

CARDUUS ACAULIS, *Dwarf Carline Thistle.* Dry Heaths and Commons in Norfolk, very frequent.

GNAPHALIUM DIOICUM, *Mountain Cat's foot,* Stratton Heath, about seven miles from Norwich.

CINERARIA PALUSTRIS, *Marsh flea-bane.* Betwixt Norwich and Yarmouth, especially at Acle and Caister.

OPHRYS LOESELII, *Dwarf Ophrys* A single specimen of this rare plant was once found at St. Faith's Newton, but it is doubtful whether it can be again found there.

OPHRYS PALUDOSA, *The least tway-blade.* For the honour of Norfolk, this plant was found in 1769, on Felthorpe Bogs, near Norwich, the place of its former growth in England, being very doubtful.

CAREX LIMOSA, *Marsh Carex.* Heydon and St. Faith's Newton Bogs.

CAREX STRIGOSA, *Loose Carex.* Sexton Wood, Bedingham.

ATRIPLEX PEDUNCULATA, *Pedunculated Orache.* Yarmouth, discovered about the year 1776.

For the preceding list of rare Norfolk plants, we are indebted to an ingenious Botanical Friend, on whose accuracy and abilities we have reason to place the utmost confidence. Those Gentlemen who are desirous of further information on this curious and fashionable study, we refer to the last edition of Camden's Britannia, vol. 2. p. 118 to 122, where the catalogue is extended to more than 700.—The first edition of Camden's Britannia, was published in 1586, in one small quarto volume, in Latin. It has often been translated into English, and augmented by successive editors, till it has, it may be presumed, arrived at maturity, under the fostering hand of Mr. Gough, who in 1789 published an edition of it in three ponderous folio volumes; but, where every thing is *put down* that comes to hand, good, bad, or indifferent, what we hoped to find consolidated, is so enveloped and obscured, by detached sentences, hearsays, conjectures, and discordant matter, of we know not whom, that in the pursuit to gratify our curiosity, we are forcibly reminded of the adage,—' Tis like searching for a ' single grain of wheat amidst a bushel of chaff.'

RIVERS AND BROADS.

The GREAT OUSE springs from Brackley in Northamptonshire, and running through Buckingham, Bedford, Huntingdon, and Cambridgeshire, and dividing this last county from Norfolk, passes by Littleport; through Denver-sluice, and falls into the British Ocean, about ten miles below Lynn Regis.—It is navigable for lighters, from Lynn to Cambridge.

The WAVENEY rises at South Lopham in this county, from what is called the Ford, though in fact it is a causeway of only nine feet in breadth, having a ditch on each side, in one of which are springs, the source of the Waveney, running Eastward by Scole, Billingford, Harleston, and Bungay, whence it is navigable to Yarmouth, Beccles, St. Olave's marshes, and meeting the the Yare and Bure, near Burghcastle, they empty into the ocean at the fort. The Little Ouse rises at South Lopham, and separating the county from Suffolk on the South-west, passes by Thetford, whence it is navigable by the way of Brandon, and joining the Great Ouse at Priest-bridge, four miles below Little-port, in the Isle of Ely, passes on to Lynn The contrary direction of these streams, rising so near to each other, and the sources of two such considerable rivers, is in this part of the country, considered as a great curiosity.

The WENSUM has its source at West Rudham, and being joined by several small streams in its course of near forty miles, passes through the city of Norwich; below Trowse it is joined by the TESSE, and at the upper end of Breydon, by the WAVENEY and BURE,* and discharges into the British Ocean, at the Fort, two miles South of Yarmouth.

The BURE rises near Hindolvestone, and running by Saxthorpe and Blickling, becomes navigable at Aylsham, whence passing Oxnead, Lammas, Coltishall, and through Wroxham-bridge, and St. Bennet's in the Holme, to Thurne, where it is joined by a river called Thyrne, or Thurne; they pass through the bridge at Acle, and are navigable to Yarmouth.

* It has not been clearly ascertained at what place this river takes the name of YARE. Some have assigned it to its junction with the Tesse, and others, where it meets the Waveney.

THE NORFOLK TOUR. 297

The NENE rifes in Northamptonſhire, dividing that county frcm Huntingdon, and running through part of Cambridgeſhire and Norfolk, paſſes through Wiſbeach, by Walpole, and falls into the Britiſh ocean at Crofs-Keys Waſh, which divides this county from Lincolnſhire.

The NAR, rifes at Mileham, and paſſing Litcham, and Caſtleacre, becomes navigable at Weſtacre, whence it takes its courſe by Pentney and Setchy-bridge, and falls into the Ouſe at Lynn.

Theſe rivers flowing through a nearly level country, their ſtreams are ſlow, and frequently diffuſe themſelves over the lower tracts in their courſe, forming ſhallow lakes, here called Broads. The principal Broads are Breyden, above Yarmouth, through which the navigable rivers Yare and Waveney, have their channel: It is three miles in length, and in moſt parts half a mile wide : Hickling-broad is a beautiful ſheet of water, about one mile over ; near to it are ſeveral ſmaller lakes of irregular form ; and about two miles Eaſt, is Horſey-broad, covering forty acres. Near to Stalham is a broad one mile long, but ſcarcely a furlong wide ; and below it is Barton-broad, of the ſame length though much wider towards the middle. Filby-broad extends a mile and a half, but is ſhallow, narrow, and ill-ſhapen. Rockland-broad is nearly of a circular form, two miles and a half in circumference. By the river Bure are ſeveral broads,. as Wroxham, Hoveton, Wood-baſtwick, Ranworth, and South Walſham, all of which are ſaid to cover 500 acres. Quidenham, Diſs, and Hingham, have each a ſmall broad. Theſe broads are plentifully ſtored with fiſh and water-fowl.

KNIGHTS *of the* SHIRE *for the* COUNTY *of* NORFOLK, *from the* RESTORATION *to the present Time, with the Number of* VOTES *polled at each contested* ELECTION.

1660.
Horatio Townshend, Bart.
Sir William Doily, Kt.

1668.
Sir John Hobart	2740
Sir Roger Kemp	2732
Sir Nevil Catlin	1987
Sir William Coke	1743

1670.
Sir Roger Kemp	1434
Sir John Hobart	1620
Sir Thomas Hare	1074
Sir Nevil Catlin	1530

1672.
Sir John Hobart	2047
Sir Peter Glean	2984
Sir James Astley	2996
Sir William Coke	2974

1676.
Sir John Hobart	3440
Sir Peter Glean	3412
Sir Thomas Hare	1735
Lord Paston	1147

1678.
Sir John Hobart	3120
Sir James Astley	2087
Sir William Coke	1730

1680.
Sir John Hobart, Bart.	3559
Sir Peter Glean, Bart.	3202
Sir Christ. Calthorp, Kt.	2517
Sir Nevile Catlin, Kt.	2549

1681.
Sir Henry Hobart	672
Sir John Holland	494
Sir Thomas Hare	3427
Sir Jacob Astley	3496

1684.
Sir Jacob Astley, Bart.	3415
Sir Thomas Hare, Bart.	3416
Sir Henry Hobart, Bart.	692
Sir John Holland, Bart.	410

1686.
Sir Henry Hobart	3027
Sir John Holland	2040
Sir James Astley	2002

1688.
Sir Henry Hobart, Bart.	1798
Sir William Coke, Bart.	1995
Sir Jacob Astley, Bart.	1670
Sir Roger Potts, Bart.	1153

1690.
Sir Henry Hobart	1370
Lord Paston	780
Sir Jacob Astley	1738
Sir William Coke	1710

1692.
Sir Henry Hobart	1127
Sir John Holland	1084
Sir William Coke	1059
Lord Paston	651

1696.
Colonel Townshend	2004
Mr. Walpole	1347
Sir Jacob Astley	1781
Lord Paston	1000

1699.
Mr. Townfhend
Sir John Holland

1702.
Sir John Holland   2702
Sir Edward Ward, Bart.   2650
Sir Jacob Aftley   2681
Sir William Coke   2662

1705.
Sir John Holland, Bart.
Afh Wyndham, Efq.

1708.
The fame

Oct. 11, 1710.
Sir John Wodehoufe, Bart.   3217
Sir Jacob Aftley, Bart.   3200
Afh Wyndham, Efq.   2783
Robert Walpole, Efq.   2397

1713.
Sir Jacob Aftley, Bart.
Sir Edmund Bacon, Bart.

Feb. 18, 1714.
Thomas De Grey, Efq.   3183
Sir Jacob Aftley, Bart.   3059
Sir Ralph Hare, Bart.   2840
Erafmus Earle, Efq.   2635

1722.
Sir John Hobart, Bart.
Thomas Coke, Efq.

1727.
Sir Edmund Bacon, Bart.
Harbord Harbord, Efq.

May 22, 1734.
Sir Edmund Bacon, Bart.   3224
Wm. Wodehoufe, Efq.   3153
Wm. Morden, Efq.   3147
Robert Coke, Efq.   3081

1736.
Armine Wodehoufe, Efq. VICE
Wm. Wodehoufe, Efq. DEC.

May 13, 1741.
Edward Lord Coke, fon of the
    Earl of Leicefter
Armine Wodehoufe, Efq.

1747.
Hon. George Townfhend
Armine Wodehoufe, Efq.

May 8, 1754.
Hon. George Townfhend
Armine Wodehoufe, Efq.

1761.
The fame

1764.
Thomas de Grey, Efq: jun:
    Merton, VICE
The Hon. George Townfhend,
    now Marquis Townfhend

March 23, 1768.
Sir Edward Aftley, Bart.   2977
Thomas de Grey, Efq.   2754
Sir A. Wodehoufe, Bart.   2680
Wenman Coke, Efq.   2610

Oct. 1774.
Sir E. Aftley, Bart. Melton
Weman Coke, Efq. Holkham

May 8, 1776.
Thomas William Coke, Efq.
    Holkham, VICE
Wenman Coke, Efq. DECEASED

Sept. 20, 1780.
Sir Edward Aftley, Bart.
Thomas William Coke, Efq.

April 14, 1784.
Sir John Wodehoufe, Bart.
Sir Edward Aftley, Bart

June 24, 1790.
Sir John Wodchoufe, Bart.
Thomas Wm. Coke, Efq.

A Concise DESCRIPTION of the PRINCIPAL TOWNS in the COUNTY of
SUFFOLK.

BURY St. EDMUND's,

IS situated on the West side of the river Bourne or Lark, which is navigable from Lynn to Fornham St. Martin's, a village about a mile North of this town. It has a most charming inclosed country on the South and South-west, and on the North and North-west the most delicious champaign fields, extending themselves to Lynn, and that part of the county of Norfolk. The county on the East is partly open and partly inclosed. It is so pleasantly situated, commands such an extensive prospect, and the air is so sharp and salubrious, that it is called the Montpellier of England. On April the 11th 1608, there was a dreadful fire in this town, which destroyed one hundred and sixty dwelling-houses besides other buildings, to the value of sixty thousand pounds. This accident though terrible in itself, in all probability was followed by this agreeable circumstance, the present regularity of the streets, which now cut each other at right angles, and the town standing upon an easy ascent, greatly contributes to its beauty.

Leland, the antiquarian-royal of England, who flourished in the reign of Henry VIII. and Edward VI.

VI. and died in 1552, gives this description of the town and monastery: "A city more neatly seated the sun never saw, so curiously doth it hang upon a gentle descent, with a little river on the East side; nor a monastery more noble, whether one considers its endowments, largeness, or unparalleled magnificence. One might even think the monastery alone a city; so many gates is has (some whereof are brass) so many towers, and a church, than which nothing can be more magnificent; as appendages to which, there are three more of admirable beauty and workmanship in the same churchyard." Now there are but two churches entire, St. Mary's and St. James's and the ruins of St. Edmund's,* the principal church in the monastery, which is supposed to have been one of the grandest Gothic structures in Europe.

The abbey which was once so illustrious, was first built by Sigebert King of the East Angles, soon after christianity was planted here by Felix the Burgundian, and being finished, King Sigebert, about the year 638 retired into it, and secluded himself from all temporal affairs.

St. Edmund from whom this town takes its name, was murthered by the Danes, near Hoxne, about the year

---

* A very curious model of this church is to be seen at Mr: Tillot's on the Angel-hill: It is ten feet long, five feet wide, and a proportionate height, containing 300 niches, and 280 windows, adorned with images and other Gothic figures. The model of St. Edmund's-shrine is ornamented with images and crowns gilt, as in its original state, and there are twelve chapels which belonged to this once magnificent church:

year 870, but not buried here till 903. On this account, and through the superstition of that age, the revenue of the abbey increased prodigiously, and the monks greedy to swallow all the prey, under various pretences secluded all the seculars, and filled their places, with those of their own order, the Benedictines: this they effected about the year 1020, in the 4th year of King Canute, who then laid the foundation of a more magnificent church, to the honor of this Martyr; the former in which his remains had been deposited being but a wooden building, or, at best, covered with wood. The expence of this fabrick was raised by an annual tax of 4d. an acre on all ploughed land in Suffolk and Norfolk. It was finished in about twelve years, and consecrated by Othelneth, or Agelnoth, Archbishop of Canterbury, and dedicated to Christ, St. Mary and St. Edmund.

Uvius, prior of Hulm was consecrated the first abbot, 1020. He first encompassed the *abbey, and a part if not the whole of the town, with a wall and ditch, the ruins of which are still to be seen in many places. Thus was the grandeur of this abbey begun; its abbots were made parliamentary barons, and its wealth yearly increased, until its final dissolution by Henry VIII. when its yearly revenues amounted to 2,336l. 16s. and the plate, bells, lead, timber, &c. yielded 5000 marks to the King. There were several Hospitals belonging to the abbey, the most famous of which was that of St. Saviour's, within the Northgate,

* Mr. King observes, that the great Gate-way of the abbey is a remarkable specimen of Saxon architecture, and was built in the time of Canute.

gate, in which the parliament met in Henry the VIth's time; and it was here that Humphrey Duke of Gloucester was murdered at the inftigation of the monks, by the hand of Pole, then Duke of Suffolk.

The civil government of the town is now lodged in the hands of an alderman, who is chief magiftrate, a recorder, twelve capital burgeffes, and twenty-four common burgeffes; who have the fole right of choofing their own reprefentatives in parliament.

Inftead of the many chapels and oratories which were formerly in this town, there are now only two magnificent and ftately churches, ftanding in the fame church-yard: The one dedicated to St. Mary, is 139 feet long by 67 feet and a half broad, and the chancel of it is 74 by 68 : The roof of the nave of St. Mary's church is truly magnificent: There is a fine afcent of fix fteps to the altar, on the North fide of which is the tomb of * Mary Queen of France, daughter of Henry VII. and afterwards married to Charles Brandon, Duke of Suffolk. This Queen of France was buried in the great church of the monaftery, and removed after the diffolution of it into St. Mary's church; her body is covered with lead, refembling an human fhape, and on her breaft is infcribed, " Mary Queen of France, 1533." Her tomb was not only fimple and unadorned, but for a long feries

* When her tomb was repaired, Sir John Cullum Bart. procured a lock of hair from the Corpfe of a bright auburn colour, uninjured by an interment of 225 years, which he prefented to the late Duchefs of Portland, and at the fale of her Mufeum, in May 1786, it fold for the MODERATE price of 6l. 1cs.

F f

series of years entirely neglected. It was even without any inscription till the year 1758, when Sir John Cullum, Bart. had the tomb repaired at his own expence, and a marble tablet inserted into it.

The other Church, dedicated to St. James, was finished in the reign of Edward VI. who was himself a contributor to it, as appears from an inscription in the church: It is 137 feet long by 69 feet wide, the chancel is 56 by 27 feet; at the West end of the South aile are two large monuments erected to the memory of James Reynolds, Lord Chief Baron of the Exchequer, and his Lady, who were buried here. In this church is an organ lately erected, and a library convenient enough, but which has no curiosities, except a M.S. of Bede's Ecclesiastical History, and Demetrius Chalcondyla's Edition of Homer.

The steeple of the church of St. James, and the abbey-gate, are buildings which must excite the attention of the curious: the former was anciently the grand Portal that led to the great church of the monastery; the arches of the tower are all round, of a Saxon form, and seem to be much older than Henry the Third's time. The abbey-gate, which conducted you to the private court of the abbot, is a masterpiece of Gothic architecture; it was built in the reign of Richard the Second, the Townsmen having demolished the former gate in his grandfather's time, upon a quarrel with the monks. The inside of it is adorned with the arms of Holland, Duke of Exeter, and of Edward the Confessor, who was the favourite Saint of Richard II.

In

In both churches there were formerly great numbers of infcriptions and effigies engraved on brafs, but they were fcandaloufly torn off and fold, in 1644, for private emolument, by the church-wardens. Nor at the diffolution of the abbey, could thefe churches efcape the plunder of the great men who were in authority under the godly prince, King Edward VI. for they fwept from the altars of them about 480l. worth of plate, and other valuahle ornaments.

On the 20th of February, 1772, fome workmen who were employed in the ruins of the abbey digging for ftone, found a leaden coffin, made after the ancient cuftom, exactly the fhape of the body. This had been enclofed in an oak cafe, which by the length of time was decayed, but the lead remained quite perfect, and enclofed an embalmed body, as frefh and perfect as at the time of its interment; the nails on the fingers and toes as perfect as when living, and the hair of the head a chefnut brown, with fome mixture of grey ones. The corpfe was done up in a pickle, and the face wrapped in a fear-cloth. A furgeon in the neighbourhood was fent for, who made an incifion into the breaft, and declared the flefh cut as firm as in a living fubject, and there was even an appearance of blood. At this time the corpfe was not the leaft noifome, but being expofed to the air it prefently became putrid and offenfive. The body was cut and mangled, the fkull was fawed in pieces, where the brain feemed wafted indeed, but perfectly enclofed in its proper membrane, the cheeks likewife were cut through, and his arms cut off and carried away.

It was soon found that the coffin contained the remains of Thomas Beaufort, third son of John of Gaunt, Duke of Lancaster, by his third Duchess Lady Catherine Swinford. He was by his half-brother, King Henry VI. created Duke of Exeter, Knight of the Garter, Admiral and Governor of Calais, and in 1410, Lord High Chancellor of England, created Earl of Perth in Normandy, and Earl of Dorset, in England. He led the rear guard at the battle of Agincourt, valiantly defended Harfleur against the French, was guardian to Henry VI. and dying at East Greenwich, Jan. 1, 1427, was (as he had in his will directed) interred in the abbey church of Bury St. Edmund's, near his Duchess, at the entrance of the chapel of our Lady, close to the wall on the North side of the choir. His monument was demolished with the rest of that grand building, at the dissolution, in 1540.

The labourers, for the sake of the lead, which they sold for about twenty shillings, stript the body of its coffin, throwing it promiscuously among the rubbish; but upon discovering whose it was, the mangled remains were inclosed in a strong oak coffin, and buried near the large North-east pillar which formerly assisted to support the belfry.

This Prince was grandson to the victorious King Edward III.—Every humane and sensible mind reflects with horror upon the savage indecency with which the remains of this Prince has been treated.

In this monastery were interred twelve of the ancient royal family.

The rest of the public buildings are the guild-hall, the grammar school endowed by King Edward VI.

the market-crofs, the wool-hall, and the fhire-houfe; nor muft we omit the butchery.

The free grammar-fchool, founded by King Edward VI. was originally in the Eaftgate-ftreet, but being inconvenient there, it was removed into the Northgate-ftreet, and rebuilt by contributions, but King Edward bears the name of the founder ftill. His buft ftands over the door in front, and under his arms at the upper end of the fchool, is this infcription:

EDWARDUS Sextus pofuit, virtutis alumnis.
Gratis difce puer, regia namque fchola eft.

The church-gate, a noble Saxon ftructure, formerly the entrance to the great church of the abbey; but fince its diffolution, has been made ufe of as a fteeple to St James's church. 'Tis very evident it was not firft intended for that purpofe, by its antiquity, and diftance from the body of the church. Between them there is a coffee-houfe.

In the church-yard is Clopton's hofpital, an uniform handfome building.

Oppofite to the hofpital, is the houfe of the late John Earl of Briftol.

Near this houfe is the fhire-hall, or feffions-houfe, lately built, in which are held the affizes for the county.

The Guild-hall gives name to the ftreet in which it ftands. It is very ancient, but has been lately much improved, and in part of it, great alterations are made. The town feffions are held here, corporation members chofen, &c.

The market-crofs is a fpacious and lofty building. the upper part is converted into a theatre, ufed only during the great fair by the Norwich Comedians.

Oppofite the crofs in the fame fquare, ftand the new fhambles, built with free-ftone, in 1761, at the expence of John Earl of Briftol, Ambaffador at the court of Spain.

On the Hog-hill, or beaft-market, ftands the common Bridewell, formerly a Jewifh fynagogue, built of flint and free-ftone.

At the Reformation there were five hofpitals, one college, called Jefus College, in College-ftreet, which is now converted into a workhoufe, fifteen chapels whofe names and places where they ftood are ftill known, though the buildings have been immemorially deftroyed, together with a hermitage at Weftgate, and thirteen other chapels, whofe places are not known, from the many alterations that time, fire, and other accidents have made in this town; fo that there have been above forty churches and chapels in all, and moft of them amply endowed, as appears from the value of the firft fruits and tenths, which afforded maintenance as well as employment for forty or fifty clergymen, under a dean and archdeacon, who officiated in the feveral churches, colleges, chapels, and hofpitals.

There are two market-days, Wednefdays and Saturdays; the chief market is on Wednefday, which is very well fupplied with all manner of provifions. There are alfo three annual fairs; the firft on Eafter Tuefday; the fecond for three days before the

feaft

feaft of St. Matthew, September 21, and three days after; but this is ufually protracted to an uncertain length, for the diverfion of the Nobility and Gentry that refort to it: The third is on St. Edmund's Day, November 20.

Bury is feventy miles from London, and forty-two from Norwich.

IPSWICH.

THE fpot on which Ipfwich ftands is fo happily fituated, that it could not fail of inviting inhabitants to fettle here, foon after this corner of the Ifland was peopled. To ftrangers who enter the town, either by what is now the London road, or by the Yarmouth road, it feems to ftand low: But when a traveller approaches the town by the ancient London road, which was over Cattiwade and Bourn Bridges, upon Wherftead-hill, he views it to more advantage; fituated, as in fact it is, on the fide of a hill, with a South afpect, declining by a gradual and eafy defcent to the Quay, where the foot of it is wafhed by the Orwell. The foil is moft healthy; it is fand, crag, or gravel. The hills which rife above it to the North and Eaft, contribute greatly to the convenience of it; not only as they fhelter the town from thofe bleak and inclement winds, but as they are well ftored with fprings of moft excellent water. The fprings from Cladwell-hills, flow in fuch abundance, that though the greater part of the town is fupplied from them, they conftantly run wafte in what is called St. Helen's and St. Margaret's wafh; and thofe

that

that rife in or near Chrift-church park, though they likewife fupply many houfes with water, do as conftantly run wafte, down Brook-ftreet. Thefe laft are of ftill far greater ufe; for the large ponds at Chriftchurch, continually replenifhed by them, through the benevolence and humanity of the owner, are always let out on any emergency; and therefore may be confidered, as perpetual refervoirs, depofited there by Providence, to fecure and protect the town from the dreadful ravages of fire.

As feveral other towns upon the neighbouring coaft, viz. Yarmouth, Aldborough, and Orford, take their names from their fituation near the mouths of their refpective rivers; fo the town of Ipfwich has its name from being feated where the frefh river Gippen or Gipping, empties itfelf into the Orwell. It is fpelt in Domefday, Gyppefwid, Gyppefwiz, Gyppewycus, Gyppewic; afterwards by dropping the Guttural, it was written Yppyfwyche; and then as our Spelling improved, by leaving out the fuperfluous letters, Ipfwich.

The names of the frefh and falt river have lately been confounded, infomuch that Mr. Kirby was unwarily led to call the frefh river the Orwell; but their names are plainly diftinct. The falt river, or to fpeak more properly, that branch or arm of the fea which flows up to Ipfwich, is called the Orwell, probably from its fpacious and commodious Haven or Harbour. Some think this was the place that the Danes failed up A. D. 1016, when they had a defign upon the kingdom of Mercia. " The Saxon "annals,

THE NORFOLK TOUR. 311

" annals call it Arwan; and as it may not be un-
" reasonable to suppose the true name of this har-
" bou may be Arwell; so do we find on one side of
" it Harwich, and on the other Arwerton."

It is certain, Henry the son of King Henry II. who was crowned in his father's life-time, when he conspired against his father, landed here with soldiers from Flanders; and taking Hugh Bigod with him, marched from hence to Norwich. Here Isabel, wife of King Edward II. landed from France, when she drove her husband into Wales. And the XX. of Edward II. [1327] Sir J. Howard had a commission to raise 500 men in Norfolk and Suffolk, and conduct them to the port of Orwell, thence to go to sea against the French.

And the Earl of Lancaster, XIV. of Edward III. had an assignment of ten ships to transport his horse from the port of Orwell to Flanders; so that we need not multiply proofs to shew that this haven and branch of the sea is called the Orwell. As to the fresh river Gipping, it has three fountain-heads: one rises at or near the little village of Gipping, by Mendlesham, to which it gives name. Another head rises near Wetherden; and the third near Rattlesden. These two last rivulets unite with the other at Stow-market; and there the Gipping, thus supplied, becomes more respectable. It is true, the Orwell is sometimes called the Orwell or Gipping, because the Gipping discharges itself into it at Ipswich; but the fresh river Gipping, cannot with any propriety be called the Orwell, because it is no part of the haven: The Thames may as well be called the Swin.

Ipswich

Ipswich strictly speaking, that is, within the gates, was not of very large extent. It was inclosed with a rampart and ditch, which was broken down by the Danes, when they pillaged the town twice within the space of ten years, about the years of our Lord 991, 1000. But this fortification was repaired and renewed in the fifth year of King John.

There are not the least remains of more than three of the gates now standing; but, it is certain, there were more. For in the ancient partition of the town into four letes or wards, as two of these were called Northgate-lete and Westgate-lete, so the two others were called Eastgate-lete and Southgate-lete.

We read likewise of Lose-gate, which stood at the ford through the salt river, by what is now the House of Mr. Trotman. Though the rampart hath in many places been broken through, and in some entirely levelled, there are still considerable remains of it; and it is easily traced from the bowling-green garden (or grey-friars walk) with a road on each side of it, to the wen, or St. Matthew's-gate.

Hence to Bull-gate, facing Westgate-street, it is levelled, and the ground built upon. But from this to North-gate, and so to the end of Cross-key street, it is almost entire. It is also visible at the back of the houses on the West side of St. Margaret's wash; and again in the yard of Christ's-hospital; so that all the parishes of St. Austin, St. Clement, and St. Heleo, and great part of the parishes of St. Margaret and St. Matthew, were not included within the

the gates; and thefe are accordingly called in old writings, the fuburbs of Ipfwich.

But if we confider the borough in a larger fenfe, as including not only the town with its fuburbs, but the four hamlets of Stoke-hall, Crooks-hall, Wikes-ufford, and Wikes-bifhop, which comprehends the whole precincts and liberties of the borough, the extent of it is very confiderable. For it reaches from Eaft to Weft, that is, from the place on Rufhmere common, where the bounds of the liberties running paft Rufhmere-hall-gate, and along the other lane crofs the Wood-bridge road oppofite to the gallows; to that place in Whitton-ftreet, where the bounds come out of the lane leading from Bramford, crofs the Norwich and Bury road, and then go into the lane leading to Whitton church, the diftance is better than four miles. In like manner, from the North to South, or near it; that is, from that place beyond Wefterfield green, where the bounds enter the road leading from Witnefham to Ipfwich, and fo to Bournbridge; it is about the fame diftance: But if, inftead of going to the Weft of the Orwell, you go from the aforefaid place through St. Clement's-ftreet on the Eaft-fide of it to Downham-bridge by John's Nefs, the diftance is greater.

The civil government of the town is vefted in two bailiffs, a recorder, twelve portmen, of whom four are juftices of the peace; a town-clerk; twenty-four chief conftables, of whom two are coroners; and the twelve feniors are headboroughs; a treafurer and two chamberlains, to collect the revenues of the town:

The

The borough sends two members to parliament, who are elected by the burgesses at large, in number between 600 and 700.

Nine churches are mentioned in Domesday-book, as standing in the Conqueror's time: There are now 12.

The trade of this town formerly consisted chiefly of the manufacture of broad cloth, by which many large fortunes were raised. But about the middle of the last century the manufactory began to decline, and at length totally ceased, and burthened the town with a vast number of poor. From hence it happened, that many of the better sort of houses were for a long time empty; and Ipswich incurred the censure of being *a Town without people*. The cause of this desertion having ceased, the agreeableness of the town invited new-comers to settle here; the number of inhabitants is increased to near 12,000; and within fifty years the rents are advanced more than fifty *per cent.* and more middling houses are daily wanted.

The chief trade is at present in corn; the malting trade is very extensive, and one hundred and fifty sail of ships belong to this port.

Here are five market days, Tuesdays and Thursdays for butcher's meat, Wednesdays and Fridays for fish; and Saturday is a general market-day for all sorts of provisions, cattle, &c.

Here are five fairs; one on Holy-rood-day, O. S. where much business is done in the two articles of butter and cheese. One on St. George's day O. S. for toys and lean cattle, chiefly home-bred. St. James's July 25, now not worth mentioning: And two fairs for cattle on May 18 and 19, and August 22 and 23; at the last of which vast number of lambs are constantly sold, to the amount of eighty, ninety, or sometimes one hundred thousand.

In this town there are five charity schools in which 116 boys, and twenty-four girls, are educated, clothed and fitted out for service, or bound out to some low trades.

This town has lately been much improved by a new pavement, and well lighting the streets.

BUNGAY.

A VERY neat market-town, 14 miles from Norwich, and containing about 2000 inhabitants, is delightfully situated upon the Waveney, which being navigable from Yarmouth, is a great benefit to its trade; the Waveney divides Norfolk from Suffolk, in the latter of which counties Bungay is built: it signifies the good Island. Here are the remains of a very strong castle, situated on a high hill, which commands the adjacent fens, and was formerly the seat of the Bigods, Earls of Norfolk, the site of it is still in the Duke of Norfolk's hands, who is also owner of the dissolved house of Benedictine Nuns, the remains of which are very few, and are standing at the East end of our LADY's CHURCH, of which the Duke is patron, but it having no tithes is of small value; this was in the abbey before its dissolution; and with the whole town, except one small street, was destroyed by fire, March 1, 1689; the loss was computed

puted at upwards of 29,8961. the town has been rebuilt and the church repaired, it has a fine double organ, neat font, and in the South aile, a handfome fquare tower fteeple, in which there is a good peal of eight bells, and a clock; the chancel was never rebuilt, fo that the altar is at the Eaft end of the church, the fteeple ftands at the Weft end of the South aile, the two ailes, nave and North porch are leaded; the feats are uniform.

TRINITY CHURCH, ftands on the other fide of the abbey, the chancel which was burnt down, was never re-built, the altar is placed at the Eaft end of the South aile, the fteeple is round and much decayed, it has no bells in it, but there is a very large one hanging in a fhed in the yard, with this motto round it, *Per me fideles invocantur ad preces*, anno domini 1608. The fteeple was deftroyed in time of divine fervice by a tempeft, which broke all the bells, and fplit it from top to bottom. On the battlements of the upper part, which is octangular, are the arms of Bigod and Brotherton, by which it feems as if the fteeple (or perhaps more likely, the battlements) was built by T. de Brotherton, Earl of Norfolk, and the church afterwards given to the abbey, for the tithes are impropriate, and were in the Crown from the Reformation, till Queen Elizabeth gave them to the Bifhop of Ely, who now leafes them, referving the prefentation of the Vicarage, which is a good piece of preferment, to himfelf. The South aile and nave are leaded, and the South porch tiled.

Upon a marble flab in this church is an infcription, in memory of Mr. Thomas Stanton, who died April 20,

20, 1691. He had been Captain of an East Indiaman called the return; and it is noticed, as an extraordinary fact, that he made the voyage to and from Surat in twelve months.

At the foot of the bridge, on the Suffolk side, there was a small chapel, the East end washed by the river, built probably for some hermit placed here: It was taken down 1732 and a granary built in its place. There are two crosses in the market-place, one for corn, on the top of which stands an old carved effigies of Justice; the other for the butter, &c. The market is on Thursday, and plentifully supplied with all kinds of provisions.

In Ditchingham parish is a neat convenient bath, and proper reception for bathing, with convenient boarding for the infirm, 'tis a very cool water, and has been found of service in several cases; it was built by Mr. John King, an apothecary here, who to recommend his Bath, published an Essay on hot and cold bathing in 1737.

The water in the pump in the King's head yard adjoining to the castle-hill, on the East side, is an exceeding strong mineral, and much drank by many people; it seems much of the same nature and quality with the mineral waters at Aylsham.

SUDBURY,

STANDS upon the Stour, which is navigable for barges from Maningtree to this town. It was anciently called South-burgh, as Norwich is said to have

have been called North-burgh. It is a very ancient town; and at present confifts of three parifhes, having three beautiful and large parifh churches; St. Gregory's, St. Peter's, and All Saints. This town was one of the firft places where King Edward III. put the Flemings whom he brought into England from the Netherlands, to teach the Englifh to manufacture their own wool, which has been carried to great extent, in the manufactory of Baize, Says, and other coarfe kind of woollens, but this is now much upon the decline, and the town is confequently burdened by a very numerous poor.

It is a town-corporate, governed by a mayor, fix aldermen, twenty-four capital burgeffes, and other inferior officers. It has divers privileges, and fends two members to parliament. His Grace the Duke of Grafton takes the title of Baron from this place.

It was made a Mayor Town by charter, ann. 1, and 2, Phil. and Mary. Q. Eliz. *Anno Regini* I. confirmed divers privileges to it, among which was that of fending Burgeffes, the firft return of them being made that year.

* Simon Sudbury, who was Archbifhop of Canterbury A. D. 1375, and beheaded by the rabble in Wat Tyler's infurrection, was a native of this town: He built the upper end of St. Gregory's church; founded a college where his father's houfe ftood, and endowed it fo well that it was of the value of 122l. 18s. per ann. when it was fuppreffed. He is alfo faid by

---

* His fcull is fhewn by the Clerk, who fells the teeth and replaces them.

by Leland, with John de Chertfey, to have founded a priory here of the order of St. Auftin; though Weaver afcribes it to one Baldwin of Shipling (Shimpling perhaps) and Mabil his wife.

WOODBRIDGE

TOOK its name from a Wooden-bridge built over a hollow way, to make a communication between two parks feparated by the road which leads by Woodbridge market-place towards Ipfwich. At the foot of the hill from this hollow-way, about a ftone's-throw from whence the bridge might ftand, is a houfe, which at this day retains the name of the dry-bridge. The river Deben on which this town is fituated, difcharges itfelf into the fea about ten miles below it, and is navigable up to the town. Here are two quays, the common quay where the chief imports and exports are, and where the fine Woodbridge falt is made; and above this is the lime-kiln qnay, where formerly the Ludlow man of war was built. Some years fince there was another dock below the common quay, where the King'-fifher floop was built; but this is now fhut from the river by a mud wall, and almoft filled up.

The church and fteeple are beautiful buildings, the former is faid to be founded by John Lord Segrave. On the South-fide of the church ftood a priory of black canons, founded by Sir Hugh Rous, or Rufus, as Weaver calls him, to which one Hanford was a confiderable benefactor. It was valued at 50l. 3s. 5d$\frac{1}{2}$.

per

per ann. and granted in 33 Henry VIII. to Sir John Wingfield and Dorothy his wife. It is a good old feat, now the Estate of Francis Brooke, Esq. The town traded much in sack-cloth; the chief manufacture now is salt. It has a pretty good market on Wednesdays. This was granted in the reign of King Henry III. There are two fairs yearly, on March 25, and September 21. In the midst of the market-place is the shire-hall, where the quarter-sessions for the liberty of St. Etheldred are holden; under which is the corn-crofs. The market-place is clean and well-built, and so is the stone-street, so called because it was the only part of the town which was paved. But the street called the thorough-fare, as being situated in the road from Ipswich to Yarmouth, is now likewise well paved, and kept so clean that it will tempt the substantial inhabitants to build and dwell there.

Here is a free grammar-school for ten boys, and an alms-house for thirteen poor men and three women.

NEW-MARKET,

AT the extremity of the county, is a well-built thorough-fare town, consisting chiefly of one long street, so situated that the North-side of the street is in Suffolk, and the South-side in Cambridgeshire. There are two churches, St. Mary's in Suffolk, and All-Saints in Cambridgeshire. His Majesty has a house here, for his residence during the races, which was built by King Charles II. and there are many neat modern houses, built by noblemen and gentlemen; and several good inns, where, though the use of figures is pretty well understood, the accommodations in general, are excellent, and, they who on a plan of œconomy, or in expectation of better entertainment, go sixteen miles further towards London, rather than stop here, will be much disappointed.

There are two annual fairs, one on the Tuesday in Whitsun-week; the other October 28. Here is also a good market on Tuesdays; and a free-school, which was endowed by King Charles II. The town is supported not by merchandise or manufactures of any kind, but by its situation upon a considerable road, and by the company which frequent the horse-races on the neighbouring heath.

About two miles West of the town is the Devil's-dyke, by the vulgar so called, who readily ascribe to him what they cannot rationally account for. It is also called Reche-dyke, from a little market-town at the beginning of it. From Reche it crosses the heath near to Stickworth. It was formerly the boundary between the East-Angles and the Mercians; and is now the boundary between the Bishopricks of Norwich and Ely. It is uncertain who was the founder of so great a work; some ascribe it to King Canute, but that cannot be true; for Abbo, who mentioned it, died before Canute began his reign: Besides, the purpose for which he is said to have done it, was far from being equivalent to the expence of such a work, viz. as a mark beyond which the King's purveyors were not to come towards Bury. It is most probable, it was cast up in the reign of King Edmund; for Matthew Florilegus declares, that the battle against Ethelwolf was fought between St. Edmund's two ditches. The other ditch is about five miles farther towards Cambridge, now called 7-mile-dyke; formerly fleam-dyke.

THOMAS CAVENDISH, efq. the second Englishman who circumnavigated the world, formerly lived at Grimston-hall, in the parish of Trimley St. Martin in this county. This gallant officer, fitted out three ships, at his own expence, against the Spaniards, viz. the Desire, burden 120 tons; the Content, of 60 tons; and the Hugh Gallant, a bark of 40 tons. On board these ships he had no more than 123 hands. With this inconsiderable force he sailed from Plymouth on the 21st of July 1586. In February following he passed through the straits of Magellan, and entered the South-seas, plundered and burnt the towns of Paita, Puna, Acapulco, Natividad, Acatler, and several other on the coasts of Chili and Peru. After which he attacked, and took the St. Anna, a large Acapulco ship of 700 tons, in his own ship, the Desire, in which he had not above 60 men; yet with these he attempted to board the St. Anna; and though he was twice repulsed, at the third attack he took her with little loss. What loss the enemy sustained is not said; but Captain Cavendish set 191 prisoners on shore at Puerto Seguro, and brought off seven with him to serve as pilots, linguists, &c. He took in this prize 122,000 pezos of gold, each pezo being of the value of eight shillings; besides a great quantity of other rich merchandise, altogether amounting to more than 60,000l. After this he touched at the Philippine Islands, and returned home by the Cape of Good Hope, and St. Helena, and arrived at Plymouth Sep. 9, 1588.

In his second voyage, 1591, after passing the straits of Magellan on the 20th of May 1592, he was parted from his fleet in the night, and never heard of since.

[323]

A LIST of the TOWNS and VILLAGES in the County of NORFOLK, shewing the Hundreds in which they lie, and their Distance in Measured or Computed Miles from the City of NORWICH.

The Market Towns are distinguished by SMALL Capitals.

Towns.	Hun.	M.	Towns.	Hun.	M.
ACLE	Wals.	11	Baffingham	N. Erp.	17
Alburgh	Ears.	15	Baftwick	W. Fl.	13
Alby	S. Erp.	14	Bawburgh	Fore.	5
Aldeby	Clav.	16	Bawdefwell	Lyns.	12
Aldborough	S. Erp.	15	Bawfey	Fr. L.	38
Alderford	Eyns.	8	Bayfield	Holt	23
Alpington	Lod.	9	Beckham (East)	N. Erp.	19
Althorpe	Gall.	24	Beckham (West)	S. Erp.	18
Appleton	Fr. L.	38	Bedingham	Lod.	12
Anmer	Fr. L.	34	Beechamwell	Clac.	33
Antingham	N. Erp.	14	Beefton	Laun.	20
Arminghall	Hens.	3	Beefton	Tav.	4
Armingland	S. Erp.	13	Beefton St. Laurence	Tunf.	10
Afhby	W. Fl.	13	Beefton Regis	N. Erp.	20
Afhby	Lod.	8	Beetley	Laun.	20
Afhill	Way.	20	Beighton	Wals.	10
Afhmenhaugh	Tuns.	8	Belaugh	S. Erp.	8
Afhwelthorpe	Dep.	8	Belaugh	Eynf.	13
Afhwicken	Fr. L.	31	Bergh Apton	Clav.	7
Aflacton	Dep.	12	Beftthorpe	Shrop.	12
ATTLEBOROUGH	Shrop.	15	Bexwell	Clac.	35
Attlebridge	Tav.	8	Billingford	Ears.	18
AYLSHAM	S. Erp.	11	Billingford	Eynf.	14
Aylmerton	N. Erp.	18	Billockby	W. Fl.	13
Babingly	Fr. L.	34	Bilney (East)	Laun.	21
Baconfthorpe	S. Erp.	19	Bilney (West)	Fr. L.	32
Bacton	Tuns.	17	Binham	N. Gr.	22
Bagthorpe	Gall.	33	Bintry	Eynf.	18
Bale or Bathley	Holt	21	Bircham (Great)	Smith.	35
Banham	Guilt.	16	Bircham Newton	Smith.	35
Banningham	S. Erp.	12	Bircham Tofts	Smith.	35
Barford	Fore.	7	Bittering	Laun.	22
Barmer	Gall.	28	Bixley	Henf.	3
Barney	N. Gr.	24	Blakeney	Holt.	24
Barnham Broome	Fore.	10	Blickling	S. Erp.	13
Barningham (Little)	S. Erp.	15	Blofield	Blo.	6
Barningham (N. wood)	N. Erp.	16	Blo-Norton	Guilt.	21
Barningham (Town)	N. Erp.	17	Bodham	Holt.	20
Barton Bendifh	Clac.	30	Bodney	S. Gr.	23
Barton Turf	Tunf.	10	Booton	S. Erp.	12
Barwick	Smith	28	Boughton	Clac.	38
Bafham (East)	Gall.	27	Bowthorpe	Fore.	4
Bafham (North)	Gall.	23	Bracon Afh	Hum.	6
Bafham (West)	Gall.	23	Bradenham (East)	S. Gr.	20

TOWNS IN NORFOLK.

Towns.	Hun.	M.	Towns.	Hun.	M.
Bradenham (West)	S. Gr.	21	Carleton	Lod.	8
Bradfield	Tunf.	16	Carleton East	Hum.	5
Bradiston	Blo.	6	Carleton Forehoe	Fore.	9
Bramerton	Henf.	4	Carleton Rode	Dep.	14
Brampton	S. Erp.	9	Castle Acre	Fr. L.	29
Brancaster	Smith.	38	Castle Rising	Fr. L.	39
Brandiston	Eynf.	9	Caston	Way.	22
Brandon Little	Fore.	9	Catfield	Hap.	14
Breccles	Way.	18	Catton	Tav.	2
Brettenham	Shrop.	22	Cawston	S. Erp.	11
Bridgeham	Shrop.	21	Chedgrave	Lod.	10
Briningham	Holt	19	Choseley	Smith.	34
Brinton	Holt	19	Claxton	Lod.	7
Brisley	Laun.	10	Clenchwarton	Fr. M.	43
Brissingham	Difs	15	Cley	Holt	25
Briston	Holt	17	Clippesby	W. Fl.	14
Brockdish	Earf.	22	Cockley Cley	S. Gr.	28
Bromehill	Grim.	30	Cockthorpe	N. Gr.	23
Bromesthorpe	Gall.	30	Colby	S. Erp.	10
Broome	Lod.	13	Colkirk	Laun.	22
Brooke	Clav.	6	Colney	Hum.	3
Brundall	Blo.	5	Coltishall	S. Erp.	7
Brunstead	Hap.	16	Colton	Foie.	7
Buckenham	Blo.	9	Colveston	Grim.	27
BUCKENHAM NEW	Shrop.	15	Congham	Fr. L.	38
Buckenham Old	Shrop.	16	Corpusty	S. Erp	16
Buckenham Tofts	Grim.	23	Costesey	Fore.	4
Bunwel	Dep.	13	Coston	Fore.	8
Burlingham North	Blo.	9	Cranwich	Grim.	27
Burlingham South	Blo.	9	Cranworth	Mit.	15
Burlingham St. And.	Blo.	9	Creak North	Bro.	30
Burgh	Holt	18	Creak South	Bro.	29
Burgh St. Peter	Clav.	14	Cressingham Great	S. Gr.	23
Burgh	W. Fl.	14	Cressingham Little	S. Gr.	25
Burgh	S. Erp.	10	Crimplesham	Clac.	38
Burnham Depdale	Bro.	34	Cringleford	Hum.	3
Burnham Norton	Bro.	33	Cromer	N. Erp.	22
Burnham Overy	Bro.	33	Croftwich	Tav.	6
Burnham Thorpe	Bro.	31	Croftwick	Tunf.	16
Burnham Ul. & Sutton	Bro.	32	Crownthorpe	Fore.	10
BURNHAM WEST	Bro.	32	Croxton	Grim.	25
Burston [GATE	Difs	10	Croxton	Gall.	21
Buxton	S. Erp.	8	Darsingham	Fr. L.	38
Caister	E. Fl.	19	Dalling Field	N. Gr	22
Caister	Henf.	3	Dalling Wood	Eynf.	14
Caldecote	S. Gr.	25	Deepham	Fore.	11
Calthorpe	S. Erp.	13	Denver	Clac.	40
Cantley	Blo.	10	Denton	Earf.	17
Carbroke	Way.	20	DEREHAM EAST	Mit.	16

TOWNS IN NORFOLK. 325

Towns.	Hun.	M.	Towns.	Hun.	M.
Dereham West	Clac.	38	Fransham Little	Laun.	21
Dickleburgh	Difs	17	Freethorpe	Blo.	11
Dilham	Tunf.	12	Frenze	Difs	19
Dillington	Laun.	17	Frettenham	Tav.	6
Diss	Difs	22	Fring	Smith.	33
Ditchingham	Lod.	12	Fritton	Dep.	11
Docking	Smith.	38	Fulmondeston	G.T.	19
Doughton	Gall.	20	Fundenhall	Dep.	9
DOWNHAM	Clac.	42	Garboldisham	Guilt.	20
Drayton	Tav.	4	Garveston	Mit.	12
Didlington	S. Gr.	28	Gasthorpe	Guilt.	21
Dunham Great	Laun.	24	Gately	Laun.	38
Dunham Little	Laun.	25	Gatesend	Gall.	25
Dunston	Hum.	4	Gayton	Fr. L.	34
Dunton	Gall.	26	Gayton Thorpe	Fr. L.	33
Larsham	Earf.	13	Gaywood	Fr. L.	40
Easton	Fore.	6	Geldeston	Clav.	14
Eccles	Shrop.	17	Gillingham All Saints	Clav.	16
Eccles	Hap.	16	Gillingham St. Mary	Clav.	16
Edgefield	Holt.	19	Gimingham	N. Erp.	17
Edingthorpe	Tunf.	16	Gissing	Difs	16
Egmere	N. Gr.	29	Glanford	Holt	22
Ellingham	Clav.	14	Godwick	Laun.	20
Ellingham Great	Shrop.	14	Gooderstone	S. Gr.	31
Ellingham Little	Way.	14	Gresham	N. Erp	18
Elmham North	Laun.	18	Greffenhall	Laun.	18
Elsing	Eynf.	13	Grimston	Fr. L.	35
Emneth	Fr. M.	50	Griston	Way.	17
Erpingham	S. Erp.	14	Gueftwick	Eynf.	14
FAKENHAM	Gall.	25	Guist	Eynf.	18
Felbrigg	N. Erp.	18	Gunthorpe	Holt	22
Felmingham	Tunf.	13	Gunton	N. Erp.	16
Felthorpe	Tav.	7	Hackford	Fore.	11
Feltwell	Grim.	35	Hackford	Eynf.	11
Fersfield	Difs	19	Hadifcoe	Clav.	16
Filby	E. Fl.	16	Hadifcoe Thorpe	Clav.	16
Fincham	Clac.	37	Hales	Clav.	11
Fishley	Wals.	11	Halvergate	Wals.	13
Flitcham	Fr. L.	37	Hanworth	N. Erp.	14
Flordon	Hum.	7	Happifburgh	Hap.	19
Fordham	Clac.	36	Hapton	Dep.	9
Forncet St. Mary	Dep.	11	Hardingham	Mit.	14
Forncet St. Peter	Dep.	12	Hardley	Lod.	13
Fouldon	S. Gr.	28	Hardwick	Dep.	12
Foulsham	Eynf.	18	Hardwick	Fr. L.	41
Foxley	Eynf.	15	Hargham	Shrop.	18
Framlingham Earl	Henf.	4	HARLESTON	Earf.	20
Framlingham Pigott	Henf.	4	HARLING EAST	Guilt.	20
Fransham Great	Laun.	22	Harling West	Guilt.	21

TOWNS IN NORFOLK.

Towns	Hun.	M.	Towns	Hun.	M.
Harpley	Fr. L.	32	Hoveton St. Peter	Tunf.	9
Hafingham	Blo.	9	Houghton	Gall.	33
Hauteboys Great	S. Erp.	8	Houghton	S. Gr.	23
Hauteboys Little	S. Erp.	8	Houghton	N. Gr.	21
Haynford	Tav.	6	Howe	Clav.	6
Heacham	Smith.	40	Hunftanton	Smith.	41
Heckingham	Clav.	13	Hunworth	Holt	18
Hedenham	Lod.	12	Ickburgh	Grim.	25
Helhoughton	Gall.	24	Illington	Shrop.	19
Hellefdon	Tav.	2	Ingham	Hap.	17
Hellington	Lod.	7	Ingoldftorpe	Smith.	39
Hemefby	W. Fl.	17	Ingworth	S. Erp.	13
Hemlington	Walf.	8	Intwood	Hum.	3
Hempnall	Dep.	10	Irftead	Tunf.	11
Hempftead	Holt	20	Iflington	Fr. M.	43
Hempton	Gall.	24	Itteringham	S. Erp.	14
Hemftead	Hap.	18	Kelling	Holt	22
Herringby	E. Fl.	15	Kempftone	Laun.	22
Hethel	Hum.	6	Kenninghall	Guilt	19
Hetherfet	Hum.	5	Kerdiftone	Eynf.	11
Hevingham	N. Erp.	8	Kefwick	Hum.	3
Heveringland	Eynf.	9	Ketteringham	Hum.	6
Heydon	S. Erp.	14	Kettleftone	Gall.	20
Hickling	Hap.	16	Kilverftone	Shrop.	26
Hilburgh	S. Gr.	27	Kimberley	Fore.	10
Hilgay	Clac.	42	Kirby Bedon	Henf.	3
Hillington	Fr. L.	38	Kirby Cane	Clav.	13
Hindolvefton	Eynf.	18	Kirftead	Lod.	7
Hindringham	N. Gr.	21	Knapton	N. Erp.	16
HINGHAM	Fore.	14	Lammas	S. Erp.	10
Hockering	Mit.	10	Landgrave	Earf.	13
Hockham	Shrop.	19	Langford	S. Gr.	29
Hockwold	Grim.	35	Langham	Holt	25
Hoe	Laun.	16	Langley	Lod.	9
Holkam	N. Gr.	31	Larling	Shrop.	20
Holme	Clac.	41	Leffingham	Hap.	15
Holme Hale	S. Gr.	10	Letheringfet	Holt	21
Holme next the Sea	Smith.	36	Letton	Mit.	15
HOLT	Holt	22	Lexham Eaft	Laun.	15
Holvefton	Henf.	5	Lexham Weft	Laun.	16
Honing	Tunf.	14	Leziate	Fr. L.	38
Honingham	Fore.	7	Limpenhoe	Blo.	11
Horning	Tunf.	9	Lingwood	Blo.	8
Horningtoft	Laun.	19	Litcham	Laun.	24
Horfey	Hap.	18	LODDON	Lod.	10
Horsford	Tav.	4	Longham	Laun.	20
Horfham St. Faith	Tav.	4	Lopham North	Guilt.	19
Horftead	Tav.	7	Lopham South	Guilt.	19
Hoveton S. John	Tunf.	8	Ludham	Hap.	13

TOWNS IN NORFOLK.

Towns.	Hun.	M.	Towns.	Hun.	M.
Lynford	Grim.	27	Norton Subcorſe	Clav.	14
Lyng	Eynſ.	13	NORWICH is a City		
Lynn King's	Fr. L.	42	and County of itſelf,		
Lynn Weſt	Fr. M.	42	including the Hamlets		
Mannington	S. Erp	13	of Eaton, Lakenham,		
Marham	Clac.	34	Earlham, Helleſden,		
Marlingford	Fore.	6	Thorpe, Trowſe, Car-		
Marſham	S. Erp.	9	rowe, and Bracondale.		
Martham	W. Fl.	17	Oby	W. Fl.	14
Maſſingham Great	Fr. L.	29	Ormeſby St. Margaret	E. Fl.	19
Maſſingham Little	Fr. L.	30	Ormeſby St. Michael	E. Fl.	19
Matlaſke	N. Erp.	16	Oſmundſton or Scole	Diſs	20
Mattiſhall	Mit.	12	Overſtrand	N. Erp.	19
Mattiſhall Bergh	Mit.	12	Ovington	Way.	23
Mawtby	E. Fl.	18	Oulton	S. Erp.	13
Melton Great	Hum.	6	Outwell	Clac.	49
Melton Little	Hum.	5	Oxborough	S. Gr.	33
Melton Conſtable	Holt	18	Oxnead	S. Erp.	9
Mendam	Earſ.	10	Oxwick	Laun.	20
Merkſhall	Hum.	3	Palgrave	S. Gr.	26
Merton	Way.	10	Palling	Hap.	16
Methwold	Grim.	36	Panxworth	Walſ.	9
Metton	N. Erp.	17	Paſtan	Tunſ.	16
Middleton	Fr. L.	38	Patteſly	Laun.	19
Mileham	Laun.	23	Penſthorpe	Gall.	23
Mintlyn	Fr. L.	38	Pentney	Fr. L.	33
Morley St. Botolph	Fore.	10	Pickenham North	S. Gr.	26
Morley St. Peter	Fore.	11	Pickenham South	S. Gr.	26
Morſton	Holt	26	Plumſtead	N. Erp.	16
Morton	Eynſ.	7	Plumſtead Great	Blo.	4
Moulton	Walſ.	10	Plumſtead Little	Blo.	5
Moulton All Saints	Dep.	13	Poringland Great	Henſ.	4
Moulton St. Michael	Dep.	13	Poringland Little	Henſ.	5
Mourningthorpe	Dep.	11	Poſtwick	Blo.	4
Mulbarton	Hum.	5	Potter Heigham	Hap.	16
Mundeſley	N. Erp.	17	Pulham St. Mary	Earſ.	17
Mundford	Grim.	30	Pulham St. Mary Mag.	Earſ.	17
Mundham	Lod.	10	Quarles	N. Gr.	31
Narborough	S. Gr.	32	Quiddenham	Guilt	17
Narford	S. Gr.	32	Rackheath	Tav.	4
Neatiſhead	Tunſ.	12	Ranworth	Wal.	9
Necton	S. Gr.	24	Raveningham	Clav.	15
Needham	Earſ.	16	Raynham Eaſt	Gall.	25
Newton St. Faiths	Tav.	5	Raynham Weſt	Gall.	24
Newton Weſt	Fr. L.	38	Raynham South	Gall.	24
Newton	S. Gr.	23	Reddenhall	Earſ.	20
Newton Flotman	Hum.	6	Reedham	Walſ.	14
Northwold	Grim.	36	Reepham	Eynſ.	11
Norton Pudding	Gall.	23	Repps	W. Fl.	14

TOWNS IN NORFOLK.

Towns.	Hun.	M.	Towns.	Hun.	M.
Repps North	N. Erp.	18	Seething	Lod.	9
Repps South	N. Er.	17	Setchy	Fr. L.	38
Reymeston	Mit.	12	Sharington	Holt	22
Riddlesworth	Guilt.	28	Shelfanger	Difs	18
Ridlington	Tunf.	15	Shelton	Dep.	14
Ringland	Eynf.	6	Sherford	Gall.	13
Ringstead	Smith.	40	Sheringham Upper	N. Erp.	20
Rockland St. Mary	Henf.	6	Sheringham Lower	N. Erp.	21
Rockland All Saints	Shrop.	14	Shernbourne	Smith	40
Rockland St. Andrew	Shrop.	15	Shimpling	Difs	16
Rockland St. Peter	Way.	15	Shingham	Clac.	30
Rollesby	W. Fl.	16	Shipdam	Mit.	19
Roudham	Shrop.	26	Sottesham All Saints	Henf.	6
Rougham	Laun.	29	Sottesham St. Mary	Henf.	6
Roughton	N. Erp.	17	Sottesham St. Martin	Henf.	6
Roxham	Clac.	36	Shouldham	Clac.	36
Roydon	Difs	23	Shouldham Thorpe	Clac.	36
Roydon	Fr. L.	30	Shropham	Shrop.	21
Rudham East	Gall.	26	Sisland	Lod.	10
Rudham West	Gall.	26	Skeyton	S. Erp.	11
Runcton Holme	Clac.	36	Sloley	Tunf.	10
Runcton North	Fr. L.	37	Smalburgh	Tunf.	11
Runham	E Fl.	16	Snarehill	Guilt.	30
Runhall	Fore.	12	Snetterton	Shrop.	17
Runton	N. Erp.	20	Snettisham	Smith	40
Rushall	Earf.	14	Snoring Great	N. Gr.	27
Rushford	Guilt.	23	Snoring Little	Gall.	26
Ruston East	Hap.	15	Somerton East	W. Fl.	19
Ryburgh Great	Gall.	18	Somerton West	W. Fl.	18
Ryburgh Little	Gall.	18	Southacre	S. Gr.	28
Ryston	Clac.	38	Southbergh	Mit.	18
Saham Toney	Way.	23	Southrey	Clac.	42
Sall	Eynf.	13	Southwood	Blo.	11
Salhoufe	Tav.	6	Sparham	Eynf.	12
Salthoufe	Holt	23	Spixworth	Tav.	4
Sandringham	Fr. L.	40	Sporle	S. Gr.	26
Santon	Grim.	32	Sprowston	Tav.	2
Saxlingham	Holt	20	Stalham	Hap.	16
Saxlingham Netherg.	Henf.	7	Stanfield	Laun.	22
Saxlingham Thorpe	Henf.	7	Stanford	Grim.	29
Saxthorpe	S. Erp.	15	Stanhoe	Smith.	33
Scarning	Laun.	18	Stanninghall	Tav.	6
Scole	Difs	20	Starston	Earf.	17
Sco Ruston	Tunf.	12	Stibbard	Gall.	17
Scottow	S. Erp.	10	Stifkey	N. Gr.	29
Scoulton	Way	17	Stockton	Clav.	15
Scratby	E. Fl.	19	Stody	Holt	18
Sculthorpe	Gall.	20	Stoke Holy Crofs	Henf.	5
Sedgeford	Smith	38	Stoke Ferry	Clac.	36

TOWNS IN NORFOLK.

Towns.	Hun.	M.	Towns.	Hun.	M.
Stokefby	E. Fl.	18	Thurning	Eynf.	15
Stow Bardolph	Clac.	40	Thursford	N. Gr.	26
Stow Bedon	Way.	10	Thurton	Lod.	8
Stratfet	Clac.	36	Thuxton	Mit.	11
Stratton St. Michael	Dep.	11	Thwayte	Lod.	11
Stratton St. Mary	Dep.	9	Thwayte	S. Erp.	14
Stratton Strawlefs	S. Erp	7	Tibbenham	Dep.	13
Strumpfhaw	Blo.	9	Tilney St. Laurence	Fr. M.	44
Sturton	Grim.	20	Tilney All Saints	Fr. M.	44
Suffield	N. Erp	13	Tilney with Iflington	F. M.	43
Surlingham	Henf.	5	Titchwell	Smith.	40
Suftead	N. Erp.	17	Tittlefhall	Laun.	22
Sutton	Hap.	17	Tivetfhall St. Margaret	Difs	15
SWAFFHAM	S. Gr.	28	Tivetfhall St. Mary	Difs	15
Swafield	Tunf.	15	Toft Weft	Grim.	23
Swainftorpe	Hum.	5	Toft Monks	Clav.	14
Swannington	Eynf.	8	Toftrees	Gall.	24
Swanton Abbots	S. Erp.	11	Topcroft	Lod.	12
Swanton Morley	Launs	13	Tottenhill	Clac.	37
Swanton Novers	Holt	18	Tottington	Way.	26
Swardefton	Hum.	4	Trimingham	N. Erp	17
Syderftone	Gall.	30	Trowfe Newton	Henf.	1
Syderftrand	N. Erp	18	Trunch	N. Erp.	16
Tacolnefton	Dep.	9	Tuddenham Eaft	Mit.	9
Talburgh	Dep.	5	Tuddenham North	Mit.	12
Tatterford	Gall.	26	Tunftall	Walf.	11
Tatterfet	Gall.	25	Tunftead	Tunf.	9
Taverham	Tav.	6	Tuttington	S. Erp.	14
Terrington St. John	Fr. M.	48	Twiford	Eynf.	15
Terrington St. Clem.	Fr. M.	46	Upton	Walf.	10
Tefterton	Gall.	19	Upwell	Clac.	50
Tharfton	Dep.	10	Weyborne	Holt	25
Thelveton	Difs	18	Wacton All Saints	Dep.	12
Themilthorpe	Eynf.	14	Wacton St. Mary	Dep.	12
THETFORD	Shrop.	29	Walcote	Hap.	16
Thirne	W. Fl.	13	Wallington	Clac.	40
Thompfon	Way.	18	Walpole St. Peter	Fr. M.	47
Thornage	Holt	19	Walpole St. Andrew	Fr. M.	47
Thornham	Smith.	40	WALSHAM NORTH	Tunf.	14
Thorpe Abbots	Earf.	17	Walfham South	Walf.	10
Thorpe	Difs.	17	Walfingham Old	N. Gr.	28
Thorpe	Clav.	13	WALSINGHAM LITT.	N. Gr.	27
Thorpe	Blo.	2	Walfoken	Fr. M.	48
Thorpe Market	N. Erp.	15	Walton Eaft	Fr. L.	33
Thorpland	Clac.	22	Walton Weft	Fr. M.	48
Threxton	Way.	15	Warham	N. Gr.	29
Thrigby	E. Fl.	15	Waterden	Bro.	26
Thurgarton	N. Erp	16	Warlington	Clac.	42
Thurlton	Clav.	15	WATTON	Way.	21

TOWNS IN NORFOLK.

Towns.	Hun.	M.	Towns.	Hun.	M.
Waxham	Hap.	18	Winfarthing	Difs	18
Weafenham St. Peter	Laun.	28	Winterton	W. Fl.	20
Weafenham All Saints	Laun.	28	Witchingham Great	Eynf.	10
Weeting	Grim.	33	Witchingham Little	Eynf.	9
Welborne	Fore.	9	Witlingham	Henf.	3
Wellingham	Laun.	22	Witton	Ble.	5
Wellney	Clac.	46	Witton	Tunf.	15
WELLS	N. Gr.	31	Wiveton	Holt	23
Wendling	Laun.	19	Wolferton	Fr. L.	39
Wereham	Clac.	38	Wolterton	S. Erp.	14
Weftacre	Fr. L.	30	Woodbaftick	Walf.	8
Weftfield	Mit.	14	Woodnorton	Eynf.	20
Wefton	Eynf.	8	Woodrifing	Mit.	15
Weftwick	Tunf.	11	Woodton	Lod.	10
Whetacre	Clav.	17	Wootton North	Fr. L.	40
Whinbergh	Mit.	13	Wootton South	Fr. L.	40
Whiffonfet	Laun.	22	Wormegay	Clac.	36
Whitwel	Eynf.	11	Worftead	Tunf.	14
Wickhampton	Walf.	12	Worthing	Laun.	14
Wicklewood	Fore.	10	Wortwell	Earf.	17
Wickmere	S. Erp.	14	Wramplingham	Fore.	7
Wiggenhall St. Mary	Fr. M.	40	Wrenningham	Hum.	7
Wiggenhall St. M. Mag.	Fr. M.	40	Wretham Eaft	Shrop.	26
Wiggenhall St. Germ.	Fr. M.	40	Wretham Weft	Shrop.	25
Wiggenhall St. Peter	Fr. M.	40	Wretton	Clac.	39
Wighton	N. Gr.	20	Wroxham	Tav.	6
Wifby	Shrop.	16	WYMONDHAM	Fore.	8
Wilton	Grim.	36	YARMOUTH	E. Fl.	22
Wimbotfham	Clac.	46	Yaxham	Mit.	13
Winch Eaft	Fr. L.	18	Yelverton	Henf.	6
Winch Weft	Fr. L.	38			

Names of the Hundreds in the County of Norfolk, as they are contracted in the foregoing Table.

Blo.	for Blofield	S. Gr.	for South Greenhoe
Bro.	Brother Crofs	N. Grim.	North Grimfhoe
Clac.	Clackclofe	Guilt.	Guiltcrofs
Clav.	Clavering	Hap.	Happing
Dep.	Depwade	Henf.	Henftead
Earf.	Earfham	Hum.	Humbleyard
N. Erp.	North Erpingham	Laun.	Launditch
S. Erp.	South Erpingham	Lod.	Loddon
Eynf.	Eynaford	Mit.	Mitford
E. Fl.	Eaft Flegg	Shrop.	Shropham
W. Fl.	Weft Flegg	Smith.	Smithdon
Fore.	Forehoe	Tav.	Taverham
Fr. L.	Freebridge Lynn	Tunf.	Tunftead
Fr. M.	Freebridge Marfhland	Walf.	Walfham
Gall.	Gallow	Way.	Wayland
N. Gr.	North Greenhoe		

ROADS
TO
NORWICH.

Road from London to Yarmouth

	Post Miles		Post Miles
WHITECHAPEL		Brought forward	66
To Ilford	7	Ipswich	4
Rumford	5	Woodbridge	8
Burntwood	7	Wickham Market	4
Ingatestone	5	Saxmundham	8
Chelmsford	6	Yoxford	4
Witham	8	Wangford	9
Kelvedon	4	Wrantham	3
Colchester	10	Lowestoff	8
Stratford	7	Yarmouth	9
Copdock	7		123
Carried over	66		

Post Roads from Norwich to London.
The following are all Post Towns or Stages.

	Post Miles		Post Miles
By *Newmarket* from NORWICH		Brought forward	81
To Attleburgh	15	Harlow	7
Thetford	15	Epping	6
Barton Mills	11	Baldfaced Stag Inn	7
Newmarket	9	Woodford	2
Bourn Bridge	12	London	8
Chesterford	4	(Whitechapel)	
Stansted	12		111
Hockerill	3		
Carried over	81		

[352]

	Post Miles		Post Miles
Another Road		Brought orward	30
To Bournbridge as before	62	Bury	12
Barkway	14	London as above	73
Wade's Mill	12		115
Ware	2		
Hoddefdon	4	*Another Road*	
Waltham Crofs or ⎱	6	To Sudbury as before	59
Enfield Highway ⎰		Caftle Hedingham	7
London		Braintree	8
(Shoreditch)	11	London as before	42
	111		116

By *Bury St. Edmunds* from NORWICH		By *Colchefter* from NORWICH	
To Tivitfhall	15	To Tivitfhall	15
Scole	5	Scole	5
Buddefdale	7	Thwaite	7
Bury	16	Stonham	5
Long Melford	13	Copdock	13
Sudbury	3	Stratford	7
Halfted	8	Colchefter	7
Braintree	7	Kelvedon	10
Chelmsford	12	Witham	4
Ingateftone	7	Chelmsford	8
Burntwood	5	London	
Rumford	6	(Whitechapel) ⎱	30
Ilford	5	See Road to Bury ⎰	
London ⎱	7		111
(Whitechapel) ⎰		*Another Road*	
	116	To Stonham as before	32
Or from NORWICH		Ipfwich	11
To Attleburgh	15	Copdock	4
Thetford	15	London as before	66
Carried over	30		113

Post Roads from Norwich to many of the Principal Cities and Manufacturing Towns in England.

N. B. Such as lie through London are omitted.

The following are all Poft Towns or Stages.

	Post Miles		Post Miles
To BATH. From NORWICH		Brought forward	41
		Newmarket	9
To Attleburgh	15	Bourn Bridge	12
Thetford	15	Royfton	13
Barton Mills	11	Baldock	9
Carried over	41	Carried over	84

	Post Miles		Post Miles
Brought forward	84	Brought forward	105
Hitchin	8	Harborough	105
Dunstable	14	Lutterworth	14
Tring	10	Coventry	15
Aylesbury	7	Meriden	6
Thame	10	Coleshill	6
Oxford	13	Litchfield	15
Witney	10	Wolsaley Bridge	9
Burford	7	Stone	12
Bibury	10	Woore	13
Cirencester	7	Nantwich	9
Tatbury	10	Tarporley	10
Petty France	8	Chester	10
Bath	15		235
	210	To BIRMINGHAM	
See another Road, p. 334.		To Meriden as above	151
To BRISTOL		Birmingham	14
To Petty France as above	195		165
Bristol	17		
	212	To LIVERPOOL From NORWICH	
To HEREFORD From NORWICH		To Dereham	16
		Swaffham	12
To Newmarket as before	50	Downham	14
Cambridge	13	Wisbeach	13
Huntingdon	16	Peterborough	21
Thrapston	17	N. B. By Thorney (to avoid the Bank)	22
Wellingborough	11		
Northampton	10	Wansford	8
Daventry	12	Uppingham	14
Southam	10	Leicester	20
Warwick	10	Loughborough	11
Stratford on Avon	8	Derby	17
Aleester	8	Ashbourn	13
Droitwich	14	Leek	15
Worcester	7	Macclesfield	13
Ledbury	16	Knutsford	12
Hereford	16	Warrington	11
	218	Prescot	12
Or To Worcester as above	186	Liverpool	8
Broomyard	14		230
Hereford	14		
	214	To MANCHESTER	
		To Ashbourn as before *	159
To CHESTER		Buxton	20
To Thrapston as before	96	Disley	9
Kettering	9	Stockport	7
Carried over	105	Manchester	7
			202

[334]

	Post Miles		Post Miles
Another Road to Derby and Ashbourn		Brought forward	109
		Newark	14
To Wisbeach as before	55	Southwell	8
Long Sutton	10	Mansfield	12
Spalding	13	Chesterfield	12
Donnington	10	Sheffield	12
Folkingham	8	Peniston	13
Grantham *	12	Huddersfield	13
Bingham	15	Halifax	8
Nottingham	10		203
Derby	16		
Ashbourn	13	**To LEEDS**	
	162	**From NORWICH**	
See another Road to Grantham, below.		To Newark, by Peterboro' as before }	125
Another Road to MANCHESTER, *(through Matlock and the Peak of Derbyshire.)*		N. B. By Spalding 122	
		Scarthing Moot	12
		Tuxford	2
To Nottingham as before	133	Barnby Moor	10
Alfreton	18	Bawtry	5
Matlock	9	Doncaster	9
Bakewell	10	Ferrybridge	15
Chapel in Frith	14	Leeds	15
Disley	7		193
Stockport	7		
Manchester	7	**To YORK.**	
	205	To Ferrybridge as above	178
		Tadcaster	12
Another Road (By Newark and Mansfield.)		York	9
			199
To Grantham as before	108		
Newark	14	**To LINCOLN**	
Southwell	8	**From NORWICH**	
Mansfield	12		
Chesterfield	12	To Wisbeach as before	55
Middleton	11	Long Sutton	10
Chapel in Frith	12	Spalding	13
Manchester as above	21	Donnington	10
	198	Folkingham	8
		Sleaford	10
To HALIFAX		Lincoln	18
From NORWICH			124
To Wansford, see Road to Liverpool }	84	*Another Road to* BATH, *See p. 332.*	
Stamford	6	To Newmarket as before	50
Greetham	7	Cambridge	13
Witham Common	4	Royston	15
Colsterworth	2	Bath as before	135
Grantham *	8		213
Carried over	109		

FINIS.

www.ingramcontent.com/pod-product-compliance
Lightning Source LLC
Chambersburg PA
CBHW020244240426
43672CB00006B/636